Leo Houck

Leo Houck
A Biography of Boxing's Uncrowned Middleweight Champion

RANDY L. SWOPE

Foreword by EDWARD B. HAUCK

McFarland & Company, Inc., Publishers
Jefferson, North Carolina

LIBRARY OF CONGRESS CATALOGUING-IN-PUBLICATION DATA

Names: Swope, Randy L., author.
Title: Leo Houck : a biography of boxing's uncrowned middleweight champion / Randy L. Swope ; foreword by Edward B. Hauck.
Description: Jefferson, North Carolina : McFarland & Company, Inc., 2019 | Includes bibliographical references and index.
Identifiers: LCCN 2018057319 | ISBN 9781476675343 (softcover : acid free paper) ∞
Subjects: LCSH: Houck, Leo F. (Leo Florian), 1888–1950. | Boxers (Sports)—United States—Biography.
Classification: LCC GV1132.H68 S96 2019 | DDC 796.83092 [B] —dc23
LC record available at https://lccn.loc.gov/2018057319

BRITISH LIBRARY CATALOGUING DATA ARE AVAILABLE

ISBN (print) 978-1-4766-7534-3
ISBN (ebook) 978-1-4766-3463-0

© 2019 Randy L. Swope. All rights reserved

No part of this book may be reproduced or transmitted in any form or by any means, electronic or mechanical, including photocopying or recording, or by any information storage and retrieval system, without permission in writing from the publisher.

Front cover image of Leo Houck of Lancaster, Pennsylvania, America's premier middleweight under direction of Jack McGuigan, National A.C., Philadelphia, Pennsylvania (Library of Congress)

Printed in the United States of America

*McFarland & Company, Inc., Publishers
Box 611, Jefferson, North Carolina 28640
www.mcfarlandpub.com*

To the memory of
Leo F. Hauck,
and to his family

Leo F. Houck (courtesy of LancasterHistory.org, Lancaster, Pennsylvania, John Hauck Collection, MG-63, JH-04-06-15).

Table of Contents

Foreword by Edward B. Hauck   1
Preface   3

Part I. The Early Years

1. Growing Up in Cabbage-Hill   5
2. Turning Professional at Fourteen   11

Part II. The Boxing Years

3. Winning at Home, 1905–1906–1907   19
4. Lightweight Champion of Lancaster County, 1908–1909   23
5. From Lightweight to Middleweight in Twenty-Eight Bouts, 1910   30
6. "Vive la Leo," 1911   48
7. Top of the Heap, 1912–1913   68
8. Baseball, the Blahs and Catchweight Battles, 1914–1915–1916   89
9. Light Heavyweight Sensation, 1917–1918   112
10. Greb and Gibbons Give Leo Fits, 1919   125
11. Grandpa Draws with Tunney, 1920   133
12. Leo and Jack Dempsey, 1921   138
13. "Triunfo en Cuba," 1922   144

Part III. The Penn State Years

14. Penn State's First Legendary Coach   151
15. Leo and the Pennsylvania State Athletic Commission   158

Appendix: Leo F. Houck's Professional Fight Record   165
Chapter Notes   175
Bibliography   187
Index of Persons   189

Foreword
by Edward B. Hauck

Leo Houck was an extraordinary athlete. He excelled as a professional boxer for twenty years and his two hundred matches included twelve opponents who held world championships. In that same time span he also played amateur basketball and football and a season of professional baseball.

But boxing was his sport, his business.

He was a classic example of that era when many young men of immigrant parents were attracted to boxing. Leo grew up in a close-knit home in Lancaster's Cabbage-Hill section, which was populated by German newcomers to America.

Early on he was drawn to boxing by watching matches at local club venues. His initial boxing experience was at a boys' club. He took to the sport with native talent and a desire that resulted in a world-class professional. He appeared in the boxing ring in many American cities and several foreign cities. In a twenty-round fight in Paris during 1911 he defeated Harry Lewis, then the welterweight/middleweight champion of Europe. A Philadelphia sports editor in attendance pronounced Houck the world's middleweight champion. Not official! One opponent he defeated five times, George Chip, won the middleweight championship, and promptly denied Houck a title match.

Toward the end of his career Leo met the celebrated Harry Greb and Gene Tunney. The Greb fights were close. Greb later reported that Leo hit him the hardest of all opponents. The two bouts with Tunney, then the upcoming contender for the heavyweight title, resulted in a draw and a loss.

In his early "retirement years," Houck was a member of Jack Dempsey's training camp, leading up to his championship bout with Georges Carpentier during 1921.

Houck was named to the original Boxing Hall of Fame created by Nat Fleischer, publisher and editor of *Ring Magazine*, the boxing "bible" in New York. The successor organization, the International Boxing Hall of Fame, based in Canastota, New York, inducted Leo Houck June 10, 2012.

In 1923, Hauck retired professionally but did not "hang up the gloves." The Penn State College director of athletics, Hugo Bezdek, was seeking a coach to establish a boxing team to join the newly established Intercollegiate Boxing Association. Leo's name was suggested. Following an interview with Bezdek, Houck was hired on the spot.

Houck thus began the making of a phase of sports history at Penn State.

Leo was a natural teacher. Most of the young men he coached never formally pulled on boxing gloves. Through his twenty-seven years at Penn State, Houck produced an enviable record. Intercollegiate championships included teams representing the military academies, West Point and Annapolis; Ivy Leaguers, Harvard, Yale, and Dartmouth; state schools, Wisconsin, Virginia, North Carolina, Syracuse, and others. Academically, the majority of student boxers graduated and went on to careers in business, law, medicine, and teaching. Two, however, moved into the professional ranks successfully, Steve Hamas and Billy Soose. Heavyweight Hamas fought his way as a top contender; Soose's career climaxed by winning the world middleweight championship.

Two other Nittany Lion boxers of the early thirties, the Epstein twins, Julius and Phillip, made their mark as screenwriters for the classic movie *Casablanca*, which won them an Academy Award.

Coaching aside, Leo Houck's personality and temperament established him as a Penn State tradition. As one professor stated, "A stranger might find it hard to believe that Leo Houck would fit into the academic picture ... he [was] a mellow daub of color. His homespun philosophy and sly humor make him one of the most quoted men on campus." Leo, the professor continued, taught the science of boxing, not slugging, street fighting or rough-and-tumble tactics.

During World War II, Houck was a member of a group representing a variety of sports. This ensemble spent four months visiting little-known military bases in Iceland, Greenland, Canada and Maine in the North Atlantic, and then in the South Atlantic, the Virgin Islands, the Bahamas, Trinidad and Azores Islands.

Keeping his connection to the professional sport, Houck, a Pennsylvania licensed referee, worked boxing programs, plus several professional championships in Philadelphia and Pittsburgh. Leo, at the invitation of the state's penal officials, held boxing clinics and programs for prison inmates at several state institutions during his college coaching years.

On a personal note: I remember Leo Houck (Hauck) best as a good and kindly father and a loving husband of my mother. And I speak for my three brothers and three sisters.

Preface

Several years ago I started to punch a heavy bag twice a week as part of my physical conditioning routine. The results I achieved were so encouraging I decided to expand my limited knowledge of boxing by visiting Terry Nye's Gymnasium in Lancaster, Pennsylvania. Terry is a former mixed martial arts fighter, boxer, and bare-knuckle brawler. He agreed to train, condition, and teach me self-defense techniques. The training focused heavily on cardiovascular endurance, learning how to deliver punches, focus mitt training, and some limited sparring in the ring.

The outstanding training I received from Terry over a one-year period improved my overall health and physical condition, and directed me naturally toward my biographical subject. I prefer to write about notable and famous Pennsylvanians, and decided to profile a boxer from Pennsylvania. The Pennsylvania Sports Hall of Fame website identified twelve inductees who had attained a superior level of achievement and brilliance in the ring during their careers. I immediately focused on one specific boxer, Leo F. Houck, from Lancaster, Pennsylvania, inducted in 1972.

Lancaster is a thriving city located only seventeen miles south of my home. I had spent five years working at the Lancaster Malleable Iron Foundry; completed a one-year independent study at Franklin & Marshall College, also located in Lancaster, while I attended nearby Millersville University; had made numerous friends who were residents of the city; and was familiar with the surroundings and streets. However, I had absolutely no inkling about the identity of one of its most famous residents, a magnificent boxer and uncrowned champion of the early 1900s.

My preliminary investigation and research into Leo Houck's life revealed that only a few feature newspaper stories, magazine articles, and detailed obituaries about his life were ever published. Discovering Leo F. Houck could certainly be attributed to my interest in boxing combined with the training I received at Terry Nye's Gymnasium. Even so, I do believe that my numerous prior experiences in Lancaster while working and studying decades earlier somehow set the stage for this later revelation that offered a once-in-a-lifetime opportunity to chronicle Leo Houck's life and career. In both boxing and life, timing is everything.

The biography comprises three distinct parts, but focuses primarily on Leo Houck's professional boxing career. I based my research exclusively on archived newspaper accounts and their reported outcomes in order to describe over two hundred of his bouts. The reader will note that throughout the biography, newspaper-decision outcomes reported for some of Leo's bouts differed on a local, regional, and national level. I have identified all the outcomes reported for each fight. Moreover, I have made no attempt to challenge or suggest the revision for any outcome previously listed on existing official fight records. Instead, I have included evidence in the biography to support the differing outcomes reported.

Meeting Leo Houck's sons, Edward and Joseph, produced a successful collaboration on the book and was, by far, the most prominent and significant event that I experienced while researching and writing the biography. Moreover, their unflagging support and patience during numerous interviews resulted in valued friendships with both of them, and produced a mutual understanding and agreement that their father would receive a fair and unbiased treatment.

In addition, I would like to acknowledge and thank the following people: Robert J. Trout, my mentor; Annetta Wells, editor; Joanne Weber, genealogical support; Cory Van Brookhoven, president of the Lititz Historical Foundation; International Boxing Hall of Fame; International Boxing Research Organization; BoxRec; Penn State Archives and Special Collections; and finally, a special recognition and thank-you to all the staff members at the Lancaster Historical Society.

PART I

The Early Years

1

Growing Up in Cabbage-Hill

In 1921, Leo Houck recounted:

Twenty years ago I joined the Cadets of the Knights of St. John.¹ At that time this was an organization of youngsters, averaging about twelve years old. We met in the old Armory, which was later the Family Theater, and later the Packard Motor Sales Room. We visited the rooms every day and played around the gym. I watched the younger boys boxing and had the desire to do some of it myself. I did not say anything, however, and spent most of my time playing the different games with the boys. Tommy Devlin, who was a master of the ring some time before this date, promoted boxing shows and trained many of the younger lads.

Here is how Carl and I happened to be matched. One evening, Tommy Devlin strolled in while a bunch of the boys were fooling with the various paraphernalia. Down in one corner of the gym Carl and I were battling away hammer and tong. Tommy stood by and watched for awhile. After a short time he came over and asked whether we would like to go on the next opening bout for the next show, for four rounds. I couldn't give him an answer right then, but came home and asked my mother and father about it. They did not know what to say. Finally, after much persuasion, I secured my dad's consent. Devlin personally instructed the Kreckel twins, Carl and Ed. I watched Tommy tell these boys many little pointers of the game, and I finally started to spar with some of the boys.

I enjoyed going to every boxing show in the city. Sometimes I would get a chance to swing the towel and on many occasions I filled up the buckets for the boxers. There were some mighty good boxers appearing in the city at that time and I learned considerably about the sport. After each show I shadowboxed and gradually the swinging of my arms became natural. I longed to get into the ring with some of the younger boys of Tommy Devlin's shows. Finally, my wish came true and I was slated to box Carl Kreckel before an audience of fans. I was only fourteen years old at the time and really thought I was about twenty. I "dolled up" for the affair and stepped into the ring for the first time in my life. Carl and I fought four rounds. Do not think we hurt one another very much, but our exhibition pleased the fans.

After this first fight, the older boys encouraged me to keep at the boxing game. They told me I would "make good" some day. I kept plugging away and worked out with the boys of my own age. Tommy Devlin took a great interest in me and taught me my first knowledge of the sport.²

Leo Houck's first fight with Carl Kreckel in 1902 resulted in a payday.³ Promoter Tommy Devlin gave each of the boys a silver dollar for his effort and a pair of boxing gloves. Devlin later revealed that the two boys' hands were so small that just before the fight he had to embark on a frantic search to find and buy children's gloves for their bout. Leo kept the pair of gloves into adulthood and stated that "they are one of my most prized possessions today."[4] Local sportswriter and boxing promoter Henry Hensel misspelled Leo Hauck's last name, changing it to Houck in the advance publicity for his first professional fight. "The spelling remained Houck for the rest of Leo's life."[5]

Leo's compensation for the fight certified his newfound status as a professional boxer. This was real money. The silver dollar Leo earned that day was more money than his father made during an entire workday. Leo continued to win purses and boxed exclusively in Lancaster, Pennsylvania, during the early years of his career. Years later, while living on 2nd Street in Lancaster, Leo saved enough money to buy the home and have his mother move in with his family. Joseph Hauck, Leo's son, referred to his father's actions by describing him as "a typical poor kid providing for his mother."[6]

After the fight with Kreckel, Leo and his father, Edward, probably walked home together from the Armory on West King Street to their row home on 654 Manor Street in the city's Eighth Ward and Cabbage-Hill section. Edward had just witnessed his son's transition from adolescence into the hardscrabble and gritty world of professional boxing. He saw Leo in action only once, the initial bout.[7] Leo did recall that his father was very much excited. "He had never witnessed a fight before."[8] Edward did approve of boxing and liked Bob Fitzsimmons, a middleweight, light heavyweight, and heavy weight champion of the late 1800s into the early 1900s.[9] On the other hand, Leo's mother and sisters regularly attended Leo's fights. In addition, Leo's younger brothers Frank and John also boxed. Occasionally, Frank or John appeared on the same boxing card with Leo.[10] "The fourth brother, Ed, never boxed but was a second for more than 80 percent of brother Leo's fights."[11]

John Hauck wrote about his mother and sister's reactions to Frank Hauck's ring battle with Rats McGrady. Here is an excerpt from Johnny's story submitted to the Lancaster press.

> My mother and sisters were the first women to ever attend boxing shows in this city. During those years it was mainly a man's sport. The night my late brother Leo defeated the giant Harry Ramsey, brother Frankie was on the undercard fighting Rats McGrady. McGrady scored a knockdown during the progress of the bout. When this happened, all eyes were centered upon my mother. The mob was curious to see how mother would take it seeing her son lying on the floor. She was the most calm person in the place, saying, "He'll get up." How true her prediction came, as Frankie, rising from the canvas, caught McGrady on the point of the jaw, knocking him out.[12]

Life for Leo was different from this moment forward. Serious conditioning, training, and sparring quickly replaced playing around the gym in the Armory with his buddies. Boxing was now serious business. Baseball, football, and basketball were sports Leo also participated in during his boxing career. Baseball was Leo's favorite sport and he remained passionate about it throughout his life.[13] While boxing professionally, he played baseball during 1911 for the Lancaster Red Roses, which was part of the Tri-State League, one of five different circuits in American minor league baseball. In addition, Leo's performance in the Tri-State League got him noticed and resulted in an offer to try out for the major leagues.[14]

Both Leo's father, Edward Hauck, and mother, Mary B. Woerner, emigrated from Germany to the United States sometime between 1870 and 1880. Edward emigrated from Langenleiten, located in the region of Bavaria, while Mary emigrated from Wurttemberg, which shared a boundary on the east with Bavaria. German immigration to the United

States occurred in three major tides. Edward may have been part of the second tide between 1865 and 1873. However, Mary was twelve years younger than Edward and may have been part of the third tide, which began in 1880.[15] "The ancestors of many of the Cabbage-Hill residents were Bavarian and Hessian German Nationals who fled to America around 1800. Almost all the residents were German for the next fifty-years."[16]

Leo Florian Hauck (Houck) was born November 14, 1888, in Lancaster, Lancaster County, Pennsylvania. There were six other siblings in Leo's family: Eleanor, born February 1882; Edward, born February 1887; Mary B., born April 1891; Frank A., born February 1893; Catherine, born May 1895; and John, born June 1898.

In order to fully appreciate Leo's early life and development, it is necessary to describe the Cabbage-Hill neighborhood where he grew up. Cabbage-Hill earned its name from the growing of cabbages to produce sauerkraut. The German-American immigrants living on Cabbage-Hill often grew cabbages in their backyards. The cabbages were harvested, combined with salts, and placed in large crocks to ferment over a period of weeks, resulting in sour cabbage or sauerkraut. During the early 1900s a sauerkraut factory, the Lancaster Vinegar Company, stood on Hazel Street in the Cabbage-Hill section of the city.[17]

The row homes on Cabbage-Hill all shared a basic and simple utilitarian configuration, but they were comfortable, having both heat and electricity. The neighborhood offered the inhabitants everything they needed to exist, including food, employment, and entertainment. Examples are the Conestoga Cotton Mills, Cheroot Tobacco Factory, Paulson's Bakery, Keiffer's Watch and Clock Shop, Fauber's Grocery, Barney Miller's Clothing Store, Kunzler's Meat Shop, Flear's Greenhouse, Peerless Umbrella Factory, Dodge Cork Company, and the Strand Theater.[18]

Cleanliness of both the residents' homes and the surrounding outdoor environments were of paramount importance, and clearly a source of pride with the German-American community. Many of the women, including Leo's mother Mary, routinely swept the sidewalks directly outside of their homes and scrubbed their porch steps every Saturday.[19]

"The most important source of identity was religious, and religious stability was maintained by St. Joseph's Catholic Church, the focal point of Cabbage-Hill."[20] St. Joseph's Church was established by a German contingent from St. Mary's Church, since that church was unable to hold the rapidly growing Catholic congregation.[21] St. Joseph's Church was the first ethnic parish in the United States, built during 1850.[22] All of Leo's family were Catholic, the predominant religion on Cabbage-Hill. Years later, Leo's youngest son Joe was bewildered upon discovering one of his friends on Cabbage-Hill had been Lutheran. "I thought everyone was Catholic. Everything your family did was centered on the church. You went to Mass, communion, baptisms, confessions, novenas, and were buried there."[23]

If you were Catholic you attended school at St. Joseph's. Leo attended the new St. Joseph's school, built in 1882 directly adjacent to the church.[24] The Sisters of Saint Francis staffed the school and provided the students with the equivalent of an eighth-grade education. This was typically the end of formal schooling for most students unless one pursued a higher education by attending either a trade school or possibly college. Leo's formal education ended with the completion of eighth grade.

Graduation from St. Joseph's at fourteen meant only one thing: joining the adult workforce, which Leo promptly did. Already embarked on a neophyte career in professional boxing, he soon discovered whether those efforts promised any real future in replacing a workingman's wages.

Many of Leo's contemporaries who boxed professionally during the same era, between 1900 and 1935, grew up in similar parochial, ethnic, and often poor working-class neighborhoods like Cabbage-Hill. One of the best-known boxers of that same era was heavyweight champion (1926–1928) Gene Tunney, often described by the press as the intellectual heavyweight champion. Tunney both read and recited Shakespeare. He shared a similar upbringing with Leo, having lived in the poor working-class neighborhood of Greenwich Village (West Village) in New York City. Gene learned to fight in the streets.

Billy Conn, a world light heavyweight champion (1939–1941), also grew up in a poor working-class Irish-American neighborhood in the East Liberty section of Pittsburgh, Pennsylvania. During an interview Billy said it best by describing what it was like to exist as a youngster in a poor working-class neighborhood. "Sure I was poor," Billy admitted to an interviewer. "Desperately poor. Not just a street kid. An alley kid. That's me. You ever see a rich kid fighting? I never did."[25]

During the early 1900s, adolescents from working-class neighborhoods who didn't pursue a higher education, worked and contributed supporting their families financially.

The Progressive Era of America emerged during the early 1900s, from 1901 to 1917, and created employment opportunities for the working class. "The opening years of the Twentieth Century were boom years for American cities. Filled with office and factory workers, shopkeepers, and immigrants, cities bulged and spread."[26] Lancaster benefited greatly during the Progressive Era. "Agriculture remained the major source of wealth in the country, but large manufacturing industries soon gave the farms some competition."[27] The city of Lancaster could boast that unemployment was nonexistent during the early 1900s. "By 1901, Lancaster could be described as a 'modern city' with a population of 46,000."[28]

During the Progressive Era in America, a small number of private citizens fostered an explosive new growth within the United States. They were called the Industrialists, and propelled the nation into becoming the leading industrial country of the world. Some of the most recognizable and well-known industrialists of the era were John D. Rockefeller, Henry Ford, Andrew Carnegie, and J. Pierpont Morgan. The fortunes they amassed compounded daily and were totally unencumbered by income taxes, which were nonexistent.

Conditions for the working class were quite different. Leo joined his father Edward, a night watchman, at the Hamilton Watch Factory in 1902, at the age of fourteen, working as an office boy in the finishing department until 1906.[29] Workers like Edward and Leo typically spent between eleven and twelve hours on the job each day. Edward worked seven days per week throughout the year, earning $9.45 weekly.[30] Many housewives on Cabbage-Hill supplemented their families' incomes by stripping tobacco at home for the tobacco factories located in the city. Their pay was based on a piecework pay scale.[31]

Leo's eighty-hour workweeks and young age conjure up images of the 1800s Dickensian workhouses. However, the long workweek did little to dampen his enthusiasm and spirit for boxing. Nevertheless, the hard work and the commitment necessary to accomplish the same, provided a solid foundation which shaped Leo's adolescent life. Work and daily hardships served as a discipline. He learned to direct and successfully apply that discipline to every challenge throughout his adult life.

Something else besides working at the Hamilton Watch Factory had also captured Leo's interest. He needed to chase his dreams and train for the next fight.

2

Turning Professional at Fourteen

My earlier fights were no pink tea affairs like some of these which beginners in the ring game have today. I took on all comers and met some tough boys.[1]

My next professional bout was Leo (Baldy) Fritsch. Harry Hensel was the promoter and the match was staged in the old Prince Street Hall. Clippings of this fight which I still have say that it was a good exhibition for beginners. It was four rounds duration and we each received $2.50 as a purse. My next appearance in the ring was October 20, 1904. I fought the preliminary with Herb (Young Warren) Eshleman of the Norwood Athletic Club. I remember the fight very well. Kid Williams, of Brooklyn, and Bobby Thompson, of Toronto, fought the windup at the Mannerchor Hall. I wanted to make good and fought like a demon. Referee Schlichter stopped the bout in the fourth round, claiming that Warren had too much weight on me. The purse this time was $5.00 so you can see I was advancing with each scrap. I fought a couple of more fights before the end of the year, but none of them of any importance.[2]

Some years before Leo's first fight, Jack Milley, a former fighter from the Fairmont section of Philadelphia, moved with his family to Lancaster. While still living in Philadelphia, Milley learned how to box from Tom O'Hara, an accomplished lightweight who fought from 1899 to 1916, amassing a total of 71 bouts. He took an interest in Jack and taught him the finer points of the game.[3]

Milley established a gym located on the southwest corner of Chestnut and Christian Streets in Lancaster, where he trained and conditioned up-and-coming boxers. He also played baseball and boxed for H.H. Hensel at the old Lancaster Athletic Club.[4] At the conclusion of his boxing career, Milley continued to attend the fights at the Armory, the Lancaster Athletic Club (A.C.), and the Maennerchor Club as both a spectator and referee. Some of the champions Milley officiated for during that era included Luther McCarthy, George Chip, Jack Dillon, and Battling Levinsky, all premier fighters of the day.[5]

After Leo passed away, his newspaper obituaries stated that Milley was present at Leo's first fight, saw promise in the scrappy youngster, and soon afterward took Leo under his wing, guiding him successfully throughout his early years of boxing. Milley's presence at Leo's first fight is entirely speculative.[6]

However, part of the reporting is true. Milley did indeed train and condition Leo, beginning sometime during 1904 and continuing until 1910. After 1910, Leo came under the management of Lew Durlacher, who managed Leo during his middleweight years.

John Hauck, Leo's youngest brother, wrote a recurring newspaper column for the

Daily Intelligencer called "Hauck's Corner." In one column titled "The Grim Reaper Strikes," John reported the most accurate accounting of Leo's first meeting with Jack Milley. The article was a remembrance of both Jack Milley and Charlie Wright, another noteworthy presence during Lancaster's thriving boxing scene.[7] This excerpt from "The Grim Reaper" describes Leo's first meeting with Jack Milley.

> One day while Milley was playing baseball, a timid youngster came up to him tugging his trousers, at the same time saying, "I am interested in learning to box, will you teach me?" Milley could not help but smile at the boy, but told him to come around to the gym the following week. Sure enough, on the appointed time the fourteen-year-old lad was there smiling to his heart's content thinking here is his chance to learn the game he loved so well. The shy youngster was saying, "I like the sport and I aim to become a pugilist." Milley then asked how he became interested in boxing. The youth answered that he went to all the boxing shows that were held at the Lancaster A.C. where he saw such champions as Jack Johnson, Joe Gans, Jack O'Brian and all the rest of the greats of that day. The boy became so fascinated by the skill of the champions that he made up his mind that he was going to try and be like them. That is how he came to ask Professor Milley to teach him the art of boxing. It did not take Milley long to see that this kid was very adept to learning. At the age of fourteen the boy was started off on a career that practically carried him halfway around the world. The youth turned out to be none other than Leo Houck.[8]

Jack Milley (standing) was Leo's first fulltime trainer. He was unquestionably one of the most influential people in Leo's life during the first ten years of his professional boxing career. Leo met Jack Milley only weeks after Edward, his father, passed away at age fifty. Jack was a surrogate father figure who venerated his young protégé. He skillfully developed Leo's natural athletic talent and boxing skills by never overmatching him early on with more seasoned opponents (courtesy LancasterHistory.org, Lancaster, Pennsylvania, MG-63, JH-04-06-27).

Unfortunately, Leo's father, Edward, passed away on March 4, 1904, succumbing to typhoid fever at age fifty. He saw Leo fight only one time. Leo's first meeting with Milley and Edward's death may have been only weeks apart. Needless to say, Leo, his six siblings, and a newly widowed mother now faced difficult emotional and financial times. Without hesitation, Leo responded to the loss of his father like a mature adult and readily accepted his new responsibilities at home. He continued to work long hours at the Hamilton Watch Factory; the income Leo earned helped to support the family throughout this difficult period. After 1906, Leo left the Hamilton Watch Factory and concentrated on boxing professionally. The purses he earned boxing quickly surpassed the day wages he earned at the factory.

"'Fighters are born, not made,' is a favorite expression amongst managers, trainers and those closely connected with the sweet science of fistiania."[9] Stanley Ketchel, the middleweight champion from 1908 to 1910, who was never formerly trained, fit that simple criterion.[10] Counter that favorite expression with a more practical theory. Almost all fighters require "being made" in order to establish a successful boxing career. The blending of talent, training, conditioning, and timing is the proven formula necessary to become a successful fighting machine. Timing is a critical element of the fight game, inside and outside the ring. Timing also includes chance meetings which suddenly introduce new, and sometimes irreplaceable, individuals into a fighter's life. The meeting of Leo, the untrained youngster, and Jack Milley, the seasoned boxer and trainer, illustrate this other type of timing. Without a doubt their relationship changed both of their lives forever. After all, not all "born fighters" will ever have their talents fully realized without someone like Milley, who was able to recognize, identify, and develop the raw innate abilities of a pure athlete—in this case, Leo Houck.

Leo's conditioning under Milley commenced sometime after the October 20, 1904, fight with Herb Eshleman, also known as Young Warren. The training pointed Leo toward a match-up on February 17, 1905, with Walter "Shorty" Groff. John Hauck's article, "The Grim Reaper Strikes," details the history leading up to Leo's match with Groff.

> Milley was so proud of young Houck that he became involved in an argument about Houck's ability. At that time Shorty Groff, the best boxer in Lancaster at his weight, was going at a terrific clip. He had just boxed Griff Jones, the American flyweight champion, in Lancaster. The fellow Milley was arguing with was very boisterous, in fact to such an extent that Milley became angry. He pulled out a roll of bills from his pocket at the same time saying, "He would bet that Houck would whip Groff." The boisterous one laughed heartily and covered the bet. Milley lost no time in arranging the match with all kinds of criticism hurled at him. The fans, believing that the boy would become injured as he only had one fight, and Groff had fought the American flyweight champion. The result was a capacity house, with the excitement at high pitch.[11]
>
> To the amazement of everyone, Milley's young champion gave the veteran Groff an artistic boxing lesson. A boy of fifteen years of age defeating a mature man of thirty was almost unheard of, but this proves that Jack Milley had a wonderful boxing mind. The writer has seen much boxing in his forty-seven years of his life, but there is always an incident that I will never forget. Forty years ago I witnessed the mastermind Milley instructing my brother, Leo. This was a thing of beauty to watch. Houck and Milley went through the moves in such a manner that it was perfection. Had these two decided to go on the stage the audience would have thought it to be a real fight. Milley left nothing unturned in his teaching. He really brought the fight out of Houck that was in him and developed his defense to such an extent that it carried Houck through a great and glorious career.[12]

Henry Hensel and Walter Schlichter, who both promoted boxing shows at the Lancaster A.C., matched Leo with Shorty Groff for the preliminary to the Joe Grimm-Dixie Kid windup.[13] One can easily imagine that the fight between Leo and Groff may have induced a bit of pandemonium for the fans attending it. Often these local fights led to fisticuffs between a few of the spectators who got carried away in the excitement, or stood to lose their wagers. In any event, many years later, Leo provided his own account of the fight with Groff in his column titled "My Twenty Years of Boxing."[14]

> My first real assignment in the ring was with Shorty Groff, another local product. He was a clever boxer and with Nev Campbell were the best boxers in Lancaster at that time. He was years older than myself and had all the advantages of experience and boxing knowledge. All I had in my favor was

youth and the determination to make good. I needed both in this bout. My youth stood me in good stead and I won the popular decision. Fifteen dollars was the sum I received for my services with the promise of other bouts.[15]

The sports fans said we have a fine exhibition. They called me a mere boy and said I was getting along fine. They gave me the popular decision over Shorty and I felt pretty good over it. "Shorty" is a local boy and will remember this fight. The older boys said our bout was not surpassed during the entire show. This was on the night of February 17, 1905.

I was then seventeen years old and started to gain weight. Was very anxious to build up my endurance. Took part in all kinds of sports. During the summer months I played baseball and kept in the best of condition. Everyone told me to take care of myself. I have always put this first in my training.[16]

Leo's account of his win over Groff is a terse recitation of the facts. His accomplishment begs for some boastfulness, but there is none. The humility and modesty Leo exhibited remained constant throughout his life. In time, those values were described by sportswriters, exalted by friends, and recognized by Leo's boxing opponents as some of his greatest attributes. His quiet self-confidence and abilities as a boxer utterly negated any reason for braggadocio. Years later, those same values of modesty, humility, morality, and honesty were imbued early on to all the Hauck children.[17] More importantly, these values were securely tethered to a fundamental belief in God and a strong Catholic faith.

Once again, Leo's youngest brother, John, understood and documented what may be the single and most important insight into the depth of Leo's and Jack Milley's friendship in this final excerpt from John's article "The Grim Reaper."

One can hardly realize this as he was always a fatherly and kind gentleman with a ready smile that made many friends for him. His pride and joy was that he was the man that taught Leo Houck the art of self-defense. He was loyal to his pupil to the last. His daughter, Catherine, told the writer that her Dad had a huge photo of Houck hanging in his bedroom, giving orders to never remove the picture as long as he lived. He saw his idol the last thing he did before he retired, and the first thing upon arising in the morning. Yes, dear readers, this is what you call real friendship. Lancaster's pioneer boxing teacher was laid to rest at a little village called Millersville. As the writer was standing graveside, he could not help but notice the wonderful rolling scenery nearby, in fact you could call it paradise on earth. A most befitting place for the beloved Milley to be laid to rest. Houck, his idol, with his brawny hands and bowed head helped lower the body into Mother Earth. If Jack knew, how he would of [sic] loved this. May his soul rest in peace.[18]

John's writing creates the poignant feeling that Milley became a surrogate father figure for Leo after his father passed away. Even though Leo fulfilled his family and work responsibilities like a mature adult after losing his father, he was still chronologically and emotionally an adolescent. All youngsters long for someone to look up to and admire, especially after the loss of a father. The timing of Leo and Milley's meeting and subsequent friendship needs to be recognized as one of the most significant and transformational moments of Leo's young life. Leo's boxing apprenticeship with Milley lasted until 1910.

Leo's metamorphosis from a flyweight to heavyweight occurred during an era in Pennsylvania when "no actual commission existed for fight promotions or boxing regulations, so all the responsibility fell on the shoulders of the newspapers. The prizefighter or manager would issue a challenge to some other fighter in the city by placing the challenge in the newspapers."[19] This led to the creation of Athletic Clubs (A.C.), Athletic Associations (A.A.) and Social Clubs (S.C.) in Pennsylvania, where boxing matches were advertised as "boxing shows." "Athletic and social clubs introduced more standardization and regulations for promoting boxing matches."[20]

During Leo's boxing career, the majority of his bouts were decided by a device called the "newspaper-decision." It worked this way. Sportswriters attended the fights, recorded and analyzed the action, returned to the office, and published their decision about who won the bout and why.

The "newspaper-decision" was a vulnerable process susceptible to reporting errors. For example, sportswriters covering boxing sometimes made incorrect decisions regarding the outcome of any given bout. At times multiple newspapers and their respective reporters published different outcomes for the same bout. In addition, "if both men were still on their feet at the end of a match, it was called a no-decision bout, with no official winner. The no-decision regulation was intended to foil crooked gamblers by making it harder to influence the boxers, referees, or judges. However, the newspaper reporters who often identified the winners of no-decision bouts were still vulnerable to payoffs."[21]

Newspaper reports of Leo's fights sometimes provided differing outcomes from those currently recorded in the official boxing records. The boxing chronology presented in Part II was based entirely on newspaper reports and newspaper-decisions from various sources throughout the United States. No attempt will be made to dispute or challenge official boxing records, regardless of what appear to be discrepancies either in the reporting or the recording of outcomes for specific boxing matches, since Leo is now permanently ensconced in the Ring Magazine Hall of Fame, the Pennsylvania Sports Hall of Fame, and the International Boxing Hall of Fame. Perhaps Charles A. Lindbergh's insightful views concerning the nature of records offers a sensible perspective for anyone while engaged in reviewing, writing, reading, and attempting to make sense of historical statistics and records.

> Records, on the other hand, illuminate the corners with which they are concerned, and surround your mind with contemporary problems. They are relatively specialized, sometimes contradictory, and often incomplete. They restrict your perspective by bringing you too close to the area they cover. But they offer in precision for what they lack in breadth.[22]

Mandatory rules and regulations governing the sport of boxing and how decisions were officially rendered only came into existence during 1923, with the creation of the Pennsylvania Boxing Commission.[23]

PART II

The Boxing Years

3

Winning at Home, 1905–1906–1907

Leo was one of the few top ring men—Willie Meehan and Georges Carpentier, were two others whose careers carried them all the way from tiny flyweights to the burley heavyweights. At the time Houck started fistic operations, there was no official flyweight class, and Leo fought as a bantam, but he didn't tote much more than 100 pounds at a time. Towards the end of his 20-year span in the ring, the Lancastrian had filled out into a light-heavy, scaling 175, but he was never one to quibble about a few pounds here and there, and several times he stepped in with the big 'uns.[1]

1905

Leo's exciting victory over Shorty Groff on February 17 did not go unnoticed by promoter Henry Hensel, who recognized that Leo had the potential to keep on winning, and hopefully attracting new spectators into the Lancaster A.C. New spectators often turned into devoted fans who continued to attend the boxing shows, which filled seats and produced larger gates. Hensel wasted no time in signing Pinky Evans for Leo's next bout on April 17. The six-round bout ended as a draw.

1906

Jack Milley, Leo's trainer, kept him busy during this year but not at an overwhelming pace. Leo boxed one fight a month up until June 4, and then had almost four months off, which allowed him to participate in the other sports that he loved—baseball, basketball, and football. Leo conditioned himself throughout his career by participating in other sports during active boxing seasons as well as any interval of extended downtime available between fights.

Leo fought almost exclusively in Lancaster during the early part of his career. Most of his opponents lived in Lancaster or the neighboring towns of Columbia, Quarryville, Harrisburg, and Reading. In addition, the northern Pennsylvania coal region towns of Shenandoah, Mt. Carmel, and Hazelton also produced some sturdy boys eager to meet Leo in the squared circle. The communities that gave birth to all these boxers "were so tough that even the canary birds sang bass."[2]

Leo F. Houck (seated, left, second row) at sixteen years of age posing with the 8th Ward Football Team during 1906, his second year of professional boxing. Leo continued to play baseball, basketball, football, and sometimes all three, during each boxing season throughout his career (courtesy LancasterHistory.org, Lancaster, Pennsylvania, John Hauck Collection, MG-63, JH-03-09-12).

These boxers represented a primordial pool of tough local fighters. Lancaster was quickly becoming an important boxing mecca due largely to the aggressive promotions of Harry H. Hensel and H. Walter Schlichter. However, Lancaster existed as a smaller satellite that revolved around the larger urban boxing universe of Philadelphia, approximately seventy miles to the east.

This year was probably Leo's first with multiple bouts scheduled throughout the year. Jack Milley's prior experience in the boxing ring as a fighter came in handy and provided a measured approach to the type of opponent Leo needed to box, and how often. Milley understood that advancing Leo too quickly was something to be avoided and paid little attention to promoters who suggested matches with seasoned journeymen fighters, intending to use Leo as a steppingstone. However, Leo was never intimidated, even early on, and quickly accepted challenges from all fighters, often disregarding warnings from Milley, concerned friends, and boxing associates about engaging opponents with notable records as knockout artists.

Leo's first three fights of the season received little if any newspaper coverage. His first bout of the year, a six-rounder, earned him a newspaper-decision win against "Young" Jack Hanlon on January 24, in Lancaster.

One month later, Leo fought Tommy Dugan in Lancaster and knocked him out during the second round.

Fourteen days later, on March 7, Leo fought and received a newspaper-decision win over Sam Parks in a six-rounder in Lancaster. Their rematch, a six-rounder, on April 18 in Lancaster ended as a draw.

Leo's next boxing show, on May 17, took on a carnival nature. Prior to his bout with Jimmy Livingston, a match between Young Watson and Jimmy Casey from Philadelphia went three fake rounds until they were chased from the ring by the referee."[3] However, all the staged fakery ended during Leo's bout when he sent Livingston to the canvas in the fourth round. The bout was recorded as a knockout for Leo.

"Gilmore Day" on May 29 in Lancaster was advertised as a day with "Plenty of Good Sport." The day's events included a parade with over thirty bands, baseball games, and a boxing show for the finale. Leo faced Hughey McCann that evening. The Caspar midgets appeared in an exhibition fight before the McCann-Houck bout. Unfortunately, McCann had little cause for celebration on Gilmore Day. Leo knocked him out in the fifth round.[4]

The next bout on October 18 with Jack Britton from Clinton, New York, produced a six-round victory for Leo. This fight was significant because Britton was the first future champion Leo defeated in the ring. Britton achieved the Welterweight Championship the first time in 1915 and held the same title from 1916 to 1917, and again from 1919 to 1922. He fought a total of 344 bouts and officially retired from boxing at age forty-four.[5]

The year ended on an up note for Leo with a December 13 technical knockout over Eddie Wallace in the fifth round. Leo's first season under Jack Milley's tutelage was a complete success. Milley arranged plenty of work for Leo but not an unreasonable number of matches. The breaks in between the bouts were sufficient, and most importantly, Milley never overmatched his fighter with seasoned boxers out of his class, but instead allowed him to gain confidence and mature in the ring gradually.

1907

The New Year started out well for Leo. On January 24 he showed Young Marshall the stars with a KO in the second round. Leo recalled this fight as his "First Kayo Thrill" and described what the experience was like.

> I'll never forget the night. The hall was packed to the rafters. In the third round Marshall rushed in wide open and seeing an opportunity I crashed my right to his jaw. Marshall went down with a thud. It was the first knockdown I had ever scored in the ring and I did not know what to do. Walter Schlichter, the referee, had to hold me off while he counted, to keep me from hitting Marshall while he was down. After Schlichter had counted the fatal ten, I only started to come to my senses. I felt very happy but at the same time I was sorry for Marshall. That kayo gave me confidence. From this time on my aim was to fight my way into the wind-up class. I reached that goal the next year.[6]

The KO over Marshall recounted by Leo was an experience that stayed with him his entire career. However, there were other bouts where newspaper reporters hinted at Leo's hesitancy to "put away" or to "carry" an opponent when he was clearly the better fighter. The experience of the Marshall knockout remained as an ever-present memory throughout Leo's career and sometimes changed his overall strategy in the ring, especially when facing a weaker or less experienced opponent.[7]

Leo's next fight, on February 24, with William Broad, aka Young Kid Broad, ended as a second-round TKO over Broad.[8] The newspaper reported that the fight lasted a round and a half, with Leo breaking his thumb on Broad's hard head.[9] Leo and Young

Kid Broad had a rematch on April 5 in another six-rounder, where Leo shaded Broad for the win.[10]

Buck Eagan faced Leo in a six-rounder on April 25 in the "hottest fight of the evening. Egan was almost out when the gong saved him."[11] This fight was a newspaper-decision win for Leo.[12]

Reddy Moore, a Philadelphia boxer, was hailed as 'the wonderful Philadelphia boy' who has never been whipped. "He met Sam Parks twice and now thinks he is good enough for Houck."[13] Leo and Moore boasted similar records regarding Parks. Moore defeated Parks twice. Leo won over Parks and fought him to a draw during 1906. Moore wanted "to show Houck that he is his master."[14] The six-rounder ended as a newspaper-decision draw.

One newspaper column called "With the Fighters" reported that Leo's next bout on October 17 against Frankie Moore ended as a good draw.[15]

Leo got his first wind-up fight this year against Frank Beaber, aka Kid Beebe, a more experienced lightweight pugilist from Philadelphia.[16] The Lancaster A.C. fight fans witnessed Leo "outgeneraling and outpunching Beebe."[17] Leo pleased the fans during the main event and did himself proud by outpointing and outboxing the Philadelphia prizefighter.[18]

After returning to Philadelphia, Kid Beebe quickly sought out the press and complained mightily to any sportswriter willing to pay attention, by stating "I clearly earned that decision and to have given it a draw [would have been] an injustice, but I feel disgusted after working as I did then have the decision given against me. Houck had a look-in one round, the fourth, but he is the only fighter they have in Lancaster and the correspondents have to plug his game along to make him such a drawing card, no matter how much they hurt the other fellow."[19] Moreover, Beebe complained to the press that Houck weighed too much for him.[20]

The publicity generated over Beebe's sour grapes necessitated another match between Houck and Beebe. They were matched again at their own request as well as the hundreds of patrons who attended the November 14 fight.[21] The accusations from the big-city fighter, looking to even the score with the less experienced country boxer, whipped up the excitement level of the fans, making the eyes of promoters Hensel and Schlichter reflect dollar bills in anticipation of a profitable gate.

All the commotion generated by Beebe in the press deserved a response by Houck. After all, he could talk to the press just as easily as Beebe. At first, Houck said "he would fight Beebe for nothing."[22] Finally, Leo took one more parting shot at Beebe by stating that he (Leo) "did the trick last time they met and will prove it more conclusively at the next show."[23] Once again, Leo received the newspaper-decision win over Beebe. Kid Beebe returned to Philadelphia a beaten and less talkative loser. Leo's two wins over Kid Beebe contributed to his growing reputation as a fighter who routinely sent those "Quaker City Lads" home holding the short end of the purse.[24]

Leo concluded the 1907 season with a total of eight straight wins and a cumulative total of nineteen straight victories since 1905.

4

Lightweight Champion of Lancaster County, 1908–1909

1908

Kid Daly, from New York City, received a severe trouncing from Leo on January 16 at the Lancaster A.C. One newspaper reported that Leo Houck "failed to put him out, though he had him groggy."[1] The fight was a six-rounder and a newspaper-decision win for Leo. After the Kid Daly win and two decisive wins over Kid Beebe in 1907, the Lancaster fans embraced Leo as a legitimate lightweight contender. Those fans were eager to see Leo move up and knew the next bout scheduled for February 20 between him and Tommy O'Keefe had the potential "to be a corker."[2] From Philadelphia, O'Keefe had a sleight weight disadvantage, but that factor seemed negligible in this match-up. He had also met Kid Beebe twice during 1907, which resulted in two wins over Beebe.[3]

The wind-up fight between O'Keefe and Houck treated the fans to a rousing donnybrook. The *Harrisburg Daily Independent* covered the fight and reported it this way:

> Lancaster's own Leo Houck was bested in the wind-up by Tommy O'Keefe. The Irishman had everything in his favor and in the last round gave Leo a sound drubbing. Houck was in no danger of going out. In the early rounds Houck gruelled [mauled] Tommy severely several times, and in the fourth O'Keefe went wild and seldom landed. Houck got rattled in the last round and Tommy pounded him hard.[4]

The six round-fight was recorded as a newspaper-decision loss for Leo.

Leo had a one-month layoff before his next fight with Percy Cove. The *Courier* reported, "Percy Cove is a stranger, but he is the goods. He comes from Seattle, is a very tall boy for his weight, and can go the route. He has been trying to match up with Houck for some time."[5] Within a relatively short period of several boxing seasons, the now twenty-year-old Houck had already garnered the attention of the West Coast boxing community. The six-round bout between Cove and Houck was scheduled for March 19. Leo described their fight in his story titled "Cove's Left Too Much for Houck."

> The fight with Cove was rather disappointing. It was expected to be a sensational affair because of the advance reports concerning the westerner. Cove had a peculiar build. He was a tall angular fellow with a mighty reach and a peculiar style. He had me either up in the air or down on the ground continually. We started after each other at the top of the opening bell, or at least, I started after Cove, but he kept me at a distance with his left hand. He was so tall I thought he was on stilts. In the sixth I

23

tore into the lanky westerner and finally had him holding on to save himself. This was the only round I could claim while Cove had piled up a lead with his long left in the other five sessions. There was no question as to who was the winner.[6]

The six-round battle ended as a newspaper-decision win for Cove.[7]

Several days after the fight, Cove went to Philadelphia, where he met and formed a friendship with Duke Kelly, who eventually became Leo's manager. Cove told Kelly that Leo had broken one of his ribs during their March 19 bout. After several more fights in Philadelphia, Cove returned to Seattle, his hometown, and eventually enlisted in the famous Princess Pat Regiment. He died in battle after being wounded thirteen times.

Next up was Willie Lucas, aka Kid Lucas, an accomplished Philadelphia lightweight scheduled to fight Leo on April 16 in a six-round bout.[8] "The *Harrisburg Telegraph* reported Kid Lucas and Leo Houck fought a hard six-round-go with honors about even."[9] The newspaper-decision was a draw.

Like the schedule of 1907, the 1908 boxing season included a total of eight fights. Leo fought one more time during April, and lost on a newspaper-decision April 25 to Phil Griffin in Philadelphia at the National A.C. After this fight Leo immediately began a several-month layoff during which he played baseball, basketball, or football. It mattered little to Leo which particular season was about to start or was currently underway. He was always sought after as a player, no matter what sport, and usually took the helm as the team captain. The Lancaster newspapers often called the team he played for "Leo Houck's Team." His increasing notoriety in the ring as a skilled boxer, combined with his other athletic gifts out of the ring, made Leo a widely recognized local and regional sports figure. Leo did two things exceedingly well no matter what the venue: he always demonstrated his best and never disappointed his fans with a lackluster performance. One thing was certain: Leo was always a great drawing card. Ticket sales for a ball game, tournament, or boxing show increased when he appeared on a team's roster or as the wind-up for an upcoming boxing show.

Participation in other sports while on a layoff from boxing kept Leo in condition all year. However, Leo never totally abandoned training between fights or before he would face a dangerous portside slinger or an expert knockout artist.

Right out of the gate on October 15, in his first fight after the layoff, Leo scored a TKO in the second round. "Harry Kegel started good but Houck soon got to his head and stomach. To avoid a knockout Referee Schlichter stopped the bout."[10]

The Kegel bout was a great confidence booster, and Leo would need all he could get for an October 19 engagement with George Decker. The newspapers touted Decker as a great "Philadelphia Boy," just like another previous opponent of Leo's, Reddy Moore, also hailed by the newspapers as the "Wonderful Philadelphia Boy." One may have started to believe all the boxers from Philadelphia were great, wonderful, had more stamina, punched harder, and owned better records than their countrified Lancaster cousins, or so touted the newspapers of the era.

Decker actually started his career in Lancaster but moved to the larger boxing arena of Philadelphia. In this case, Decker was still a favorite with the Lancaster fans. He previously fought in New York at the Roman Club, and at the Armory Athletic Association in Boston, and was soon to meet Charley Griffin, the Australian champion. This particular match-up between Decker and Houck on November 19 took over a year to arrange. The *Courier* reported that "he [Decker] will find Houck better than ever."[11]

The outcome was a newspaper-decision draw. "Leo Houck the champion in his class in Lancaster County stood off George Decker, of Philadelphia, in the wind-up. The Lancaster boy was full of fight and the Philadelphian had his hands full from the start to finish."[12] Decker was touted by the newspapers as a viable contender in his class prior to meeting Leo. The fight result, even though it was a draw, telegraphed a message to Leo's brain that he was clearly on his way to becoming a contender too, possibly a season or two away from a top-ten nationwide ranking.

Each boxing fan of that era anticipated a just redemption for his favorite boxer whenever he suffered a defeat by some out-of-town rival. Everyone lied if he told you otherwise. On the other hand, redemption for a boxer is just a euphemism for retribution. Leo had a solid fan base in Lancaster and his fans' collective patience while waiting for the Griffin rematch was soon to be rewarded. Approximately seven months after the loss to Griffin on April 25, Leo concluded the 1908 season on December 17 with a newspaper-decision win over Griffin. "Houck had by far the best of the argument and Griffin had all he could do to stay on his feet."[13]

The 1908 boxing schedule yielded three wins, three losses, and two draws for Leo from a total of eight bouts.

1909

Eddie McAvoy, a Philadelphia fighter, visited the Lancaster A.C. on January 14 for a six-round bout with Leo, the new lightweight champion of Lancaster County. The *Harrisburg Telegraph* reported that McAvoy cleverly blocked any rushing attempt by Leo, and both excelled at a tough give-and-take during any infighting. "McAvoy's infighting was particularly severe, but Houck's stiff punches on the jaw balanced matters. Early on in the last round McAvoy appeared in danger under Houck's repeated rushes, but he managed to last the round."[14] The *Harrisburg Telegraph* reporter described this bout as "finishing even."[15] Leo received a newspaper-decision loss for it.[16]

Jack Britton may have been one of the best boxers Leo met early on in his career. Their next bout, scheduled for February 4, was their second meeting since Leo's win over Britton in 1906. "From start to finish they were at it with both fists, putting it all over each other. In the fifth round Houck went to the mat on one knee but recovered instantly. The last round was Houck's, who on the whole had the better of the battle."[17] The newspaper-decision was a win for Leo.[18] Once again, Leo bested Britton, a future welterweight champion.

During the second round of Leo's next fight at the Lancaster A.C., on February 18, Leo drew first blood on Rosario Lucas, aka Kid Locke. Two rounds later Locke planted a dazzling right hook to Leo's jaw. He immediately dropped to the mat and took a full count.[19] The knockdown occurred in the fourth round of the six-round bout. Lightning-fast double jabs and a punishing infighting style were the underpinnings of Leo's fundamental style of boxing. Locke cleverly avoided any infighting during this match. While Leo "was looked upon as having received the worst of last night's bout at Lancaster, his admirers here claim that he worked under a slight disadvantage because of a minor illness. Leo admitted he caught a cold during training prior to the fight but fulfilled his engagement anyway because he did not care to disappoint his friends and fans."[20]

One thing the fans did not know about the fight was just how close Leo came to being knocked out during the fourth round. Leo described the experience in detail in an article titled "Locke's Right Taught Houck to Be Cautious."

> Jack Milley, my manager, and my brothers Ed and Frank were in my corner. They advised me to keep alert, but I became careless after the first two rounds. We were sparring around in the center of the ring, when suddenly someone turned off the huge arc light which hung over the ring or at least that is the sensation I had. What really happened was that Locke plugged me on the chin with a terrific right hand punch. In a few seconds I began to recover and I realized what happened. I could hear referee Schlichter counting and my brothers and Milley yelling to take the count. At the count of nine I got to my feet and rushed into a clinch, for further time to recover. That right hand smash taught me not to run into an opponent with my hands down.[21]

The *Harrisburg Telegraph* and the *Harrisburg Daily Independent* fight reports seemed to promise a loss for Leo—even Leo believed Locke would get the decision—yet the newspaper-decision rendered it a draw.

Over 2,500 fans were expected to attend Leo's next bout against Grover Hayes of Chicago on February 23 at the Harrisburg Boxing Club. Hayes had stayed twelve rounds to a draw in two fights during 1908 with the formidable English champion Jim Driscoll, who ended his career with an astounding 47 percent knockout rate.[22] Needless to say, the matchup was a distinct bump-up in class for Leo, although he was not picked to come out on top over Hayes, who was considered the more skillful pugilist. The *Harrisburg Telegraph* said this about Leo: "If he succeeds in whipping Hayes it will place him in line to meet the best men in the country at his weight."[23] Lew Durlacher was to referee the fight. Houck knew that Durlacher managed a few boxers from Philadelphia and he had refereed a few of Leo's earlier bouts. At this time, Leo had no idea that Durlacher would soon play a prominent role in his life.

The *Harrisburg Daily Independent* published a detailed account of the Hayes-Houck fight titled "Hayes Meets Foe Worthy of His Steel." Excerpts from the story follow.

> Leo Houck, than whom there is no greater personage in the vicinity of Lancaster, discovered to his immense satisfaction that he could fight a first class pugilist for six rounds without striking his colors. He and Grover Hayes formed the stellar attraction and when it was over and done critics awarded him a tie with Hayes. That is going some for Leo.
> At the completion of each round Hayes walked to his corner, seated himself, and was languidly fanned by two trainers like an Oriental beauty. There was no throwing of water, gulping down of stimulants, and so on.
> With Houck it was different. His seconds worked hard to get him in fighting trim. He showed unmistakable signs of fatigue, but bobbed up the next round and took his medicine unflinchingly. Also he delivered some of the same dose.
> Machine-like precision marked every movement of Hayes. Not once did he strike out that it did not seem he had carefully calculated each blow. There was no hurry or fussing. Everything was done with calm and sober consideration, it seemed. There was very little to choose from in the first two rounds. Hayes when he got close quarters worked his hands like piston rods, landing blow after blow on Houck's body. In the sixth Hayes started out as if he would like to finish Houck, but the game Lancasterian blocked neatly.[24]

Seventeen years later, Leo provided his own account of the fight.

> My first out of town bout in the wind-up class was in Harrisburg in February of 1909. Grover Hayes of Philadelphia was my opponent.
> I was timid during the first round, but after that I forgot all about the crowd and would never have known there was anybody around save myself and Hayes, had it not been for the cheering. I wasn't certain I had won, but when the Harrisburg papers gave me the decision I was very happy. I had

defeated one of the best lightweights of the day and realized greater things were in store for me as a boxer.[25]

Nine days later on March 4, Leo faced Young Kid Broad at the Lancaster A.C. in another six-round bout. The newspaper-decision win over Broad set Leo up perfectly for the next fight against a tenacious Jack Britton. The March 18 bout with Britton was their third and last time in the squared circle. Britton always gave Leo a fast-paced six-round fight, and this fight was no different. The *Philadelphia Item* reported the fight as a newspaper-decision draw.[26]

Once again, Leo looked forward to a five-month layoff, which started on May 15. First, he needed to get past a rematch scheduled for March 27 against Grover Hayes. This fight occurred approximately one month after Leo's initial win over Hayes. They fought the semi-wind-up bout at the National A.C. in Philadelphia.[27] "Grover sustained a cut over the eye in the fifth round, which bled considerably in the last two rounds. He did not box as cleverly as usual, and seemed bent on trying to knockout Houck with hard punches to the head and stomach."[28] The fight outcome was a newspaper-decision draw.

Leo started to dream about manicured baseball diamonds and the lush emerald green outfields that waited for him. However, there was one last bit of business before his layoff, which was Tommy O'Keefe, an accomplished lightweight from Philadelphia.[29] Their six-round engagement was held on May 14 at the Lancaster A.C.

"Tommy O'Keefe found more than his match in Leo Houck, in a rattling six round battle. Houck had the better of every round, and at the commencement of the first rushed Tommy to the ropes. O'Keefe slipped away, however, and the fight went the limit. Houck was continually after his man, and Tommy several times saved himself by clinching at critical points. He appeared unable to hold his guard under Houck's sledge-hammer blows."[30] Leo's bull-rush, double jab, and close infighting worked and earned him another newspaper-decision win.

Jack Milley looked out for his beloved protégé and approved of the layoffs for Leo during the boxing season. Layoffs produced a strengthened reconstitution of flesh, bone, and blood. Milley played baseball himself and knew that the benefits of playing other sports during a layoff also helped to maintain Leo's conditioning. This strategy gave Leo time to recover or rehabilitate from any nagging injuries sustained during his ring battles. However, Leo occasionally received new injuries during layoffs that sometimes delayed his scheduled return to the ring. Many fighters of that era fought at least one or two times a week throughout an entire year.[31]

The Lancaster fans watched Leo return from the five-month layoff to win a newspaper-decision over Mike Fleming on October 14 at the Lancaster A.C.

Joe Sieger, from Denver, Colorado, the strongest man Leo had ever been against, was his opponent on November 11 at the Lancaster A.C.[32] Both Houck and Sieger met and defeated common opponents Tommy O'Keefe and Young Kid Broad. The *Courier* claimed the Sieger-Houck matchup would be a grudge fight, reporting "Houck and Sieger are bitter enemies. Once they fought rough and tumble for an hour in a pool room."[33] There is no way to validate if or where the donnybrook may have occurred, so the authenticity of the story is questionable. However, the Lancaster fans loved this type of build-up, especially any scuttlebutt about Leo, their favorite boxer. Promoters Hensel and Schlichter wrote the advertisements for all the Lancaster boxing matches and may have been responsible for scripting this dubious urban legend.

Seiger could be described as a "journeyman boxer" since his career was littered with numerous losses and draws when compared to total wins.[34] However, he was still a threat to Leo and capable of an upset win. On November 11 at the Lancaster A.C., "Leo Houck, Lancaster County's lightweight champion, had a slight advantage over Joe Sieger. Clinching was frequent; both men were badly mauled before breaking."[35] This fight outcome ended as newspaper-decision draw, Houck's third and last draw for the season.

The Lancaster A.C. was in the middle of a profitable season during 1909. Promoters Hensel and Schlichter had a star boxer in Leo Houck, the Lancaster County Lightweight Champion. "Houck is attracting the attention of all managers by his good work and it will be no surprise to see him at the top ere long."[36]

Harrisburg fans routinely attended the boxing shows at the Lancaster A.C. and comprised a significant part of Leo's growing fan base. So far, Leo visited Harrisburg for only one engagement, his second fight with Grover Hayes. Hensel and Schlichter often visited cities like Harrisburg and Columbia, as well as smaller towns like Lebanon, Pennsylvania, prior to a boxing show in order to sell tickets and make arrangements to reserve seating space on the train for fans traveling to the shows. Later on, in 1910, when Leo started to fight in Philadelphia on a routine basis, accommodations for rail transportation were always secured by Hensel or Schlichter. Typically, up to one hundred or more fans from Lancaster traveled to Philadelphia to support their local pugilistic hero, even more so when Leo was matched against a highly touted Quaker opponent.

Leo had four more fights scheduled for the season after the draw against Sieger. Joe Hirst, "The Fighting Italian" from Philadelphia, met Leo on November 25, Thanksgiving Day, in Philadelphia. "Houck had the Quakers on their toes on account of his unexpected showing."[37] However, the *Philadelphia Record* awarded all but one round, the first, to Hirst, making the fight's outcome a loss for Leo.[38]

This particular fight provides a great example of multiple newspapers reporting differing outcomes for the same fight. The *Courier* and the *Philadelphia Item* both reported the fight as a draw.[39] The newspaper-decision and no-decision era was a shoddy deal when it came to deciding fights, but it was the only deal available at the time.

Young Kid Broad met Leo on December 2 at the Lancaster A.C. in another six-rounder, his fourth and final mill with Leo. Houck received the newspaper-decision win.[40] Since 1904, Leo had fought a total of eight different fighters using an aka of "Young so and so," or "Kid so and so," even a "Young Kid so and so." There would be more of the same.

Leo's next scheduled six-round bout on December 16 at the Lancaster A.C. against Kid Locke surely triggered memories for Leo about what almost happened to him when he became overconfident in the ring. Ten months earlier, Kid Locke had nearly put Leo to sleep in the fourth round. Leo clearly remembered the overhead arc light directly above the ring and how it grew dim instantly after Locke clobbered him on the chin with a stunning right.

> The Kid held his own in the first round, but the next two were easily Houck's. He gave Houck a severe battering on the ropes in the in-fighting. Honors were even in the fourth but the Kid was apparently weak in the fifth and saved himself from Houck's dangerous left by frequent clinches. In the sixth Houck gave the Kid a severe beating all over the ring, but the gong found the Philadelphian strong and fighting hard to avoid a knockout blow.[41]

The fight ended as a newspaper-decision win for Leo.

The final bout of the 1909 season was held at the Academy Hall in Reading, Pennsylvania, on December 20 against William Nitchie, aka Young Nitchie. This particular fight was scheduled for ten rounds, Leo's first bout past six rounds. Up until then, he was accustomed to fast-paced six-rounders. Any adjustments required for the additional rounds were minimal for a well-conditioned boxer like Leo. Over one hundred fans from Lancaster and an equal number from Philadelphia traveled to Reading for the fight.[42]

> Nitchie tried desperately to beat Houck. When the bout opened he tried to get close to Houck, but the latter staved him off with fast left jabs and sent in hard swings to the body. In the close fighting Houck beat Nitchie on the kidneys. At the outset these thumpings apparently did no damage, but about the fifth round they began to show the effects, for Nitchie looked weary. The Philadelphia lad came back fast however, in the sixth and about held his own. It was in this round that Nitchie, seeing he could not get to Houck, was puzzled for only a moment. He blocked high and then contented himself with body punches. In two rounds Houck rushed Nitchie against the ropes and beat him unmercifully on the body. In summing up the fight, Houck had the best of it in every round except the seventh and ninth, and then Nitchie was almost even. For eight rounds Houck was the aggressor and landed the greater number of blows, and all were clear and hard. The Lancaster lad showed that he is a persistent hard worker and willing at all times to mix it up. There is no doubt that if Houck continues to develop rapidly during the next few years he will have attained a national standing in the boxing game. What he wants is discreet guidance at the hands of some master of the sport.[43]

Leo was awarded a newspaper-decision win over Young Nitchie.

The *Reading Times* story reported, "Houck had the best of it excepting the seventh and ninth, and then was about even."[44] However, Nitchie got Leo's attention in the fifth and rallied in the sixth, which forced Leo to employ a bit more defense during the sixth. As Leo's own account about what happened to him during the fifth round of the fight states:

> This was my first ten-round fight and it was one of the fastest of my career. For four rounds we battled on even terms, but in the fifth session Nitchie sure did cock me with a left hook for which he was noted. The blow did not floor me but it certainly did daze me. However, I had enough sense to fall into a clinch. By the time we parted I was entirely myself. From then on I had the advantage and won the newspaper decision. Only my wonderful condition saved me in that fifth round.
>
> This bout taught me more than ever to acquire more of the defensive art of boxing, which the boys of today seem so glaringly lacking.[45]

Leo spent the brief one-month layoff at home recuperating from an attack of quinsy (known today as tonsillitis) before his next scheduled bout in 1910.[46]

5

From Lightweight to Middleweight in Twenty-Eight Bouts, 1910

Hensel and Schlichter's advertisement promised "One Swell Bill" for the January 20 boxing show at the Lancaster A.C. Leo had recuperated from his bout of quinsy and now looked forward to his second meeting with Joe Hirst, a formidable lightweight who was anxious to knock off any low-hanging fruit on his way toward a challenge of Oscar Nielson, aka Battling Nelson, the current lightweight champion. Frankie Hauck, Leo's younger brother, fought Charles Harris in a preliminary bout during the same show.

Hirst was a son of immigrant parents and part of the early wave of young boxers from many ethnically diverse backgrounds—Irish, German, Italian, and Slavic. The prize ring was their way "up and out" of poverty and the stifling neighborhoods known as ghettos. Although Hirst never attained a championship title during his career, he was one of many Jewish boxers who fought during the years 1910 to 1940, which produced twenty-six Jewish world "championship titles."[1] Today African Americans, Hispanics, and other races dominate the sport as their key to rise "up and out" of poverty.

The *Harrisburg Telegraph* provided a brief report about the Hirst-Houck bout.

> Leo Houck, Lancaster's champion, and Joe Hirst, of Philadelphia, broke even last night in a rattling six-round bout. During the first five rounds the advantage lay with Joe, who did most of the leading and proved himself Leo's equal at infighting. The latter appeared tired at the end of the fifth, but he began the sixth with a fierce rush and pursued his old-time whirlwind tactics until the gong sounded, putting it over Joe almost at will.[2] The newspaper-decision was Leo's second loss to Hirst.[3]

Although Hirst scored another win over Houck, he needed to get past Mickey Gannon, a Philadelphia lightweight and dangerous knockout artist, in order to get a match with Battling Nelson, the current lightweight champion. Gannon had previously beaten Battling Nelson on November 23, 1907, the only year between 1905 and 1910 when Nelson did not hold the lightweight championship title.[4] For whatever reasons, Hirst never got the chance to fight Gannon, but Leo did on January 29 in a six-round bout at the National A.C. in Philadelphia.

The opportunity and decision to fight Gannon was detailed many years later by Leo in a series of columns he titled "My Twenty Years of Boxing," which appeared in the *Lancaster Daily Intelligencer*.

> After my fight with Joe Hirst on the 21st of January I was booked to fight Tommy O'Keefe in Lancaster, February 10. Not anticipating any fight before that time, I rested a few days before resuming

my training. George Goodhart held a party one night during the week of the 24th and had invited many of the fighters and fans to his home on the "Hill." During the festivities I received a telegram from Lew Durlacher asking me if I could be in shape to fight Mickey Gannon in Philadelphia, January 29. When I read the message to the boys they were all excited. They tried to discourage me from taking on this important battle. Mr. Hensel said "the time was not ripe for me to meet a boy like Gannon." He thought I would be knocked out. Most of the fans were figuring it that way but I decided to take the fight and wired Lew to this effect.

Mickey Gannon was the pride of Philadelphia at that time and had defeated the best men that could be secured to fight him. Cyclone Johnny Thompson was the most prominent contender for the lightweight crown and Mickey had decisively defeated him. Jack McGuigan wanted to match him with "Battling Nelson" and it was said the Dane was afraid of him. In fifty-two contests that Gannon fought in three years, he knocked out twenty-six men in less than six rounds, had twenty-five no-decision contests of six rounds and the Thompson bout was for twelve. I was to meet the best man of my career, but [I was] eager for the match. The "ifs" were running through my head thick and fast. I made up my mind to be in the best shape and give Gannon something to think about.

Every Philadelphia paper gave me the decision and [said] that I gave a severe drubbing to Gannon. I had Mickey in danger several times and watched his wicked left constantly. He worried me in the second round but after that I knew I could whip him. My best rounds were in the third and sixth. He was groggy and held onto me as if for his life. In the last round when we came together in the center of the ring I extended my hand to shake and Mickey struck me without acknowledging the usual courtesy. I became just as mad as he after this unsportsmanlike act and waded in for all I was worth.

The Philadelphia *North American* had this account of the fight. "While Gannon had weight over Houck, the boy from the land of the Red Roses showed his mastery from the start. Gannon, the hard hitter who is seeking a match with Nelson, had him in danger only in one round. In the second he staggered Houck with a series of lefts, but the boy from up-state came back strong and with a left jab and right hook gave Gannon the beating of his life. In the fourth he put Gannon down for the count of five with a terrific right to the jaw. In the sixth Houck smothered Mickey with blows and had the latter holding and befuddled at the finish. It was a great triumph of Houck over the toughest lightweight that Philadelphia can boast."

Before the fight with Gannon I bought a new pair of shoes and afterwards posed for my pictures at one of the newspaper offices. While donning my attire I noticed I had two right shoes. I told Lew Durlacher about it. Lew always took the humorous side of things and remarked, "Great, simply great, Leo my boy. It surely means everything will be all right tonight, but I would have the blues if they had been left-hand shoes." Durlacher's prediction came out right and I kept the shoes.[5]

Lew Durlacher arranged the Gannon fight as a favor to Leo. He requested a contest with a superior out-of-town rival, a boxer who could test his mettle and answer one simple question—did he possess the ability to become a contender?

Soon after the Gannon victory, Durlacher took charge of Leo's affairs. The business end of Leo's career improved tenfold after the Gannon win. "After my decisive victory over Mickey Gannon, Lew had no trouble getting all kinds of fights for me. The promoters were very anxious to put me on their card. The bouts started to come in thick and fast and kept me busy in the ring."[6] From this point forward, every fight Durlacher arranged for Leo paved the way toward one single goal: a title bout.

Less than two weeks after the Gannon victory, Durlacher matched Leo with Tommy O'Keefe, a Philadelphia lightweight, on February 10 at the Lancaster A.C. The *Harrisburg Telegraph* reported that Leo had already defeated most of the leading fighters Philadelphia offered.[7]

O'Keefe may have strongly objected to the *Harrisburg Telegraph*'s broad generalization about Leo's mastery over the Philadelphia boxers. O'Keefe was a boastful and tough lightweight from Philadelphia, who "ate gunpowder and nails for breakfast." He had no losses in his last eight bouts since May 14, 1909—his last engagement with Leo. Moreover,

O'Keefe had posted a win over Joe Hirst during 1909, something Leo had failed to accomplish twice between November 1909 and January 1910. O'Keefe promised his friends that he would lick Leo with his left hand.[8] This third and last engagement with Leo must have been a great disappointment for O'Keefe. Leo explained, "It was a hard fight for three rounds and then in the middle of that chapter I floored O'Keefe for a nine count. He never recovered completely and during the remainder of the fight I had things my way."[9] Both men stayed on their feet at the end, but Leo owned the six-rounder from the first to last gong, which resulted in another newspaper-decision win for Leo.[10]

Durlacher challenged and tested his protégé's skills, conditioning, and temperament. He had dramatically increased the number of fights for Leo during the remainder of the 1910 season. Many bouts were scheduled only days apart. Leo was lucky if he had a week layoff between fights. The *Courier* totally endorsed Durlacher as Leo's new manager by stating, "Lew Durlacher is the man, and Houck should listen to all he says."[11]

Leo thrived under Durlacher's management and adapted to the increased number of fights during the 1910 boxing season. The most outstanding reason for Leo's success in the ring was his attention to conditioning, an integral component of his overall makeup as a boxer, which sustained him when he was pushed physically and fatigued by the rigors of Durlacher's new schedule.

On February 12, two days after his battle with O'Keefe, Leo fought Yi Yi Erne. Sixteen years later, Leo described his first engagement with Yi Yi Erne and his propensity to "wax and wane" from one bout to another.

> I was on the edge for this, my greatest fight up to this time. Erne was called the "Rube" Waddell of the ring. When he "was right" he was unbeatable, but when he wasn't most any novice could beat him. On this occasion, Erne "was right." The fight was nothing of the sensational. Erne used all his tricks and waited for me to lead. When I did he caught me coming in. Another favorite trick of his was to flash at the end of the round and even though he looked poor in the early minutes this flash made him look good to the fans. He did this throughout the fight. In the sixth round I caught Erne with a right hook and floored him for a five count. He leaped to his feet and started his dance tactics which I believe won for him the decision.[12]

The *Pittsburgh Daily Post* reported the fight as a newspaper-decision win for Erne.[13] Conversely; the *Reading Times* reported a newspaper-decision draw.[14] Official records list the fight as a newspaper-decision draw.

Four days after the fight with Yi Yi Erne on February 16, Leo fought Patrick Stynes, aka Paddy Lavin, at the Academy Hall A.C. in Reading. Lavin was based in Buffalo, New York, and had a succession of nine fights in Pennsylvania between September 12, 1908, and May 8, 1909. For the most part, Lavin was known regionally in Pennsylvania, and fought either at the National A.C. in Philadelphia or the Reading A.C. during this period.

This was Leo's third fight in seven days. Facing up to three different opponents within a one-week period was commonplace for boxers during the early 1900s era of boxing. Today some may define it as machismo, when in fact it boiled down to paying the rent and putting groceries on the table.

Detailed interviews and first-person accounts of fights by boxers from the early 1900s are somewhat rare. Leo's own account of his ten-round bout with Paddy Lavin, written for the *Lancaster Daily Intelligencer*, is another installment from a series of boxing recollections he wrote that today may rightfully claim their significance as authentic boxing history.

5. From Lightweight to Middleweight in Twenty-Eight Bouts, 1910

About one-hundred fans accompanied me to Reading the following Wednesday, February 16, where I fought Paddy Lavin of Buffalo, in a ten-round draw. Levin was a heavy middleweight and I had barely entered the welterweight class. Paddy was taller, heavier, and had a lengthy range. I fought out of my class when we staged the clash. One thing that kept me in the running with the New Englander was that I fought him close at all times. I tried to be the aggressor and kept within his long range. In order to do this I took considerable punishment, but proved to myself that I could stand considerable rough treatment. I used my right hand pretty well and opened up his eye in the eighth. My best round was the last. I put forth every bit of energy that remained in me and by this performance gained the draw.

"The Buffalo lad's long reach prevented Houck from using his lightening [sic] fast left jab, which generally is so effective, and on the other hand, Lavin excepting for an occasional registered punch, could not break through the guard of the Lancaster man. What made the fight look in favor of Lavin was the blood that flowed from Houck's nose. This was opened in the second round but careful attention in the intervening rounds prevented it from cutting off Houck's wind. In fact, when the bout ended Houck was breathing little harder than usual. The Lancaster man must be credited with being the aggressor all through the fight. Lavin's left eye was almost closed in the eight round, but it did not inconvenience him. On the whole a draw would only be fair."—*Reading Times*.

After this series of fights in rapid succession I decided to rest for a short time. Durlacher did not schedule me for a fight until March 8 with "Young Nitchie" in Lancaster.[15]

There is a high probability that Edward Hauck, Leo's older brother and one of his seconds, stopped the nosebleed that Leo suffered during the second round of the bout. Edward served as a second for more than eighty percent of Leo's fights.[16]

The *Reading Times* reported the fight as a draw.[17] However, the *Harrisburg Telegraph* story titled "Houck Got His," reported Lavin's win as a shade over Hauck.[18] Official records list the fight as a newspaper-decision loss for Leo.

After a two-week rest, Leo returned to the ring on March 3, refreshed and ready for his second six-round reunion with Young Nitchie at the Lancaster A.C. Nitchie had posted two wins and a loss since December 1910, his last engagement with Leo. Nitchie was three inches shorter than Leo and possessed a reputation as an out-and-out brawler. Leo was aware of Nitchie's ability to surprise and worry an opponent. The memory of being clobbered on the chin by "Kid Locke," which almost resulted in a knockout, constantly rattled around in Leo's brain and put him on alert for that single devastating blow one never sees coming.

Leo shared his thoughts about the Nitchie fight with the public years later.

> Nitchie and I were both outclassed as contenders for the title and the bout was one of the hardest I ever fought. We used as our style of boxing—infighting. I had it all over Nitchie in this department and it gave me the fight. He forced me to fight at close quarters and I continued to punish him with short jabs to the stomach. I had never seen a Lancaster audience go so wild over a six-round bout. Both Nitchie and myself knew we were fighting and evidently pleased the fans. The newspapers gave me the popular decision, and a number of the fight fans who had seen many of the big scraps said it was the best short-distance fight they had ever witnessed.[19]

Six days later on March 9, Leo fought another ten-rounder, his third, against Jack Cardiff, a boxing instructor and occasional referee, at the Academy Hall in Reading. At this time Cardiff, from Reading, had a total of but seven wins in thirty-eight bouts. The match looked like a tune-up fight for Leo prior to his next engagement with a much tougher opponent named Young Loughery.

> As usual Houck was on the attack. Cardiff attempted to box but slipped to his knees twice during the first round. Houck employed his stock in trade during the second round by fighting inside and landing numerous stinging blows to Cardiff's stomach and kidneys. Houck never allowed Cardiff to fall

into a clinch during the entire fight. During the third round Cardiff managed to land a right hand blow to Houck's jaw but he quickly recovered and immediately renewed his attack and landed even heavier blows. By the fourth round Houck brawled and bulled Cardiff around by combining left jabs to his head and neck and followed up with gut wrenching blows the midsection before returning to the head and bloodying his nose. Cardiff rarely delivered a blow but his conditioning was superb. He needed it to survive this battle. During the fifth Cardiff managed to land a clumsy blow lacking any pizzazz. This annoyance sent Houck to work beating on Cardiff's stomach like a drum. During the sixth round Houck's barrage of overhand rights spun Cardiff around the entire ring, which gave Cardiff an opportunity to see and greet all his supporters sitting ringside with a grunt, groan, or gasp for breath. There was no change in fortune for Cardiff during the seventh, eighth, and ninth. Cardiff's midsection appeared red and swollen and he saved himself only by covering up. Houck put Cardiff down on his knees twice with left hooks and jabs during the tenth, but had no luck putting his opponent to sleep. Overall, the offensive boxing skills demonstrated by Cardiff were negligible, but the conditioning and recuperative powers he displayed were outstanding. One common thread between these boxers was superb conditioning.[20]

There was a backstory to the Cardiff fight that became public only years afterwards when Leo recollected the match. This account by Leo reveals another side of his nature, which included some humorous ridicule combined with elements of Old Testament punishment.

> After the Nitchie fight, I bucked up against Jack Cardiff, the veteran instructor and boxer of Reading. We fought the ten-round wind-up before the Academy Hall, on March 9. He looked more like a light-heavy than anything else. He refereed the fight between Paddy Lavin and myself sometime before this date and did not handle the bout in a satisfactory manner. I remembered the little incident and promised myself I was going to try and take him down a peg or two. A crowd of Lancaster fans and myself were standing in front of the club when we heard a band coming down the street. Following the musical organization was Jack Cardiff reclining comfortably in an automobile. They were escorting him to the clubhouse. You would think he was another Jefferies.[21]
>
> He came out to the ring accompanied by six or seven seconds when the time for the windup arrived. In addition to these towel swingers, he had many friends in the audience who insisted on telling him how to handle me. One red-haired gentleman yelled out during the fracas, "Keep away from him." That would have been a good plan for Jack to follow, for I was determined to give him a severe lacing. He seemed an easy target for me and had I had little trouble in defeating him. He surprised me, however, by offering such a stubborn constitution. I could not floor him and he stayed the entire distance.[22]

Leo enjoyed a six-day respite after the fight from which he had emerged totally unscathed. Cardiff had landed hardly any blows, and the punches that did connect lacked oomph.

Once again, the Quaker City boxing community dipped into their deep reservoir of fighters and matched Leo with another new opponent named Thomas Loughlin, aka Young Loughrey, a welterweight from Manayunk. His third match this season, against Leo on April 7, was held at the Douglas A.C. in Philadelphia.

Leo recognized that Loughery was the more experienced fighter since he had already boxed many of the leading lightweights. He was regarded as an out-and-out brawler who occasionally boxed. Jack Hanlon, his manager, was grooming Loughery for a future match with Battling Nelson, who currently held the lightweight crown.[23]

The *Harrisburg Telegraph* provided a cursory report about the fight that was totally devoid of any descriptive boxing jargon. "It was one of the hardest bouts seen in this city in a long time. Loughery led in the early rounds but Houck sported at the finish and was entitled to the decision, had one been given. Houck did not have much to spare at the finish, but he was the stronger."[24]

A description of the fight reported by the *Public Ledger* provided a more detailed account of this raucous fight.

> Leo Houck of Lancaster fought the most sensational bout of his career in the wind-up at the Douglas Athletic Club last night. His opponent was Young Loughrey of Manayunk, conceded to be one of the best sluggers in the East. Houck not only out boxed, but outfought the Manayunk welterweight at his own game. Each of the six rounds was a thriller.
>
> The fifth had the entire crowd on its feet. Loughrey had his opponent in one corner of the ring, swinging his left and right wildly for the Lancaster boy's jaw. Houck took the blows and never winced.
>
> Suddenly he saw an opening and drove his right into Loughrey's solar plexus. The latter doubled up from the blow; his head sank, and while in this position, Houck drove him completely across the ring and the ropes saved him from a knockout.
>
> The bell rang while he was hanging onto the ropes and he staggered to his corner. There was no fight in Loughery in the sixth round and referee O'Brian was kept busy tearing him from the clinches.
>
> Loughery fought a foul contest being repeatedly warned by the referee from hitting in the breakaways and using his head unfairly in the clinches.[25]

The fight resulted in another newspaper-decision win for Leo.

Two days later on March 17, Leo fought Joe Hirst for the third time at the Lancaster A.C. The *Harrisburg Telegraph* reported the fighters shared a bitter rivalry toward each other and stated that a chance meeting between them on the street may provoke spontaneous fisticuffs.[26]

The prior two fights with Hirst were losses for Leo. However, this time Hirst faced a more seasoned opponent since their last engagement on January 20.

Eleven years after the fight, Leo recounted their third bout in his newspaper column, "My Twenty Years of Boxing."

> Two days after the Loughrey fight I fought Joe Hirst for the third time in a six-round wind-up in this city. Joe had not improved very much since our last meeting, but always gave me a fierce fight. I seemed to worry him with my left hand and he frequently fell in close. I had learned considerable about infighting and proved to have something on him in this department also. Joe shaded me in the second and fourth rounds. He broke through my defense and kept me out of reach. He landed some mighty hard blows on my jaw and I certainly felt them.[27]

The fight ended as a newspaper-decision win for Leo, his sixth so far this season.

Yi Yi Erne had been winning consistently since February 10, his last engagement with Leo. Within a thirty-two-day period, he won over Jack Britton, Mickey Gannon, and Willie Fitzgerald. Fortunately, Leo had a thirteen-day layoff to rest and train for his second six-round bout with Yi Yi Erne on March 31 at the Lancaster A.C.

Promoters Hensel and Schlichter expected a full house. They upped the ticket prices and erected an additional platform to seat more fans. Prominent boxing supporters and fight managers from New York, Philadelphia, and Baltimore were also expected to attend. The eastern lightweight championship title was on the line. The *Harrisburg Telegraph* quoted an excerpt from the *Philadelphia Ledger* regarding the importance of the fight for the winner.

> All of the winter the fistic fans of Philadelphia have witnessed a series of elimination contests in the clubs in order to determine who the best lightweight in the East is. Hugh F. Calvin of Greys Ferry, known to the fistic world as Young Erne, has emerged from the series of bouts with only one boxer disputing his title. Leo Houck, of Lancaster, who has rapidly come to the front, made Erne extend himself to the limit recently, and was only nosed out at the finish by a hairline decision.

Just why there is so much eagerness manifested in the outcome of the bout or the relative ability of the two men is explained by the fact that the man who wins decisively and proves himself the best lightweight in the east will have first call on one of the preliminaries to the Jefferies-Johnson battle on July 4.[28]

The fans witnessed four preliminary fights prior to the Erne-Houck wind-up. However, the largest crowd ever at the Lancaster A.C. was disappointed with Yi Yi's performance. Even more so because of the higher-priced tickets they purchased in advance.

Yi Yi attempted to rush Leo throughout the fight and often swung wildly without landing a blow. By the second round Yi Yi constantly fell into a clinch and kept his body covered up. The battle was completely one-sided in Leo's favor except for the fifth when Yi Yi rallied and went for broke ending the round about even. The fans witnessed Yi Yi at his worst while Leo finished completely unscathed. The *Harrisburg Telegraph* reported an interesting observation about the fight, "Erne was not knocked out, but he was not far from it, and had it been a fight for a big purse Houck would have shown his superiority earlier in the game."[29] Yi Yi was "not right" for this fight, and Leo knew it immediately. "When he [Yi Yi] was right he was unbeatable but when he wasn't most any novice could beat him."[30] There was no reason for Leo to punish Yi Yi severely when he "wasn't right."

Leo provided a hilarious anecdote titled "Whipped Erne Twice" about this second meeting with Yi Yi. "After the first round, which was even, I tore right into Yi Yi and won handily, receiving the decision. Erne gave out the alibi that the ring was on a slope and that I was used to it, while he was handicapped."[31]

The newspaper-decision win and title of lightweight champion of the East were awarded to Leo. Feeling cheated, Yi Yi clamored for a rematch and a level ring.

Leo had one week to rest and prepare for his third engagement. Young Loughrey had had only one fight, a win over Dave Ryan on March 22 at the Fairmont A.C. in the Bronx, since his last engagement with Leo on March 15. Loughrey was primed by his recent win over Ryan, and intended to detach Leo from his newfound status as lightweight champion of the East.

Leo provided the best account of this fight.

Young Loughrey and I met for the second time of the season at Reading, April 7, 1910. It was a rough and tumble fight. Time and again Loughrey rushed me and I had to hang on for fear of going out of the ring. It was more like a football game than anything else. The newspaper reports disagreed on the decision, but Billy Rocap, of the *Philadelphia Ledger*, refereed the ten-round fight and his account follows:

"After ten of the most sensational rounds ever fought in this State, Leo Houck, of Lancaster earned the decision tonight over Young Loughrey, of Philadelphia. It was a rough bout from start to finish. There was a constant mixture of wrestling, hugging, and clinching at which each did his share. Houck sent Loughrey to the floor with a right uppercut early in the fight. Leo was outside the ropes half a dozen times during the bout, being driven by Loughrey's rushes. He earned a decision simply because he landed the greatest number of blows. His right hand uppercuts were well timed and caught Loughrey under the chin in breakaways."[32]

The fight ended as a newspaper-decision draw despite referee Billy Rocap's assessment of the fight.

The referee, often called the third person in the ring, has the best vantage point to decide the true outcome of a fight. The reporter and judge sitting ringside are close, but still somewhat removed from the action. On the other hand, the referee is inside the ring and witnesses every blow that lands, and those that miss. In addition, he notes the impact of the blows and how they affect each boxer.

Yi Yi Erne had two weeks to train for his third and final six-round bout with Leo on April 15 at the Douglas A.C. in Philadelphia. Yi Yi and Kid Beebe, who both fought Leo several times, always provided excuses to the newspapers after losing to him, stating that Leo was the hometown favorite and always received a newspaper-decision win for his bouts held in Lancaster, or claiming that Leo had too much weight over them, or that the ring had an unlevel surface. Leo's corner remained consistent for all of his bouts with Yi Yi–Lew Durlacher, Todd Parr, the noted English wrestler, Duke Kelley, and Leo's brother Ed.[33]

Leo described his third and final bout with Yi Yi.

> On April 15 I met Young Erne in Philadelphia for the second time in two weeks. This time I defeated him handily. Yi Yi ran me a merry chase around the ring. Must admit that Erne out sprinted me. Erne practically fought the contest with one eye after the second round. I caught him a stiff short right hand jolt, which closed the looker. Once in the third I sent him through the ropes with a vicious left hook, which landed flush on the jaw. The majority of the ten rounds were a combination of leading, countering, and clinching. Every time I pushed my left into the face of Erne he grabbed me. There was only one round where he showed any real fight. He landed on me with both hands and drove me across the ring. He surprised me somewhat and I could do nothing the rest of the round. In the fifth I came back with all I had and dived in with uppercuts in rapid succession and repeated the same dose in the last session.[34]

Anyone reading Leo's narrative about his fights with Yi Yi may believe that his boxing abilities seemed diminished as he struggled to counterpunch, and frequently clinched, in order to survive. On the contrary, one month later on May 16, 1910, Yi Yi started to win again and reeled off eleven consecutive wins until November 5, 1910.[35] Yi Yi had regained his form and once again "was right."

Leo's next fight occurred in New Haven, Connecticut, his first professional fight outside of Pennsylvania. Leo shared the long train ride to New Haven with his manager Lew Durlacher and corner men Todd Parr and Duke Kelly. They all took up residence at the Hotel Taft, where Leo trained for his April 21 engagement with welterweight Dick Nelson at the New Haven A.A. Nelson, from Frederiksberg, Denmark, began his boxing career on May 28, 1905, in Copenhagen, and by 1906 had moved to New York City. During his career he often returned to Europe, fighting a total of twenty-eight bouts in Demark, along with numerous other matches held in Sweden, the United Kingdom, Germany, Belgium, and Norway.[36]

At this time, Leo sometimes experienced difficulty in making the weight requirement for his bouts. He penned a story titled "Curious Crowd Saves Weight Forfeit for Leo Houck in New Haven Bout," where he described a diversionary pre-fight tactic at the weigh-in, which happened hours before the fight with Nelson.

> Dan Fitzgerald, who since has become quite famous as a boxing referee in New England, had charge of the weighing-in. I had to force my way through the crowd to reach the scales. Durlacher and Kelly were already there, and with the crowd packed in tight right up to the platform. I stepped on the scales. Durlacher knew that I was over weight and as I stepped on the scales I made my arm rigid and Durlacher held me up. Needless to say, I did not move the beam. "All right," shouted Fitzgerald and I hopped off with a sigh of relief. The crowded weigh-in helped save my weight forfeit of $250.00.[37]

The bout between Leo and Nelson was very evenly matched, and both boxers had difficulty scoring clean points from the second to the twelfth round. They both landed repeated body blows and clinched often. Houck, who appeared to be the stronger of the two, had the better style of fighting, but was no match for Nelson, who constantly offset

Leo F. Houck had one of his busiest years in 1910 while under the management of Lew Durlacher. Leo had successfully segued from a lightweight to a middleweight during 1910 and had established himself as a recognized middleweight contender by the end of the season (courtesy the *New Haven Union*, April 20, 1910).

Houck's work by landing the most telling blows. The bout ended as a draw, Leo's third and last draw during the 1910 boxing season.

Durlacher extended Leo's visit in New England and arranged an April 26 match with Dave Deshler at the Armory in Boston. Leo was over weight and Deshler refused to meet him; so Frank Perron, aka Kid Perron, was selected as Deshler's substitute. On the surface the fight with Perron looked like an easy win for Leo. Perron had struggled from the very beginning of the 1910 boxing season. His first six fights, between January 13 and April 13, resulted in a disappointing record of five consecutive losses counterbalanced unequally with one salvation draw.[38] One had to admire Perron for jumping into the breech as a substitute for Deshler. There was a very slim possibility that Perron could improve and win over Leo.

After six days in New England, Leo was eager to return home. Extended periods away from home made Leo homesick for his family and Lancaster.[39] He needed to put Perron to sleep before the end of the third round and return home.

> Leo stalked and rushed Perron throughout the first and second round and easily dominated the offence by in-fighting. During the third round Leo slammed both rights and lefts into Perron's

midsection. Perron deflected one of the blows directly onto his groin. There was no response from the referee or warning to Leo about a low blow. Seconds later Leo pelted Perron with a glancing left that made full contact with his groin, which dropped him. He rolled over in agony face down on the mat. The fight was stopped in the third round, which disappointed the fans who were eager to see Leo in action. This was Leo's first and last disqualification during his entire career.[40]

Leo did return home early from the fight, but not the way he anticipated.

Frank Perron received a win over Leo the hard way. He continued to fight in twenty-eight more bouts but won only four more times before July 3, 1916, the end of his career.[41]

During the next four days, Leo traveled from Boston to Lancaster, enjoyed a brief visit with his family, packed his bags again, and departed town for an April 26 six-round engagement with Johnny Willetts at the National A.C. in Philadelphia.

Willetts had made his debut on February 22, 1907. Within three years he had fought and won over many of the same opponents Leo had boxed—more specifically, Kid Locke, Young Loughrey, Young Kid Broad, Young Nitchie, and Joe Hirst. "Willetts and Houck figured prominently in the controversy regarding an elimination contest to select the logical opponent for the lightweight world champion, Battling Nelson."[42]

The *Lancaster New Era* published an excerpt from the *Philadelphia North American* about the Houck-Willetts fight in an article titled "Bell Robbed Leo Houck of Kayo Victory Over Famous Quaker."

> It was Houck's bout by a large margin and the Lancaster boy was loudly cheered as he left the ring. By his timely punches Houck took the lead and held it until the third and Willetts took the fourth, bringing the claret from Houck's nose in this round.
>
> In the closing rounds Willetts swung a right around the neck of Houck and Houck hooked a left to his wind. They exchanged body blows in the clinch, but Houck managed to free himself and landed a right heavily on Willett's head, staggering him. Houck again shot a right to Willett's jaw and dropped him for the count of nine. When he arose Houck dropped him again for a nine count. Willetts pulled himself up only to be dropped again and this time the bell ended the contest.[43]

Leo had scrapped four times during a two-week period since his last meeting with Young Loughrey on April 7. During those two weeks he traveled from Philadelphia to Connecticut, then to Massachusetts, and back again to Philadelphia. Four days after the Willetts fight on April 30, Leo hit the road again and battled Young Loughrey in a fifteen-rounder on May 4 in Wilmington, Delaware. This was Leo's first fight over twelve rounds.

In contrast, Young Loughrey had only one fight during the same period, a win over William Mellody, aka "Honey Mellody," at the Armory in Boston. Mellody was a welterweight from Charleston, Massachusetts, who boasted an overall knockout record of twenty-seven percent.[44]

By now Leo had established himself as a seasoned boxer and legitimate lightweight contender. He was ready to fight Battling Nelson for the championship if an opportunity arose. However, Loughrey was in line to knock off Leo and derail that possibility. Loughrey already had a win over Leo and a recent draw on April 7 in Reading, and reckoned that he deserved the opportunity to fight Nelson first.

> Leo attempted to rush and in-fight but was neutralized by Loughrey's defensive counterpunching. At times the fight looked like a wrestling match. Both opponents rushed and grappled each other. Loughrey pushed Leo through the ropes twice. Around the middle of the fight both clinched and fell through the ropes together. Loughrey forced the fight for twelve rounds but Leo was credited with a strong finish the final three. The referee had an almost impossible task breaking the fighters when they clinched. Overall, the fight belonged to Loughrey all the way.[45]

One could argue that the rigors of the last four fights within a two-week period were telling on Leo. Certainly, fatigue was one factor that may have contributed to the loss.

Durlacher, Leo's manager, demanded a rematch with Loughrey. Promoters Hensel and Schlichter immediately scheduled a rematch and had no difficulty peddling tickets to Leo's fans in Lancaster and Harrisburg, who were eager to see Loughrey "get his."

First, Leo needed to heal. The numerous blows and cumulative wear and tear that Leo, or any other boxer, receives in the ring often results in some type of injury that requires either a layoff or medical attention. In Leo's case, surgery was required to correct an injured ear that had already started to bother him during his May 4 bout with Young Loughrey.[46]

The May 9 newspaper report was the first public mention about Leo's injury. In retrospect, one can understand why Leo always put the quietus on the press. He felt it was important to never reveal any injuries received in the ring. Leo never allowed an opponent to know where it hurt or if he was nursing an injury. Imagine fighting one or two bouts a week throughout an entire year. Inevitably, one or multiple body parts are going to be sore or injured, at least some of the time.

The citizens of Lancaster celebrated on May 24 with a Knights Templar parade in the morning, baseball during the afternoon, and boxing in the evening. However, the fight scheduled between Leo and Hirst that evening at the Lancaster A.C. was postponed until June 16. Leo's ear had not healed entirely, but he did participate in the boxing show as a referee.[47] Later in life, Leo was ranked among the leading referees of the country and promoted fights locally in 1932. "His reputation for honesty was such that he was the only man in the entire state to hold both a promoter's and a referee's license at one and the same time. That privilege was granted him by the State Athletic Commission and his high reputation was cited at the time the grant was made."[48]

The Hirst-Houck bout finally took place on June 16 at the Lancaster A.C. This was their fourth and last meeting.

> In the fourth and final bout Houck vs. Hirst, Leo gave his opponent a boxing lesson. During the first three rounds Hirst tried to lead but Houck simply parried each punch and forced him into the ropes. Near the end of the third round Leo launched a barrage of crushing punches that overpowered Hirst. He retreated to his corner with a severely cut mouth. During the fourth canto, Houck swung and connected a hard right hook into Hirst's soft left ear. His corner men worked feverishly to stem the blood that seeped from his mouth and ear. Hirst tried clinching to ward off an incoming tide of blows throughout the fifth. During the sixth round Houck switched tactics by concentrating hard shots to Hirst's midsection. Leo had Hirst groggy several times during the fight but Hirst remained upright and always came back. The final gong found Hirst still game but in a bad condition. He had "suffered greatly."[49]

Joe Hirst was deeply respected by Leo, who paid him a wonderful tribute: "I will never forget my four fights with Joe Hirst as long as I live. He was one of the hardest and cleanest fighters I have ever met."[50] Hirst died tragically at the hands of some thugs in a Philadelphia restaurant during an argument that escalated into a deadly brawl.[51]

After the Hirst fight, the *Harrisburg Telegraph* suggested "Houck May be in One of the Preliminaries at Reno." Since Leo's star had risen as one of the premier fighters of the east, arrangements were necessary to have him spend about month out west in order to have him gain further exposure in successively better bouts. Sam Langford, an uncrowned heavyweight champion, and Stanley Ketchel, a middleweight champion from 1908 to 1910, had made a tentative arrangement to fight each other on July 4 in Reno, Nevada.

5. From Lightweight to Middleweight in Twenty-Eight Bouts, 1910

There was a possibility for Leo to appear in the preliminaries during the morning, prior to the Langford-Ketchel match that afternoon.[52] Unfortunately, this event never transpired and Leo remained in the east, but eventually traveled westward during 1914 when he faced Billy Murray in Dale City, California.

Young Loughrey wanted Leo's title as the lightweight champion of the east and believed his last win over Leo proved that he deserved the accolade. The actual geographical boundaries that encompassed the eastern lightweight territory were never completely defined by the sporting news or any official organization. Perhaps the east was a region that included several eastern states and New England to the north, or it may have been a smaller area that included only Pennsylvania and New York. Maybe it defined a specific locale that merely included the cities of Lancaster and Philadelphia. No one really knew for sure which areas were included or excluded when describing the eastern lightweight championship territory.

Both Loughrey and Leo wanted to take a break for the summer, but the promoters begged for a rematch.[53] Their respective managers agreed and a fourth meeting, a six-round event, was scheduled for June 23 at the Lancaster A.C.

> I was never in better condition. Loughery appeared easy for me in this set-to. I knocked him down twice and decisively defeated him. He used some of his characteristic rough tactics and came through my guard. My best round was the last. I came back strong and gave him an awful beating in this final session The bell saved him from taking a knockout.[54]

The newspaper-decision win for Leo was glorious. "My friends rushed into the ring and carried me to the dressing room on their shoulders. I was very well pleased with myself, for I had defeated one boxer who always claimed the decision."[55]

After a two-month layoff, Leo fought Harry Lewis, a Jewish welterweight champion from Philadelphia, for the first time. "Lewis has been training in Atlantic City and declares that he is in prime condition."[56] The twelve-round fight was held on August 23 at the Armory A.A. in Boston.

Naturally, Lewis was riding high after his European tour from February 19 until June 27, 1910. Lewis fought eight bouts in Paris and one bout in London, a tour that included four consecutive knockouts, followed by one technical knockout.[57] The record was impressive even though most of the fans in the United States were unfamiliar with his foreign opponents or their records.

Lewis seemed overconfident and looked beyond the upcoming bout with Leo. Instead, he was more intent on squeezing in another fight immediately after the fight with Leo, before setting sail for France to begin another European campaign.[58]

Johnny Hauck, Leo's youngest brother, recollected the circumstances that surrounded this match and exactly how Leo received and accepted the offer to box Lewis in Boston.

> I was a kid then and I used to tag along with Leo wherever he went. On this particular day ... it was a Saturday.... I went along with him to the baseball diamond at Fourth and Coral Sts. Leo was a pitcher for the old Jolly Rovers and they were playing there that day.
>
> While Leo was batting to the outfield, this man came across the field to approach him. They got into a conversation and I learned later the man was Lew Durlacher of Philadelphia, who used to manage Leo. Seems as though he had just got an offer to have Leo fight Lewis, then the welterweight champion, in Boston.
>
> Now it was Saturday and the fight was scheduled for the following Tuesday. In these days a modern boxer, a fighter, would never think of accepting a fight on such short notice, especially not an important bout against a champion. But Durlacher told Leo this was his big chance and Leo never hesitated

> to accept. He signed right there and then, finished the ball game and went home to get ready to go to Boston.
>
> Since the next day was Sunday, there was no chance for Leo to do any extensive training. Besides, he had to leave for Boston that night. How well I remember my mother and brothers going to the train station, then on North Queen St., to see him off. All of us had begged Leo not to take the fight on such short notice, and all of us were crying when he left. Even big husky Teddy Bowman, who was one of Leo's closest friends, had tears in his eyes when the train pulled out.
>
> We were convinced Leo had made a big mistake and would suffer for it in the ring. After all, Lewis was the champion and for a guy to go against him without any special preparation was asking a lot; too much, we thought.[59]

Leo was twenty-one years old when he signed for the Lewis fight. Johnny's mention of the family crying as Leo departed underscores his importance to the family after his father had passed away. They all looked up to him, adored him, and now returned to their home on Cabbage-Hill to worry about him.

Just before sunrise, the day after the fight, Leo's brothers, Frank and Johnny, raced each other to the nearest newsstand to purchase the morning edition newspaper. They quickly thumbed through the pages of the *Harrisburg Telegraph* and discovered the fight report titled "Leo Houck Is Now Welterweight Champion."[60]

Eleven years later Leo provided a personal recollection about the Lewis engagement.

> Harry defeated me badly in the first round. He drove me all over the ring. The audience yelled for the sponge and thought I was out many times. In the latter part of the fight I evened matters out and outclassed the Philadelphian, gaining the decision. Billy Rocap, sports editor for the *Ledger*, was a spectator, as was Mike Donnelly from this city. Rocap's account of the fight follows:
>
> "Leo Houck, of Lancaster, won a sensational victory over Harry Lewis of Philadelphia after twelve hard rounds at the Armory Athletic Association, Boston, on Tuesday night. Referee Flaherty gave the Lancaster boy the decision at the finish and the crowd shouted their approval. Houck was carried from the ring on the shoulders of Parr, the English wrestler.
>
> "The bout was sensational from the fact that Houck from sheer pluck averted losing the fight by a knockout in the first round. Lewis sent him reeling to the ropes with a left hand hook on the jaw and Leo was helpless. He clinched the round out and recuperated wonderfully by the minute's rest. In the succeeding rounds he never left Lewis get set. He met Harry's rushes with straight right punches, which shook the latter up and soon had his left eye in mourning. Lewis tried shifts, only to be met with straight rights or an upper cut.
>
> "Houck had all the better of the infighting and three times Lewis fell to the floor by missing leads. In the last three rounds Lewis tried hard for a knockout and had Houck bleeding at the mouth and nose, but was unable to land the punch on the right spot."[61]

The *Harrisburg Telegraph* reported that the bell saved Lewis in the final round. "In the last round Houck had his opponent on the ropes and was hammering him hard. Just as the bell rang Lewis fell to the floor and was carried to his chair."[62]

After the fight, Lewis said he lost because he was out of shape. He demanded a rematch, telling his fans via the press that he would handle Leo the next time they met.[63] Lewis rejected any casual mention from the press that his title could be taken away by a boxer from such an unsophisticated neighborhood as Cabbage-Hill in provincial Lancaster.

Lewis's reason for the loss united him with the Philadelphia boxers Kid Beebe and Yi Yi Erne, who were also handy with excuses after Leo thrashed them.

Early in September Lewis said "he held the Lancaster boy too cheaply, and that he did little or no training for the event." The same newspaper story reported that Leo said "his victory up Boston way was no fluke, and he declared that he will repeat it, with the chance of winning ahead of time if Lewis does not stall."[64]

There were twenty-four days for Lewis to get in shape before his next six-round engagement with Leo on September 17 at the National A.C. in Philadelphia.

Approximately one hundred fans traveled with Leo from Lancaster to Philadelphia for the fight. All of the Leo fans had secured ringside seats, and he knew he just had to win.

Lewis tried to change his tactics for this fight, as recounted by Leo years later.

> Harry was careful the entire show and I was forced to do most of the leading. He feinted with his right to try and score a knockout, but I continually crossed him with my left and countered with my right to his face. I rarely permitted him to get set. The first round was grueling and both of us went to our corners bleeding. Lewis started to rush me in the second, but at the end of the round I had him on the ropes. I had Harry worried in the third and fourth and always sent my blows home first. I landed many blows in rapid succession under his heart and he came back in the fifth in weakened condition. He clinched repeatedly in the last two sessions and at the final bell limped to his corner "all in." Every paper in Philadelphia gave me the fight by a good margin and claimed that I had justly earned the welterweight championship.[65]

Leo returned to the Lancaster A.C. eleven days later on September 28 for a six-round wind-up fight with Joe Sieger from Denver, Colorado.

The 1910 boxing season was a difficult one for Sieger, who fought fifteen times and won only twice.[66] He was in the tank and tired of the short-end money. Sieger and his manager hatched a scheme to "hold up" the Lancaster A.C. and demanded more compensation for the fight, but promoters Hensel and Schlichter flatly denied their pitch for more money and promptly fired Sieger. Jimmy Dolan, a welterweight from Trenton, New Jersey, was quickly substituted.[67]

Jimmy Dolan boxed from December 21, 1908, until September 3, 1920, and posted only five wins from a total of thirty-five career bouts. Dolan, a game journeyman fighter, possessed boxing skills, determination, and toughness, but never came close to being a contender. It took a lot of guts for him to get into the ring with Leo, who by now seemed unbeatable. The substitution of Dolan for Sieger looked like a "set-up" fight, where one boxer has an extremely low probability of producing a win or draw. In this case, a "set-up" seemed unlikely since Dolan may have been the only fighter available on short notice.

Even the first-time spectator totally new to the sport of boxing could predict Dolan's fate before the first round ended.

> Dolan rushed Leo and attempted to lead. His offence was shredded and countered by Leo who landed every blow. This forced Dolan to cover up and listen for the gong. During the second round Leo whacked Dolan at will, which bounced him off the ropes and into every corner of the ring. By the third round Dolan was knocked groggy but managed to sleep walk until the bell. Dolan was doomed. Leo floored Dolan seconds into the fourth round. He took a long count, regained his footing, and was immediately knocked down again. After the second knockdown Dolan's corner men threw in the sponge.[68]

The newspaper-decision win was a technical knockout for Leo.

Three days later on October 1, Leo fought Arthur Susskind, aka Young Otto, in a six-rounder at the National A.C. in Philadelphia. Otto boxed a total of 159 career bouts and had a phenomenal knockout record of thirty-six percent. Between January 2, 1904, and March 3, 1906, Otto boxed thirty times and scored an incredible nineteen knockouts.[69]

Leo wrote a brief account about his fight with this knockout artist.

> Young Otto, of New York City, was reported as possessing one of the most successful knockout punches of any fighter in the game at the time. It was only a report, for I saw nothing of the big city scrapper. We met at the National Club, Philadelphia, October 1, in a six round bout. I started at him from the first gong and was afraid he might slip this wonderful punch over on me. I took the first two rounds easily. I repeatedly pushed my right to his face and staggered him to the ropes. In the third he started to wrestle and I could not shake him off. The last two rounds were very uninteresting. I led with my left and he clinched. He stalled around until the sound of the final bell, much to the dissatisfaction of the crowd.[70]

Of course, the fans felt cheated by Otto's nonperformance and no-show "Sunday Knockout Punch," but agreed unanimously that Leo had earned the newspaper-decision win.[71]

After six days' rest, Leo fought Young Loughrey for the fourth time this season on October 7 at the Nonpareil A.C. in Philadelphia. Loughrey's manager was not satisfied with the decisive defeat Leo had over Loughrey on June 23 and insisted on this rematch.

"He smiles like a baby but bites like a gator."[72] That statement summed up Young Loughrey, who loved any opportunity to get set and slug it out with an opponent.

Leo provided a brief narrative about their fifth and final bout.

> We had met a half dozen times, more or less, and I proved to be the more superior in the more recent battles. This particular fight was a stubborn affair. We both took considerable punishment and the bout was considered one of the best ever staged in the club. We did very little clinching, standing up and peppering one another with both hands. I had the better of practically every round and knocked Loughrey off his feet in the sixth. He was up like a flash, however, and came back for more.[73]

Five years later, Leo revisited his boxing history with Loughrey and provided the fight fans with a newspaper article titled "Bouts with Tom Loughrey Were Hardest, Declares Houck."

> Frequently I meet up with some of the older boxing fans and they ask me what fights I consider the hardest of my career as a boxer. It requires no pondering to reply, that those with Tom Young Loughrey of Manayunk were the hardest and not only the hardest but the roughest.
>
> Five times we met, one match following almost on top of the other and all were fought hard. Strange to say, I enjoyed every one of them, for Loughrey loved to fight. He wasn't a boxer, he was a fighter.[74]

Four days following the last fight on October 11, Leo fought Tommy Quill, an average fighter and welterweight, from Brockton, Massachusetts, at the Armory A.A. in Boston. The match looked like a "set-up" to keep Leo busy and in condition.

Leo was overweight by six pounds and did not meet the weight specifications for the match. Quill seized an opportunity to wrangle a hokey deal over this triviality. Leo accommodated Quill and agreed to waive the weight difference on one condition. If both fighters were on their feet at the end of the twelve rounds the referee would declare a draw.[75] This manipulation of the fight rules meant that Leo had to knock out Quill for the win.

> Houck had all the better of the milling. He knocked Quill down in the very first round with a short upper cut to the chin. During the next several rounds Houck "made a xylophone out of Quill's short ribs."[76] Quill managed to block at times but was clearly out gunned. Houck accelerated the pace in the sixth and staggered Quill with a right overhand cross in the seventh. Houck delivered a gorgeous left jab right onto the tip of Quill's jaw in the eighth which crumpled Quill into a heap on the canvas. His corner men knew he was knocked out and threw in the sponge.[77]

One day before Leo's next scheduled match with Jimmy Gardner on October 16, the boxing world reeled in disbelief that middleweight champion Stanley Ketchel was shot and killed on his farm at Conway, Missouri. "He died with a bullet to his lung, shot by a jealous hired hand who claimed the handsome prizefighter tried to steal his lady friend."[78]

Stanley Ketchel, aka the Michigan Assassin, is still considered one of the best middleweight champions in boxing history. Nat Fleisher, a pre-eminent sports reporter, writer, and authority on boxing during this era, lists Ketchel in his all-time division rankings as the number one middleweight.[79] Today, boxing authorities and historians have replaced Ketchel at number one with more contemporary fighters, but he still remains prominent on most top-ten rankings.

Ketchel's sudden death immediately changed and muddled the middleweight division. The *Scranton Truth* reported that "four claimants to the title stand out prominently, and of these three have faced the former champion in the ring. Former champion Billy Papke, of Keewanee, Illinois, now in Australia; Frank Klaus, of Pittsburg; Hugo Kelly, of Chicago; and Leo Houck, of Lancaster; are now in line."[80] In addition, the *Washington Post* also provided a similar ranking of four middleweights who deserved an opportunity to go after the title. "They are Frank Klaus, Hugo Kelly, Jack (Twin) Sullivan, and Leo Houck. Klaus is the best and by his recent form Houck stands second."[81] The ranking and recognition of Leo Houck as a legitimate middleweight contender was a significant bump-up for him and his camp.

Some of the other middleweight contenders who populated the division after Ketchel's death included Billy Papke, Mike Gibbons, Eddie McGroorty, Bob Moha, Jimmy Clabby, Jeff Smith, and Jack Dillon.

Since the beginning of the 1910 season, Leo had steadily gained weight and segued naturally from a lightweight into a welterweight and finished the latter part of the season as a middleweight. His next six-round bout on October 17 against Jimmy Gardner, a middleweight from Lowell, Massachusetts, was held at the National A.C. in Philadelphia. Gardner, like Leo, also had two wins over Harry Lewis. This fight was Leo's first in the middleweight ranks.

> The fight was a rough and tumble affair from the very first round. At times both boxers used wrestling tactics. Houck easily took the second and last round. Gardner demonstrated superior pugilistic skills and out boxed Houck during the fourth. Houck belted Gardner mightily during the sixth round and both continued to exchange blows after the final bell rang. The boxers were finally separated by their seconds.[82]

Leo was always ahead on points throughout the fight and received the newspaper-decision win.

The Fighting Italian, Fred Corbett, a middleweight from Philadelphia, fought Leo in a six-rounder on October 17 at the Lancaster A.C. This match was a tune-up for Leo before his next scheduled bout against Frank Klaus, the top-ranked middleweight contender.[83] Tad McGeehan, sports editor for the *New York Herald Tribune*, had coined a humorous sports epithet for these types of boxing mismatches: "The Battle of What of It."[84]

> In the first round Houck knocked Corbett to his knees twice. During the second round Corbett tried to box but failed to land any blows and survived the round by clinching. Thirty seconds into the third round Corbett woke up and rallied. Houck responded and pounded his opponent all over the ring.

Houck's final blow, a right cross onto Corbett's jaw, floored him just as the gong sounded the end of the round. Corbett was carried to his corner unable to answer the bell for the fourth round.[85]

The newspaper-decision was awarded to Leo as a technical knockout.

Philadelphia matchmaker and boxing manager Jack McGuigan recognized that Leo Houck's recent victories over Harry Lewis, Tommy Quill, Jimmy Gardner, and everyone else who entered the ring with him since June had made him into a boxing sensation and more importantly, a legitimate ranked middleweight contender. McGuigan and Lew Durlacher, Leo's manager, both knew this was an opportune moment to match Leo with Frank Klaus and arranged a six-round bout between the fighters on October 29 at the National A.C. in Philadelphia.

This was the same Frank Klaus, aka the Pittsburgh Bearcat, who battled Stanley Ketchel, the middleweight champion, to a draw during a six-rounder on March 23 at the Duquesne Garden in Pittsburgh. One thing was certain: Klaus was emboldened by the draw with Ketchel and three consecutive wins directly thereafter. Moreover, Klaus knew he was top of the heap in the middleweight "Scrambled Egg Brigade."[86]

Johnny Hauck provided some details about this particular fight in an article titled "The Middleweights of Leo Hauck's Day."

> During this time many great middleweights were coming to the front. In fact, at this period it is believed and records prove that there were never as many great fighters in one division. Klaus was meeting and defeating the best of them. He was picking up where Ketchel left off. During this time brother Leo was graduating from the welterweight class into the middleweight division when they proposed a match between him and the "Bearcat."
>
> Many thought that this match should not be made as they feared the Lancaster boy was too young and immature for such a test. He was only twenty-one at the time but he wanted to meet the Pittsburgher.[87]

Johnny Hauck's article mentioned that Leo was only twenty-one and that some believed too immature to face the Pittsburgh Bearcat.[88] However, Klaus was only one year older than Leo. Therefore, any speculation about Leo's young age, immaturity, or both should be dismissed as a wash when compared to Klaus. They had comparable records, fought common opponents, and shared an equal status as middleweight contenders.

Sixteen years after the Houck-Klaus bout, the *Lancaster New Era* published an account of the fight as reported by a Philadelphia newspaper in an article titled "Houck's Bouts with Klaus Were Hardest of His Career."

> Houck rather surprised Klaus with his showing, putting up one of the best fights of his career. He used the best judgment when in tight places and always managed to get out of them without serious damage. While Houck did the best work at long range, Klaus was the better at close quarters, but received many stiff jabs in working in close. The bout was nip and tuck all the way and in the sixth round both men mixed it up. Klaus as in the previous rounds played for Houck's ribs and kidneys. Houck played for the head and sent stinging blows to Klaus's face. At the final bell Klaus was fighting Houck on the ropes and then continued to swap until separated.[89]

Official records list a newspaper-decision win for Leo. However, in an article written by Leo's brother, Johnny Hauck, for the *Lancaster Sunday News* many years later on November 27, 1960, he recollected that the fight "was one of the most terrific fights ever fought in the ring, and it ended as a draw."

The 1910 boxing season ended prematurely for Leo on November 11 at the Rhode Island A.C. in Thorton, Rhode Island. Leo fought Frank Mantell, a German-American middleweight, from Pawtucket, Rhode Island.

5. From Lightweight to Middleweight in Twenty-Eight Bouts, 1910

Mantell felt confident and had some recent notable decisions to his credit. However, he was clearly outclassed in this bout with Houck. He tried to jab and exchange blows at close quarters but failed dismally. Houck jabbed repeatedly and looked for an opportunity to end the fight early. That effort was comprised after Houck threw a left hook in the sixth round that Mantell ducked into, which broke a bone in Houck's hand. Houck showed true class and continued to fight, which thrilled the crowd of two-thousand spectators. He ignored the pain and belted Mantell at will whenever and wherever he desired. Houck received the newspaper-decision win.[90]

The Rhode Island A.C. surgeon applied splints to Leo's injured hand before he left the fight club.

An exhaustive X-ray examination conducted in Lancaster revealed a bone bruise that had plagued Leo for at least several years. The pus collected by this injury was finally relieved by the break. Physicians who witnessed the operation on Leo's hand delivered a welcome prognosis that the broken bone, when knit properly, would produce a perfect and stronger left hand.[91]

During the next several months Leo's manager, Lew Durlacher, was besieged with matches for Leo, which included offers from London clubs, Parisian amphitheaters, the Alhambra Club of Berlin, and numerous boxing clubs in California, anxious to have Leo box for the middleweight championship of America.

The 1910 boxing season was Leo's longest and most arduous campaign during his lengthy career. He boxed a total of twenty-eight times and averaged two to three fights a month with a career-high record of six bouts during October. On a national level Leo Houck ranked second to another German-American fighter, Valentine Braunheim, aka Knockout Brown, who engaged in a total of twenty-nine battles during 1910.[92]

6

"Vive la Leo,"
1911

American boxers invaded the French capital of Paris early in 1911. Harry Lewis arrived first and had already defeated Jeff Thorne on December 14, 1910, at the Salle Wagram Boxing Club in Paris. During the winter of 1910, international contests featuring English and American boxers were very popular.[1] Before the end of January, fighters Jimmy Clabby, Frank Klaus, Billie Papke, Tommy Burns, and Sam Langford planned to arrive in Paris. Leo Houck was expected to be among this crowd, but his trip was delayed by several months while he rehabilitated his left hand after an operation to repair a broken bone. In addition, his manager had already committed Leo to six boxing engagements early in the season, which further delayed his journey to Europe.

In the meantime, Lew Durlacher, a clever promoter and manager, used the press to publicly challenge Joe Woodman, the manager of middleweight Sam Langford, to prepare his boxer and make weight in order to fight Leo and settle all arguments about the next middleweight champion. Durlacher was infuriated with Joe Woodman and believed that he bluffed and made too many left-handed assertions, which sounded as if Langford already owned the middleweight title.

Sam Langford, one of many top black boxers of the early 1900s, could be described within the pages of a "Who's Who of Pugilism" as a fighter's fighter. With over three hundred bouts to his credit, he faced racial discrimination in the ring, which effectively thwarted any opportunity for him to participate in a championship bout. Sportswriters respectfully bestowed him with the title "Uncrowned Champion."

The *Washington Post* reported that Sam Langford of Boston believed that he could easily claim the middleweight honors over any of the current crop of contenders.[2] Langford lost a controversial decision to middleweight champion Stanley Ketchel in April 1910, although the final verdict could have gone either way.[3] Langford may have figured that after Ketchel's death in October 1910, he now deserved the middleweight title.

The quarrel between Durlacher and Woodman over Langford's middleweight ranking ended with a public challenge. Durlacher said, "If Langford will make even 158 pounds at 6 o'clock Houck will knock him out of the ring. This talk of Langford's and Woodman's about Sam being the middleweight champion is all rot."[4]

Langford and Woodman ignored Durlacher's direct challenge to fight Leo. Instead, Woodman and Langford promptly departed the United States early in January 1911 for two matches in Europe, one in London, and one in Paris.

By January, Leo's hand was much improved, so much so that he played basketball for the Jolly Rovers of Lancaster against the Cardinals on January 14 at the York YMCA in Pennsylvania.[5] The basketball games helped to rehabilitate and strengthen his injured hand.

Leo needed to fulfill six engagements before sailing for Europe. His first six-round bout of the season was against middleweight Barney Lebrowitz, aka Battling Levinsky, from Philadelphia, who anglicized his given Jewish name to Barney Williams. This was a common practice with Jewish boxers during this era since anti–Semitic discrimination was pervasive in the boxing world. Jewish boxers sometimes adopted Irish, Italian, or German-sounding names in order to secure fights.

Levinsky held the World Light Heavyweight Championship title from 1916 to 1920. His official career record lists approximately two hundred eighty-eight bouts from 1910 until 1930, but the total number of both unrecorded and recorded fights is estimated at four hundred to five hundred fights during his entire career.[6]

Leo's first six-round bout on February 2 at the Lancaster A.C. against Battling Levinsky initiated a lengthy rivalry, which finally concluded eight years later in 1918, on Christmas day.

The *Harrisburg Telegraph* provided a brief synopsis of the fight, Leo's first after a two-month layoff spent rehabilitating his left hand after a surgery late in 1910.

> Houck initially had trouble knocking off the rust after a two month layoff and looked disadvantaged by Levinsky who was a foot taller and easily outreached his opponent. Houck received some stiff jolting punches from Levinsky. Houck reeled backwards but looked unfazed. By the third round Houck was in charge and almost put Levinsky to sleep only seconds before the bell signaled the end of the round. Houck received the newspaper-decision win and a standing ovation. After the fight, Houck promised his fans that he would provide a good accounting of himself during his trip to Europe.[7]

Two days after the Levinsky fight on February 2, Leo battled a newcomer from Pittsburgh named Tom McMahon, aka the Pittsburgh Bearcat, in a six-rounder at the National A.C. in Philadelphia. McMahon had started his professional career in 1910 and had only fifteen bouts to his credit. The local fans quickly dismissed McMahon. They believed this fight was a tune-up bout for Leo and predicted that McMahon "was being led to the slaughter."[8]

The *New Castle Herald* provided an exciting description of the fight, which included several unexpected surprises for Leo and some controversial opinions regarding the newspaper-decision outcome.

> McMahon opened up on Houck during the first round and clobbered him with a left hook above his right eye. Houck was caught off guard and driven backwards into the ropes where McMahon delivered a volley of lefts and rights to his opponent's midsection. Houck managed to clinch and recover. Seconds before the gong signaled the end of the round McMahon caught Houck flush on the jaw with a left, which left Houck draped over the ropes. McMahon moved in to finish the fight but Houck was saved by the bell.
> During the second round Houck kept his jaw down and repeatedly worked his left jab into McMahon's nose and mouth. McMahon countered with a steady attack to Houck's body and managed to drive him across the ring with rights and lefts to the head.
> McMahon looked for a knockout in the third round but missed with lefts and rights aimed at Houck's head. Houck kept jabbing away and bloodied McMahon's nose. The round ended about even.
> Houck staggered McMahon with a right to the jaw early in the fourth round and followed up with a series of rapid fire left jabs. McMahon held on and belted Houck severely in the stomach. The fourth round went to Houck by a shade.
> The fifth round was totally devoted to head hunting as both boxers looked for a knockout.

McMahon punched harder and had Houck on the ropes by the end of the round. McMahon took the round by a wide margin.

The sixth and final round was a total slugfest from the first to last gong. Both boxers punished each other but McMahon was clearly the most successful while he attacked Houck's midsection and drove him from one corner of the ring to the other.[9]

The Philadelphia newspaper-decision win went to Houck by a shade.

Controversy surrounded the fight's outcome. Bert Cowhurst, a prominent boxing figure in charge of the ticker ringside at the National A.C., was involved in the promotion of Leo's European tour and believed the potential financial returns overseas might be diminished if the newspapers reported that Leo lost to a relatively unknown boxer. "Thus the report was sent out to boost the native son."[10]

Of course, McMahon's performance against Leo caused quite a bit of commotion in the boxing world. He was immediately touted as the next Stanley Ketchel. Jimmy Dime, a Philadelphia fight promoter who attended the fight, believed that Leo had received a thorough lacing and was lucky to have avoided a knockout. Dime also promoted McMahon, and immediately received numerous offers from the New York promoters to sign his boxer. In addition, Dime boasted that he would make McMahon a champion within a year and offered Leo another match and a side bet of $1,000 or more.[11]

Even Lew Durlacher, Leo's manager, believed McMahon could beat any middleweight in the world as well as most heavyweights, and further asserted that within a year he would be in a class all by himself. McMahon was a formidable threat to the middleweight division and was proclaimed as the hardest-hitting middleweight in the country.[12] Dime's predictions about McMahon's future as a middleweight champion never materialized. One of McMahon's most notable achievements in the ring occurred during 1915 when he was awarded a newspaper-decision win over Jack Dillon, the light heavyweight champion from 1914 to 1916.[13] Since there was no knockout and both boxers were on their feet at the end of the fight, Dillon's ownership of the light heavyweight title remained intact.

There was no reason for Leo to reflect about his controversial shade over McMahon. After all, McMahon was a newcomer who had just started his boxing career and needed to build a reputation as serious contender within the middleweight division. Certainly McMahon deserved high praise for his day of parity in the ring with Leo, a much more experienced fighter.

Several days after the McMahon bout, Leo traveled to Boston with Lew Durlacher and Jack Leonard, a Philadelphia lightweight, and made their headquarters at the Castle Square Hotel. The early arrival gave Leo a week to train for his second engagement with Frank Klaus, a twelve-round bout, on February 14 at the Armory A.A. in Boston.

The *Boston Globe* reported that Klaus and Leo both weighed in under 158 pounds at the six o'clock weigh-in. The 158-pound maximum weight was, by now, a limit that many promoters and boxers had set for the middleweight class. This changed in 1915 to a limit of 160 pounds.[14]

> Each boxer gave a lot of attention to the other's body, but the blows that Klaus sent to the wind and ribs had Houck distressed early in the contest. Some good countering was done by both and Klaus excelled in blocking.
>
> It was the work that Klaus did at close quarters which practically won the battle though in the third round he put Houck down on the mat in his own corner with a right and left on the jaw.
>
> Houck appeared to be afraid to take many chances in letting his right go when he had the opportunity of landing on the face and body. Several times he used it for upper cutting and he landed some

stiff punches on Klaus's jaw. In some of the rounds he caught Klaus with a good right counter on the jaw but Klaus did not appear to be troubled. Klaus had Houck doing a lot of holding and while Houck was thus engaged Klaus would keep banging the right and left to the wind and ribs until separated by the referee.

In most of the rounds Houck jabbed or hooked Klaus in the face with the left and while that sent Klaus's head back, many of the punches did not seem to have much steam behind them, especially during the latter part of the bout. Every time Houck did land a punch it only made Klaus bore in much harder, and while Houck blocked some blows to the body Klaus planted some stiff lefts and rights into his wind and under the heart that made Houck wince and slow up.

There were many hot exchanges and most of the blows sent to the body. Often Klaus would push Houck's head back with the opened left glove and then try to send the right to the jaw. He managed to get a few of those rights on Houck's face but most of them Houck caught on the back of his head.

In the last round Houck made quite a flash and while he caught Klaus with some lefts on the nose and rights on the face and body, Klaus countered with both hands to Houck's body.

Both men were pretty tired when the bout ended, but referee Flaherty pointed to Klaus as the winner as soon as the bell rang ending the contest. Lew Durlacher, Houck's manager, agreed with the referee in his decision and so did most of the spectators.[15]

There was no disgrace in losing to Klaus, and Leo's status as a contender remained solid. He was still a viable threat in the ongoing battle for a new middleweight champion.

Klaus's win over Leo was noteworthy, but Billy Papke still remained at the "top of the heap" in the middleweight division. He claimed the middleweight title in 1910 after Stanley Ketchel's death, and defended it by knocking out Willie Lewis in three rounds on March 19, 1910, in Paris. On February 11, 1911, Papke fought Cyclone Johnny Thompson in Sydney, Australia. Thompson won on points in twenty rounds, but within a year outgrew the middleweight class and Papke reclaimed the crown. During 1911 all ranked contenders within the middleweight division were chasing Papke and Klaus.[16]

After two successive and difficult fights on the road, Leo returned to Lancaster and prepared for his next six-round bout on February 23 against the English boxer Harry Mansfield at the Lancaster A.C.

The *Harrisburg Telegraph* reported, "Mansfield has long been hankering for a match with Leo."[17] Mansfield was a seasoned middleweight from London who had battled with Frank Klaus, Harry Lewis, Jack Dillon, Frank Mantel, and Bob Moha. Mansfield was confident and promised the public that he would easily whip Leo.[18]

Probably Leo's oddest fight was the Mansfield fight, when the Englishman's shenanigans revealed him to be a modern day reincarnation of the "Werewolf of London."[19]

> Strange tales are told of ring happenings in the days gone by, but no stranger incident has been recorded that which occurred to me right here in Lancaster on February 23, 1911, when I fought Harry Mansfield, the famous English boxer.
>
> Harry Hensel, who at that time was promoting shows in Prince Street Hall in partnership with Walter Schlichter, had to pay a huge purse to bring Mansfield to Lancaster.
>
> Mansfield was a cocky Englishman and was quite boastful. Prior to the match in Lancaster with me he spread the news that he would knock the Lancaster farmer from his health and a lot of other things. It is one of the fights I will never forget and I doubt if any of the fans present at the time will ever forget it, either.[20]

On the night of the fight the Lancaster A.C. was packed to the rafters. The fans were all excited, because Mansfield had a reputation for delivering a crushing left-hand blow and they wanted to see just what he could do. Al Lippie, who managed Harris Lewis when he battled Leo in Paris for the middleweight championship, had discovered Mansfield in England and brought him to the United States to campaign. Lew Durlacher, Duke

Kelly, and Ed, Leo's brother, were in Leo's corner, while Walter Schlichter was the third man in the ring.

During the first round both fighters circled each other tentatively. In the second round Leo had no problem getting set and started to punish the English braggart. Leo delivered numerous lefts, followed by right crosses and an occasional right uppercut. Mansfield was incensed after he discovered that Leo was such a tough customer. Soon blood flowed from Mansfield's nose and mouth and he immediately switched to an offense of foul tactics. Schlichter noticed and warned Mansfield to start fighting fair. During the third and fourth rounds Leo doled out more punishment to his opponent, who continued using foul tactics. Leo's unrelenting onslaught during the fifth round had completely exasperated Mansfield, so he sunk his teeth into Leo's shoulder. Ed Hauck, Leo's brother, immediately leapt through the ropes into the ring and tried to swing for Mansfield, but Schlichter, the referee, quickly interceded and threw a vicious kick toward Ed, which chased him from the ring and restored order. Mansfield was a beaten man before the end of the sixth. This was Leo's first and last fight with an opponent who used his teeth as an offense. Leo was awarded the newspaper-decision win.[21]

The *York Daily* and the *Harrisburg Telegraph* both reported that the Mansfield bout was Leo's farewell fight prior to sailing for Europe. The departure time frame reported by the newspapers was premature.[22] Durlacher had scheduled two more fights for Leo before their journey overseas, one with Harry Ramsey and the other against Battling Levinsky. The surgically repaired broken bone in Leo's left hand was an unknown factor early in 1911 when he returned to the ring. The six fights prior to leaving for Europe provided enough time for Durlacher to observe Leo in the ring and ensure that he was one hundred percent, especially when he used his left.

In the meantime, prior to Leo's overseas journey, the *Washington Post* reported, "Harry Lewis, now on his second European boxing campaign, might become quite unsettled to learn that Leo is headed for London to seek him out and more." Leo, who was typically reticent with the press, boldly announced that his principal object in going abroad was to show the Londoners that Lewis is not such a "holy terror as they think he is." The newspaper inflated and reinforced Leo's rhetoric by stating, "There will surely be a peck of trouble brewing for Mr. Lewis when Leo lands in London town."[23] Moreover, the *Wilkes-Barre Record* joined in and challenged Harry Lewis, who was already in France and claiming to be the middleweight champion, to first whip Hugo Kelly, Frank Klaus, Leo Houck, Jimmy Gardner, Billy Papke, Jack Sullivan and Mike Sullivan before making such a conclusive assertion.[24]

After the bizarre Mansfield fight, Leo enjoyed a seventeen-day layoff before his next six-round engagement on March 16 with Harry Ramsey, a Philadelphia middleweight, at the American A.C. in Philadelphia. Ramsey had a brief and difficult professional boxing career that lasted three years. He faced and lost against many of the best middleweights in the nation during that time frame.[25] Ramsey never had the time required to season and mature in the ring. He was moved up too rapidly in the middleweight ranks, and subsequently was outclassed early on by far more experienced pugilists.

The *Harrisburg Telegraph* covered the Houck-Ramsey fight and provided the details for this vicious battle.

> Ramsey had a clear advantage over Houck in both height and reach but was unable to figure out his opponent's defense. Ramsey swung wildly at Houck and missed repeatedly. Houck countered, stepped in close, and landed hard left and right uppercuts to Ramsey's jaw. Houck used his infighting skills

and whapped Ramsey's body in double time with both fists. During the third round Ramsey missed with a haymaker that was swung so forcefully he caused himself to slip and fall onto the mat.

During the last round Ramsey flashed brilliantly and outpointed Houck but it was too late. Ramsey managed to connect a series of well timed rights to Houck's jaw and staggered him momentarily but the blows lacked the stuff necessary to get Houck in trouble. The fight was Houck's all the way.[26]

The *Harrisburg Telegraph* reported that Ramsey received the worst beating in his career. The loss to Leo abruptly ended any practical aspirations for Ramsey to enter the current middleweight melee for the championship title.

Three days after the Ramsey bout, Leo fought Battling Levinsky on March 16 at the Lancaster A.C. Levinsky had stewed about his loss to Leo on February 2, and decided to take a layoff until his next scheduled bout with Leo. On the other hand, Leo had fought four difficult matches leading up to the March 16 Levinsky fight.

Hugo Kelly, a middleweight contender from Chicago, was also available during this same time, and Leo was offered a bout with him in Pittsburgh. The purse would have netted Leo more money, but he preferred to remain in Lancaster and fight Levinsky.[27] This may have been a carefully calculated decision. Kelly's record from June 25, 1909, until March 21, 1911, lists six consecutive wins in which he defeated Frank Klaus twice along with Tommy Sullivan, Eddie McGoorty, Tony Capone, and Bill MacKinnon.[28] At this juncture Kelly was ranked about even with Klaus, and Leo needed to avoid a possible loss or knockout by Kelly before his much-anticipated European tour. Selecting Levinsky as his opponent was smart. Leo had beaten Levinsky early in 1911 and he was a familiar commodity in the ring.

Leo's second fight with Levinsky, a six-rounder, was Leo's last bout in the United States before departing for Europe and provided the local fans with enough excitement to tide them over until they received the wire reports about Leo's overseas adventures.

> Both fighters stalked each other during the first round, which ended about even. After the first round Houck started to knock Levinsky all around the ring with right and left hand swings that landed adroitly on his head. There was more of the same from Houck during the next two rounds. Levinsky was unable to muster any defense and counterpunched ineffectively. He clinched repeatedly after each attack by his opponent. By the end of the fourth Levinsky looked dazed and weary. Houck attempted to belt Levinsky out during the fifth but he was miraculously saved by the bell. In the sixth round Levinsky surprised and staggered Houck with a solid right to the jaw. Houck repaid Levinsky with two drives to the face that threatened to put him downwards onto the mat. Somehow Levinsky managed to stay on his feet until the round ended. Levinsky was soundly trounced by Houck who left no doubt about his superior conditioning and total rehabilitation from a surgery to repair a broken bone in his left hand at the end of the 1910 boxing season.[29]

On March 22, Leo Houck, Lou Durlacher, his manager, Billy Rocap, boxing editor for the *Philadelphia Ledger,* and Philadelphia boxers Tom and Frank Loughrey, all boarded the pride of the Cunard Line, the luxury ocean liner *Lusitania,* for Paris, where Harry Lewis was waiting apprehensively for Leo "on the other side."[30]

The Houck-Lewis fight in Paris on May 3 was advertised as a world middleweight championship bout. The *Harrisburg Telegraph* reported, "The winner will be conceded to be the premier in his class and acknowledged by the leading sportsmen of Europe."[31] The advance publicity about the twenty-round fight prompted the Salle Wagram Boxing Club to rent the Hippodrome in Paris, which easily accommodated 20,000 people.[32]

William H. Rocap of the *Public Ledger* provided a news report that included an almost forgotten but significant event that occurred prior to Leo's arrival in France. Jim Sullivan, who held the British middleweight title, had refused to battle Harry Lewis in

London, so Lewis's manager, Al Lippe, quickly claimed the European championship title for his fighter. No one challenged either Lewis or Lippe to this unexpected and bold proclamation. In addition, Lippe went on to state publicly in England that Leo Houck's wins over Lewis in the United States were flukes. False news reports always infuriated Leo. Lippe had overstepped the boundaries of common sense while talking with the press. Lippe and Lewis had no inkling that Leo was now totally committed to driving both of them into the bunker.

Leo and Durlacher stopped in London first and spoke with the National Sporting Club. They hoped to meet and arrange a fight with Jim Sullivan at 160 pounds. Sullivan was aware of Leo's two decisive wins over Lewis and declined the meeting. Leo and Durlacher immediately left London, traveled to Paris, and gave Lewis an ultimatum—fight or flight.[33]

While in France, Lippe continued to publicly debunk and play down Leo's decisive wins over Lewis. This hogwash from Lippe was successful and created a veil of skepticism about the reliability of the facts, even after the French press accurately reported that Leo had beaten Lewis twice in America.[34]

Lippe and Lewis were on the spot and knew it. They had painted themselves into a corner and to save face agreed to fight Leo on May 3 in Paris, but first a series of preliminary conditions leading up to the fight needed to be settled by both sides. Several days of negotiations and arguments between Leo's manager Durlacher and Lewis's manager Lippe ensued.

The Houck camp was so anxious to fight Lewis they conceded on practically every condition Lippe wanted for his fighter. The first condition required both fighters to weigh in at 158 pounds the day of the fight, and a $1,000 deposit was required as a penalty for being overweight. The second condition imposed by the now increasingly overbearing Lippe was a side wager of 1000 franks to 500 franks that Leo would weigh in at 156½ pounds. The Houck camp readily accepted this condition and the fight was mutually agreed on to last a total of twenty rounds, the longest bout of Leo's career. The final condition involved the selection of a referee. Lippe wanted his man, Dr. Luis Phelan, a Chicago physician and physical culturist. The Houck team accepted Phelan and believed they had now eliminated the last condition presented by Lippe. Unfortunately, Phelan was a greedy referee who envisioned a lucrative bouquet of money that a colossal fight like this would produce, and demanded an additional 500 franks from Durlacher in advance of the fight. Leo made it plain that under no conditions would he now accept Phelan as the third man in the ring and "that was that." Finally, both sides agreed to accept Monsieur Maitroit as the referee. Of Maitroit it was said, "He wanted the men to box fair and he would protect both, giving the decision to the man whom in his judgment had earned it."[35]

Over 10,000 spectators were in the Hippodrome on the evening of May 3. All were eager to finally lay their eyes on Leo Houck and take a full measure of the man who defeated Lewis, their popular champion and favorite for two seasons in a row.

Lewis entered the ring first with Lippe, his manager, and Phil Reese, his trainer. Within moments Leo entered the ring with his manager Lew Durlacher. Both fighters weighed in under the contracted weight, but Lewis, who weighed in at a lower weight than his opponent, looked larger. A closer inspection of Leo's physique revealed an athlete carefully trained to the moment. Another day or two of training for Leo may have easily dulled the entire effort.

All eyes in the Hippodrome were on Leo. He was an unknown factor and somewhat enigmatic to the French fight fans, who embraced boxing like a second religion. They had little information about Leo's personal demeanor and comportment inside or outside of the ring. Forty-six years after the fight, the *Lancaster New Era* published an article titled "Houck Won Paris Fight 46 Yrs. Ago," which included a story from the *Mirror of Life,* a London newspaper that described Leo's quiet and utterly confident nature as he prepared himself for the first gong. The *Mirror of Life* story is clearly one of the best-written and basic observations about Leo the boxer. He had no idea how his simple and quiet pre-fight ritual would impact and preface his introduction to the French spectators, and twenty rounds later endeared him to a new multitude of fans thousands of miles away from his home in the working-class neighborhood of Cabbage-Hill.

> He entered the ring fully aware of the importance of the contest and meant to win, quite confident that he could do so.
> After a curt nod in acknowledgement to the public's welcome he gave himself in Durlacher's care, kissed the small crucifix that never leaves his corner when he fights, and waited, his eyes closed for the gong to call him to the center of the ring.
> From that moment, not a single glance did he cast outside the roped arena and not a single flutter did he indulge in to attract the gallery's attention.
> As the gong sounded he rose calmly from his chair, solemnly and religiously made the sign of the cross and taking small steps advanced, his guard quite closed, towards his antagonist.[36]

The Fight by Rounds

Rd. 1: Lewis led with a right to Houck's jaw and clinched. Houck pasted the kidneys and ducked a left. Lewis made suspicious use of his elbow at close quarters. Two rights from Lewis landed on Houck's neck and ear. Houck scored with several straight lefts.

Rd. 2: Lewis reached Houck's stomach with a left and battered his body with lefts and rights at close quarters. Houck landed a left flush on Lewis's mouth twice. Lewis tried a right but missed.

Rd. 3: Both fighters got together and smashed away at each other's body. Houck scored with a rat-tat or postman's knock on the nose. Houck gets home on the ribs during in-fighting. Lewis pays attention to his opponent's stomach. Houck connects a left onto Lewis's jaw.

Rd. 4: Lewis took a slight lead and pawed around Houck with feints, rushed twice, and punished his body. A left and right sent Houck to the ropes. Houck slips and catches a hard left on the jaw.

Rd. 5: Lewis landed a right to Houck's neck and followed up with a right downstairs. Houck pounded Lewis with a hard left to Lewis's heart. Houck continued to in-fight and concentrated on Lewis's stomach. Houck jolts Lewis with two lefts to the jaw, slips, and catches a hard left on his opponent's jaw. Lewis clobbers Houck with lefts and rights to his ribs.

Rd. 6: Lewis attacked but misses every blow. Houck receives a hard left on the jaw and counters with a right to Lewis's jaw. Both fighters manage to simultaneously land lefts to each other's jaw. Houck drove a hard left to Lewis's heart and missed inside with an uppercut. Houck executes a perfect right hand uppercut to Lewis's jaw and receives much applause from the spectators. Soon afterwards Houck lands a stinging left and receives more applause.

Rd. 7: Houck takes the lead. Lewis slips while sidestepping and catches a right from Houck while hanging on the ropes. Durlacher yells at the referee and demands that Lewis's gloves need to be wiped off. Both fighters tried lefts and fell into a clinch. Lewis pummeled Houck's body and he countered with punches to the kidneys. Lewis landed a left onto Houck's neck. Houck, full of energy, ran to his corner at the end of the round.

Rd. 8: Houck's accuracy is remarkable and he proves to be the quicker opponent. He belts Lewis in the stomach with a left and neatly averts an incoming left from Lewis. Houck scores again with a double left, one more left, and ducked Lewis's returns. Lewis got busy late and attempted an unsuccessful one-two punch seconds before the gong ended the round.

Rd. 9: Houck fights furiously and lands a left followed immediately by a right to Lewis's jaw. The punches make Lewis groggy and he clinches in desperation for over fifteen seconds, which prevented

Houck from getting his arms free to finish the job. Lewis was in serious trouble but recovered slightly in the latter part of the round. He rushed Houck into the ropes while belting him in the body.

Rd. 10: Lewis, fully recovered from the last round, gets home with a hard straight left followed by a savage attack to Houck's midsection. Houck brilliantly ducks Lewis's looping swings and connects with a left to his neck. Both fighters engage in a severe mix-up of blows to the body. Lewis shades Houck and earns the better part of the exchange.

Rd. 11: Houck takes command and sends Lewis's head straight back with a jolting right uppercut. Lewis retaliated with two hard blows to Houck's stomach. Undeterred, Houck scored with two flawless straight lefts and a right uppercut to the heart. Another left from Houck lands flush on Lewis's jaw and bloodies his mouth. Houck ends the round with a hard right, two lefts, and a right uppercut to Lewis's jaw.

Rd. 12: Houck earns more points with an extraordinary display of boxing skills. Houck planted another blow directly onto Lewis's injured mouth. Lewis was rattled and resorted to his repeated defense, an attack on Houck's body. Houck stopped Lewis's challenge and clipped him twice under the chin. The jolt to Lewis's head produced an audible clicking sound. Lewis attempted to knockout Houck with three wild swings and missed each time.

Rd. 13: Houck deftly placed a hard right onto Lewis's jaw. Lewis countered with a crunching blow to Houck's ribs. Houck swung right and missed but rattled Lewis's kidneys after they fell into a clinch. Houck received applause when he expertly ducked a forceful left from Lewis. Houck punched Lewis directly on the nose and once again, cleverly ducked an incoming right. Houck skipped lightly to his corner at the end of the round.

Rd. 14: The momentum of the fight now belonged to Houck who delivered another short arm right uppercut to Lewis's chin. Lewis went limp and clinched. He was clearly in trouble and alternately held down Houck's arms or elbowed while in the grasp. Lewis rebounded slightly and landed with a right uppercut and one-two to Leo's body. The in-fighting was all Houck's advantage.

Rd. 15: Houck continues advantage. He lands a right on the ear, ducks Lewis's return, and counters him with a left to the face. Houck sent a straight right to Lewis's jaw and snaps his head backwards with a stiff right uppercut. Lewis goes to the body and later scores with a hard left to Houck's face. Houck continued to jab with the right and get several lefts home but was abruptly steadied by Lewis with a stinging left.

Rd. 16: Lewis improved and sent Houck into the ropes. He nearly fell out of the ring. Lewis assisted Houck back into the ring and peppered him with lefts and rights but a right uppercut from Houck stymied Lewis's renewed action. Houck threw two well executed lefts followed by a stinging right. The round ended about even.

Rd. 17: Both fighters threw lefts and rights without much success until Houck finally connected with a left and left Lewis shaken. Lewis recovered quickly and pummeled Houck's body.

Rd. 18: The fight slowed up considerably and Lewis tried several lefts. Houck nimbly stepped back and averted the swings. Houck landed a right onto Lewis's ear and he countered with a left to the throat.

Rd. 19: Greatest round of the battle. Harry Lewis, behind on points, rallied and swarmed all over his opponent. He mustered up a superhuman effort and waged a battle royal in an effort to drop Houck. After one prolonged spar between the fighters Lewis broke out anew in a fierce onslaught and caught Houck with a terrible blow to the jaw that shook him to his foundation. Lewis's devastating blows continued to rain down upon his opponent who was hurt and in trouble. Houck then managed to steer clear of Lewis and avoided any serious consequences. Houck looked flushed with anxiety as he returned to his corner at the end of the round.

Rd. 20: Fully recovered Houck looked calm as he mounted his attack. He missed with a right uppercut but connected on the next attempt. Lewis looped with a right but Houck ducked and hammered in a hard left. Lewis covered up after Houck clobbered him on the head with a hard right. Lewis jabbed and scored twice on Houck's cheek. Houck hustled his opponent to the ropes and proceeded to wipe out his deficit from the last round with a merciless bevy of rights and lefts to the body. Houck secured the final round and winning decision.[37]

The fight took place on a Wednesday evening. Public interest in Lancaster was extraordinary and people started to gather early in the evening at the *Lancaster Intelligencer* office in anticipation of the cablegrams from Paris which would arrive sporadically throughout the fight. Two individuals among the crowd were Leo's younger brothers, Frank and Johnny. They were determined to be the first to carry the news of the fight decision home to their mother. The initial cablegrams contained unfavorable news about Leo's early progress during the fight and this news spread throughout the crowd, but the brothers remained unfazed and waited patiently until the final cablegram arrived. The last cablegram proclaimed their brother as the new middleweight champion of the world. "After this favorable cablegram they jumped with glee and scampered to their home to carry the glad tidings."[38]

The victory was acknowledged by a standing ovation of over 10,000 cheering spectators at the Hippodrome as Referee Maitroit announced that Leo was the new middleweight champion of the world. William Rocap, boxing sports editor of the *Public Ledger*, immediately sent a cablegram to the United States proclaiming that Leo Houck was now the new and undisputed middleweight champion of the world.[39]

Rocap also provided an exciting accounting of what happened directly after the fight.

> A great demonstration followed the decision. Attaches of Grognet's School of Boxing where Houck did his gymnasium work jumped in the ring at the end of the bout and carried the winner off triumphantly on their shoulders. On reaching the main aisle they were aided by a score of spectators. Men and women by the hundreds gathered about the young hero of the great fistic battle and almost smothered Houck with congratulations. A force of gendarmes and a dozen soldiers of the Republic were necessary to get him to his dressing room.
>
> After a rub down, the new champion dressed for the street, and despite the fact that the contest was not over until nearly 1 o'clock (the next morning), Place Clichy, the site of the Hippodrome, was congregated with people. Napoleon, in his palmy days, received no greater demonstration. France had proclaimed a new world champion. The news had flashed to the clubs and cafes. As Houck and his immediate friends, with manager Durlacher, wormed their way through the crowd to a waiting auto, men and women taking a late supper at the sidewalk cafes stood up and cheered, "Bravo Leo! Bravo Houck!" A score of taxicabs followed the whizzing auto to the Excelsior Café, on the Avenue de la Grande Armée, where Houck had promised to celebrate his victory with the American colony. Businessmen from London, in fact, all who had met the blushing, modest Lancaster boy, joined in the jollification. Houck was again a surprise, as he ate plate after plate of strawberry glace, which seemed to satisfy his parched lips and mouth better than anything else.
>
> On his return to the hotel at 2:30 a.m., there were waiting for him special messages and cards from many Americans that witnessed the contest. N.H. Goodwill, manager of the Paris office of the Pierce-Arrow automobile; William Dodsworth, of the American Express Company; editor Robert Guerin, of *La Matin*; F. Hurdman Lucas, of the *Mirror of Life*, and Andre Augustin, editor of *La Radical*, had already left congratulatory cards before breakfast this morning. It is not likely that a champion in any branch of sport has ever received so much spontaneous commendations from men of all walks of life.[40]

Leo earned the largest purse of his career, a sum of $8,000, and received numerous lucrative offers to remain in France and continue to fight, appear in exhibition matches, or make personal appearances. Instead, Leo decided to return home.

One hundred and four years after Leo's triumph in Paris, his sons Edward and Joseph pondered and questioned their father's decision to abandon this golden opportunity to remain in France and earn a small fortune, capitalizing on his popularity and new role as a middleweight world champion.[41]

The *Parisian News & Notes* stated that Leo was very homesick and his manager, Lew Durlacher, was determined to keep him free from temptation while in Paris. These two things are most likely the reasons for Leo's rapid departure from France.[42]

Both Edward and Joseph Hauck agreed with the *Parisian News & Notes* story that reported their father was prone to homesickness. This condition precluded any genuine interest on Leo's part to remain in France regardless of the offers. Leo always preferred to fight close to home, but was not completely averse to going on the road for short periods. Prolonged travel, training, and fighting on another continent were, to a certain extent, a hardship for him. There is no evidence available to reveal what his manger thought about their rapid departure after the fight, or the missed chances for income which would have provided an enhanced level of financial security for both of them.

Six days after Leo's fight, Sam Langford once again attempted to jump headfirst into the muddled middleweight division. Langford was preparing to leave for Australia and decided to claim the middleweight title before he left. He offered to defend it at 158 pounds, weighing in at 2 p.m. the day of the fight. In addition, he offered a side bet of $2,500 and insisted the winner receive seventy-five percent of the purse, while the loser takes home a paltry twenty-five percent.[43]

This tomfoolery about the middleweight title first surfaced early in January 1911, when both Langford and his manager, Joe Woodman, publicly asserted in the *Washington Post* that Langford already owned the middleweight title. Americans wised up to Langford's repeated bluffs, but the British sportswriters feasted on the claptrap and started to belittle the established middleweight contenders who were, for the most part, unimpressed with Langford's mischief.

There was one middleweight who took issue with Langford's bluffs and that fighter was Leo Houck. For the second time, Langford managed to get under Leo's skin and thoroughly aggravate the usually taciturn boxer. Lew Durlacher let the Langford camp know there would be a substantial forfeit on the day of the fight if either fighter were unable to make the 158 pound weight. This proposed match had more significance to Leo than a considerably more lucrative engagement with Billy Papke.

The Boston Armory A.A. offered to stage the bout, but it was no soap. Langford found out the deal was legitimate and immediately left for Australia. The *Williamsport Sun Gazette* reported, "Houck has now driven him out of England. The time of heavyweights masquerading as middleweights is now at an end."[44]

Leo returned from Paris on May 19, 1911, and was greeted at the Lancaster railroad station by a large crowd. The *Harrisburg Telegraph* also reported that Leo was homesick while in Paris and refused to stay any longer even though he received an offer to remain and fight Billie Papke on June 24 for a purse of $6,000. Papke was fighting in Sydney and London during 1911, and certainly may have been available for the match. "Durlacher said that he may accept the offer of $4000.00 and all training expenses to return to Paris to fight Papke."[45] Leo never returned to Paris, but in due course fought Papke in 1912.

There were several other offers for Leo to return to Paris, but he wanted to remain in Lancaster until the cooler weather arrived, and trained for his next bout at the Rossmere ball grounds in Lancaster on June 16 with Joe Thomas, a middleweight and California native, who now resided in Lowell, Massachusetts.[46]

Leo had returned from Paris in superb condition and told the press he never felt better. Thomas had to face the facts that his odds of winning were in excess of twenty to one. The ring was built directly over the baseball diamond and fully illuminated for the night's boxing matches.

The *Harrisburg Telegraph* described their six-round wind-up fight.

Houck landed two hard punches to Thomas's jaw seconds into the first round. The remainder of the round was difficult for Houck as Thomas constantly clinched and covered up. By the second round the fans started to grow restless with Thomas's lackluster performance. Suddenly in the third round Thomas connected a blow to Houck's face and cut his lip. After that Houck took complete command and led every round after. Thomas worried constantly about Houck's infighting and covered his body constantly. After a session of infighting Houck reverted to the jab and effectively drove his opponent into the rope a dozen or more times. Thomas only escaped a premature ending by using clinching tactics whenever possible. During the fourth Thomas stepped up and threw a wicked uppercut, which Houck easily avoided. By the fifth Houck rushed again and connected with four successive solid jabs, which whipped Thomas's head and snapped his neck violently backwards. Houck's onslaught continued with punishing left and right blows to Thomas's body until the end of the round. The sixth and final round produced a renewed attack by Houck to Thomas's body. Thomas stumbled and sleepwalked through the round but managed to save himself from a knockout by clinching.[47]

Leo looked forward to a splendid layoff after the Thomas bout so he could pitch and play left field with the Lancaster Cincoes. Always an attraction on the baseball diamond, Leo was regarded as one of the best amateur pitchers in Lancaster County.[48] In addition, Leo agreed to referee boxing shows throughout his summer break for promoter Henry Hensel of the Lancaster A.C.

In the meantime, Leo's recent victory over Lewis in Paris was recognized by James J. Corbett, heavyweight champion from 1892 to 1897, in a weekly letter he wrote for the *Chicago Sunday Tribune*. He commented about the current mixed-up situation in the middleweight division and announced his great admiration for Leo Houck, stating that while he believed him to be one of the best of the bunch, he needed to settle the case of supremacy with Billy Papke. Corbett further stated, "Leo is only a youngster and has proved his worth by the defeat of Harry Lewis and a number of others. Better string with the young blood when class is there."[49]

Whether or not Leo read about Corbett's high praises and advice to go after Papke, one thing is certain: Leo did read the newspapers and kept abreast of the boxing scene, especially the current state of affairs in the middleweight division. Sure enough, Leo's ire for Papke surfaced after he read about his knockout of Jim Sullivan on June 8, 1911, in London. Sullivan was considered to be the English middleweight champion and Papke immediately claimed the right to the championship title. Leo was incensed and made no bones about how he felt when interviewed by the *Harrisburg Telegraph*, "Papke must fight me at the American limit, 158 ringside," said Houck. "When I was in Paris I learned that Papke was a heavyweight—at least he didn't want to reduce below 160. He can't call himself champion until he had beaten me and I'll camp on his trail until he fights or crawls."[50] In addition, Frank Klaus found little humor in Papke's claim to the middleweight honors and offered his own protest. "Papke cannot claim the middleweight championship without beating me," said Klaus in California yesterday. "I can do 158 ringside easily and when Papke comes here he will have to make that weight or forfeit."[51]

Close to the end of July, Leo decided to give up baseball for the season and resume training. He enjoyed a two-week yachting trip and returned ready to meet all comers. Of course, the fighter on top of the list as a possible opponent was Billy Papke, and Leo stated that he would meet him at 158 pounds or: "Any old weight will suit me. Just so I can get him into the ring."[52] Durlacher was unable to match Leo with Papke during 1911, but Leo would get his opportunity to do battle with Papke in September of 1912.

Now that Papke was eliminated from Leo's 1911 schedule, he changed his focus and prepared for a September 16 six-round fight against George Chip at the National A.C. in

Philadelphia. Chip was a promising middleweight from New Castle, Pennsylvania, who started his professional boxing career on January 30, 1909. Within a two-year period Chip was already an established threat who had routinely fought more seasoned boxers out of his class.

Three days before Leo's scheduled fight with Chip, an unforeseen circumstance was reported by the *Harrisburg Telegraph*, stating that Houck would schedule the remainder of his fights for the 1911 season by himself because he was displeased with his manager, Lew Durlacher. The abrupt shake-up was a shocker. Durlacher had masterfully guided Leo through a triumphant 1910 season and twenty-eight fights, during which Leo successfully transitioned from lightweight to welterweight to middleweight, and entered the 1911 season as a legitimate middleweight contender.[53]

On September 16, the night of the Houck-Chip fight, two reporters from different newspapers covered the fight. Their observations were, and are, most interesting.

The *Harrisburg Telegraph* reported the brawl this way: "Houck Wins from Chip at National."

> During the first two rounds Houck neither led nor rushed but waited to see what his opponent had. Houck discovered early on his jab worked with remarkable effect and he followed up with short left hooks. The blows were landing and telling on Chip by the third round. Houck easily out boxed Chip and continued to lead from the third to the final round.
>
> Houck used some clever footwork to avoid Chip's wild Sunday punches. Houck, the more experienced boxer, was far too clever for Chip.[54]

The fight was reported by the *Pittsburgh Post-Gazette* under the headline "Chip Is the Winner."

> Houck accomplished nothing during the first four rounds. He held constantly and appeared dull. Houck was taking it easy and made little attempt to improve his performance. During the final two rounds Houck knew he had to wake-up and start throwing punches.
>
> Both fighters appeared lackluster except for one exciting moment during the fourth round when Chip connected a rapid right upper-cut to Houck's jaw, which shook him up briefly. Chip relied on an ineffective straight lead but used them in combination with stinging right upper-cuts that landed squarely on Houck's chops. Both fighters abandoned boxing at times and resorted to brawling. They focused on each other's body as the intended target. Houck did flash in the last round and drove a left jab into Chip's face in combination with a series of rights to his body.[55]

The contrast between the fight descriptions and conflicting outcomes for the same fight as reported by the newspapers is humorous and occurred frequently during the newspaper-decision era. Official records show Leo was awarded the newspaper-decision win.

Only five days remained until Leo's next bout, a ten-rounder on September 21 against Frank Mantell at the National S.C. in New York City. Leo continued to train as hard as ever and needed to defeat both Mantell and his next opponent Harry Ramsey within the next two weeks, in order to match with Frank Klaus. The *New York Times* reported, "The followers of Frank Mantell are not too confident of their man, and believe he will be forced to show his best against the rugged Houck."[56] In contrast to the *New York Times* report, Mantel appeared to be well prepared for the fight. He had two recent victories prior to his match with Leo: a knockout over Ted Nelson and a technical knockout over Connie Schmidt.

On the night of the fight, Houck received a large round of applause from the crowd as he crossed the ropes and stepped into the ring. He looked about eight pounds lighter than Mantell, but this condition had never bothered Leo in the past, nor did it that night. Newspaper fight descriptions are often brief and lack important details, but this special report submitted to the *Harrisburg Telegraph* is a great example of early 1900s fight reporting written by a seasoned professional boxing sportswriter:

> Round 1: Mantell opened with a left to the neck. In a clinch both were holding and the referee separated them. Mantell landed a terrific right on the ear and Houck was jarred. In a half clinch Mantell put in body blows, but when he rushed Houck uppercut him on the jaw with a heavy right. Mantell swung another hard right to the neck and did enough forcing to take the round.
>
> Round 2: Mantell worked into a clinch. Breaking away Houck put in a sharp blow, which pushed Mantell down. The latter leaped up and ran in for a mix. Houck landing a right hook on the neck. They exchanged straight punches and clinched both landing short body blows. Houck jolted his man with a clean left on the jaw and met another rush with two rights under his chin. Mantell mixed it but Houck fought him off and had the round.
>
> Round 3: Houck tore in with a left in the stomach. Then he waited for a lead and ripped in uppercuts with great power. In several half clinches Houck used a free right hand on the body, but Mantell, breaking away, drove his man to the ropes. Houck at long range shot lefts and rights to the neck, after which they hit in several clinches. Mantell had the Lancaster man on the ropes when the bell rang but the round was about even.
>
> Round 4: Houck's right for the jaw was high. They went into a mix and traded swings on the head until locked. Mantell missed a dangerous right for the jaw, and Houck jumping in close rocked him with a couple of heavy hooks in the face. Mantell fought wildly for a moment but Houck kept cool and delivered the harder blows, reaching the body and neck until Mantell clinched. Houck's round.
>
> Round 5: Houck met advances with solid jabs and hooks. Then he rushed with a couple of body smashes. He beat Mantell to the punch three or four times, and landed with increasing strength. As Mantell rushed Houck uppercut him in the wind and then shot a left to the ear. They got into a hard clinch, but worked with free hands until broken. Houck landed half a dozen quick blows at close range and Mantell was clinching at the bell. Houck's round.
>
> Round 6: Rushing to close quarters Mantell received numerous short hooks in the neck and face. Houck blocked another rush and whipped in body punches. He jarred Mantell with a straight left to the jaw and also jumped in with a hard body blow. Mantell in a half clinch worked both hands to the ribs, Houck fighting him off and driving him to the ropes. More clean lefts in the face made Mantell's left eye puff. Houck's round.
>
> Round 7: Houck drove in lefts to offset Mantell's attack and they all landed. Mantell received a left on the mouth and Houck followed with more effective leading. At short range Houck did the better work. Mantell landing on him in several clinches. Mantell slugged at close quarters but Houck paid him back in his own coin, Mantell finally holding. Houck did the leading the rest of the way and had the round.
>
> Round 8: Houck opened up with a right over the heart. Mantell mixed in at close quarters, punching the body. Houck did some body punching too, but Mantell clinched. Houck stood off and put in clean blows with both hands until Mantell tried to rough it. Then Houck slugged and Mantell hung on. Houck did the cleaner work after that and the round belonged to him.
>
> Round 9: Houck blocked a dangerous left and swung a punch to the ear. Mantell tore in for a mix and Houck fought him to a clinch. Houck sailed in with quick jabs and drove Mantell to the ropes. The latter returned the compliment but was blocked. A straight left jarred Mantell and a stomach blow made him hold. Houck mixed it and Mantell rallied in great style. Houck had the round, however.
>
> Round 10: Houck tore in with hard smashes to the face and body. Mantell mixed in a landed a right on the eye. The referee tore them apart and Mantell ran in to receive a right uppercut. He forced Houck to the ropes and the latter drove in a corking blow to the ribs. Mantell mixed it again and in a half clinch they used short punches. Houck also scored on a knockdown with a left on the jaw and with a right on the stomach. He had Mantell clinching at the bell. Houck's round and bout.[57]

An interesting observation and newspaper opinion was offered about Leo's performance in the ring. During the fight, Leo had numerous opportunities to knock his opponent out, but instead delivered lighter punches. The reporter also noted that Leo had "not put one man to dreamland in two years but frequently could have done so if he so desired."[58] Leo never developed a penchant to needlessly punish a less experienced boxer. Conversely, Leo never extended any ring courtesies or allowances beyond the routine to a rival like middleweight contender Frank Klaus.

On September 28 at the Lancaster A.C., seven days after the Mantell bout, Leo matched with Harry Ramsey in a six-rounder, their second fight during 1911. The newspapers touted Ramsey, from Perth Amboy, New Jersey, as a candidate for the middleweight championship. The buildup of Ramsey as a middleweight contender was premature at this point in time, and the *Harrisburg Telegraph* incorrectly reported that he earned wins over Mickey McDonough, Joe Thomas, Jack Fitzgerald, Tommy Sullivan, Billy Berger, and Mike Glover.[59] Ramsey started his professional boxing career on March 28, 1910, and had a total of sixteen professional fights prior to his second meeting with Leo.

There was plenty of pugilistic action prior to the Houck-Ramsey wind-up. Even Frankie Hauck, Leo's younger brother, who now billed himself as Young Frank Hauck, appeared during the preliminaries.

The *Harrisburg Telegraph* reported that the wind-up fight was a letdown for the fans of the "Cauliflower Industry" who expected a much better performance from Ramsey.[60]

> Houck did most of the leading throughout the fight and attempted to knockout Ramsey before the third but was stopped by his constant clinching tactics where he tied up Houck's hands under his arms. In the fourth round Houck released a solid left to Ramsey's face and puffed up one of his eyes, which left it barely open. Ramsey bulled Houck into the ropes but was ineffective when he tried to punch and punish him. Houck had no difficulty with the tactic and drove his opponent away under a steady shower of blows. Ramsey managed to bounce a succession of feeble blows off Houck's head. Both fighters flashed and delivered in the sixth and final round. Houck pummeled Ramsey and he almost fell. Ramsey recovered then clinched and sleepwalked until the final gong.[61]

Leo easily earned the newspaper-decision win over Ramsey in what looked like a set-up fight in preparation for a much tougher opponent.

Frank Klaus was next on Leo's schedule in another six-rounder, on October 18 at the American A.C. in Philadelphia. A lot had changed for both fighters since their first meeting on October 29, 1910. Now they were both vying for the middleweight championship title. Klaus was destroying everyone in his path. The East Pittsburgher had amassed a string of ten consecutive wins from February 7 until October 10, 1911, which included three knockouts and two technical knockouts. During 1909 Klaus had wins over both Harry Lewis and Billy Papke.[62]

Klaus and Leo were perfectly matched middleweight specimens weighing in at 158 pounds each, with only a half-inch difference in height between them. The expectations for this match combined with the anticipation of a much-ballyhooed session of fisticuffs, without a doubt rivaled the Houck-Lewis battle in Paris and reached a crescendo the evening of the fight; but what happened next baffled the fans and sportswriters.

The fight verdicts reported by several newspapers on October 19 all offered contradictory evidence as to what had really happened. The *Harrisburg Daily Independent* reported, "Houck Won from Klaus" while the *Harrisburg Telegraph* reported, "Leo Houck Had His Troubles," and gave the win to Klaus.[63] The *Pittsburgh Daily Post* published its version titled, "Leo Houck Shows Better Than Klaus," but the *Pittsburgh Post-Gazette* viewed the fight differently and printed their story titled, "Klaus and Houck Draw."[64] The only outcome missing was a disqualification or forfeit by either fighter. Some of the sportswriters may have argued that neither fighter was entitled to a decision.

The *Harrisburg Daily Independent* reported that the fight fans were at times upset with both fighters' performances in the ring and hooted at them several times for their poor work. In fact, each boxer was over-anxious to knock the other out and often clinched and grappled around the ring until separated by the referee.[65]

Probably the best account of the fight, their last, was published by the *Harrisburg Daily Independent*.

> Houck had the best of the long range exchanges, using a left straight to the face to good advantage, often sending Frank's head back with a jolt. The Pittsburgh fighter did his best work in the clinches and at close quarters, welting Leo hard around the body. Houck had the advantage of the first three rounds, although little damage was done. The fourth and fifth were in favor of Klaus, Houck either tiring or saving himself for the last round. In the last round Houck cut loose and jabbed Klaus many times in the face. Once he followed this up with a right hand punch that was aimed at Frank's jaw, but went high and caught him over the eye, opening an old cut, from which the blood flowed freely.[66]

Official records all credit Frank Klaus with the newspaper-decision win.

Leo had six days to forget about his lackluster fight and performance against Klaus prior to leaving for his next bout with Jack Dillon in Boston. Dillon, a middleweight from the Midwest, was a powerhouse and compact package of muscle and sinew who had accumulated an impressive collection of knockouts. He believed that any middleweight contender "in his road" was just a temporary impediment as he slugged his way toward the middleweight championship. Naturally, Dillon considered Leo part of this befuddled middleweight mix. Moreover, Dillon was so confident in his abilities that he alleged all roads for a middleweight contender ultimately lead to himself.

Jack Dillon, the "Hoosier Bearcat," who was sometimes called "Jack the Giant Killer," loomed large in the current middleweight muddle. On October 24 he was scheduled to fight Leo at the Armory A.A. in Boston. The engagement was billed as an elimination bout to determine who would be entitled to the middleweight championship. Unfortunately, Dillon injured his hand on October 23 against Battling Levinsky and notified the club that he was unable to honor his commitment. Battling Levinsky, who lost the fight, agreed to substitute for Dillon and fight Leo the following day.

To illustrate the point of sheer toughness and determination of the early 1900s boxers, one should think about Battling Levinsky's condition one day after being beat up by Dillon, who was unquestionably the hardest hitter in any division up to and including the heavyweights, whom he often fought successfully out of his own weight class. Levinsky was already sore from the fight and stiffened up considerably more on the train ride from Philadelphia to Boston. Yet, there he was, one day after the Dillon fight, present and accounted for the evening's wind-up, which was no whirlwind six-rounder but rather a twelve-round slugfest.

Levinsky, like Leo and many other fighters of the early 1900s, was born during the "Gilded Age," an era of material excesses contrasted with conditions of extreme poverty. These future fighters, for the most part, discovered boxing early on and were only marginally aware of this "Gilded Age" dichotomy. They were, by and large, considered poor and part of the working class who were accustomed to the struggles and hardships of the times. As professional fighters they learned to survive by fighting often. Substituting on short notice was commonplace and looked upon as a bonus fight. The guarantee of an additional purse provided an extra bit of security in an unpredictable and not so secure career. For these boxers the gritty reality of the times was anything but glamorous. Those who wanted to become champions and make a living fighting discovered the career choices or trade-offs were as plain as black and white. A boxer had to take the one to three fights a week and practice "The Manly Art of Modified Murder," or quit boxing and accustom himself to the stupefied monotony and low wages of factory life.[67]

The *Harrisburg Telegraph* hardly covered the fight but claimed that Leo was all in by the end. The *Boston Globe* provided a more detailed account about Leo's performance with Levinsky in their third meeting during the current season.

> In the first round Levinsky connected with left jabs onto Houck's face. The jabs seemed to lack any real power but the hooks to both Houck's kidneys and wind were effective. The round ended with Levinsky clinching. During the second round Levinsky walloped Houck squarely with an overhand right and dropped him flatly onto the mat. Houck recovered and Levinsky delivered some more overhand rights that landed clumsily and too high to score another knockdown. Throughout the remaining rounds Houck took the lead and tried for a knockout but found it difficult to connect the punches to Levinsky's head. Instead, Houck went to work on Levinsky's kidneys while infighting and later had some effect with repeated jabs to his face and jolting punches to his body. The fighters often clinched but it worked in Houck's favor as he continued to punch Levinsky in the kidneys and body. Houck found enough room in the clinches to get his left and right hands free and land blows to Levinsky's face and jaw. Overall, the fight did little to stir up much excitement in the crowd and Houck won on points largely due to his clever boxing during the final four rounds.[68]

After the Levinsky fight, Leo planned to sign with a local team to play basketball during November and December, between his scheduled boxing matches. Before his first basketball game he faced Harry Ramsey in a six-rounder on November 3 at the Nonpareil A.C. in Philadelphia. This was their third and last engagement. Ramsey had been idle since his loss to Leo on September 28. One thing for certain, Ramsey had a devoted fan base. They claimed that he had to take off too much weight, and too quickly for his second bout with Leo in September. Moreover, the devotees of "all things Ramsey" claimed this weakened condition sapped his strength and prevented him from building up a decent head of steam until the final round, when he finally woke up. Leo told the newspapers prior to the match that he did not care if Ramsey weighed a ton. Leo's manager, Lew Durlacher, occasionally made bold and premature public predictions about Leo's fights and stated, "Houck will win decisively."[69] Gamblers took the bait and the short-end odds on Leo. The public comment by Durlacher indicated that he was once again actively managing Leo's career. The earlier schism between the men, which had resulted in Durlacher's dismissal by Leo on September 13, appeared to be mended and officially over.

For whatever reason, there was only a scant amount of publicity for this bout. The *York Daily* showed its lack of interest by describing the fight result in the stingiest of ways: "The fight was fast and hard throughout but neither man was able to gain a decided advantage."[70] Official records list the fight as a draw.

After the Ramsey bout, the devotees of boxing still remained convinced that the middleweight championship title needed to be settled between Klaus and Houck. Interestingly enough, sportswriters were now perceiving Papke, who currently claimed the middleweight championship title, as an outgrown middleweight and under duress late in 1911, when he suffered losses in his last two fights of the season to Sailor Burke and Bob Moha.[71]

Leo wasted no time after the Ramsey bout and quickly resumed his training regimen.

He had two weeks to prepare for Buck Crouse, his next challenger, who was a legitimate threat to his top-ranked status. However, Leo needed to settle another matter, which required his immediate attention. He made arrangements to play basketball between boxing engagements, and signed on with the St. John's Catholic Club of Lancaster. His first game was on November 9, only six days before his scheduled six-rounder with Crouse at the Duquesne Gardens in Pittsburgh. Basketball and baseball continued to provide an enjoyable reprieve for Leo, which temporarily interrupted the constant physical punishment of boxing.

Buck Crouse was Pittsburgh's middleweight phenomenon. His boxing achievements in 1911, in combination with his thirty-six percent knockout rate, put him squarely in the hunt for the middleweight championship. One could easily argue that he deserved to be ranked equally with Klaus and Leo, or any other middleweight contender in the current middleweight championship skirmish. Crouse, like Leo, rapidly ascended the middleweight ranks during 1910, and was the third-busiest boxer in the United States that year when he fought a total of twenty-seven fights, only one less than Leo.[72]

Of course, Leo was aware of Crouse's record from January 17 until November 11, 1911, when he won eighteen times, which included ten knockouts plus four technical knockouts. The same time frame actually included a total of nineteen fights, but Crouse's win streak during this period was interrupted by a draw with Billy Berger on August 22, 1911.[73]

The stage was set and the fans were sufficiently whipped up by the press, who described the bout as "almost a championship battle in itself."[74] Newspapers now described Leo as the "Lancaster Terror," but his reign of terror ceased outside the confines of the squared circle. Leo was always a gentleman on the other side of the ropes, and professionally acknowledged Crouse beforehand as "the best man he ever faced."

The *New Castle News* claimed that Crouse won all the way, yet the fight was not one-sided.[75] The *Boston Daily Globe* reported that Crouse won by a good margin and sensationalized their report by stating that Houck was now eliminated from the middleweight championship chase. Their account, titled "Crouse Gives Houck Enough," detailed the fight round by round.

> Crouse started round one with a series of left jabs that landed effectively and worried Houck. Both fighters exercised some caution during this round and took a full measure of one another. Crouse continued to throw jabs and box while Houck took it easy and did little if any counter punching. Crouse connected some blows to Houck's face and head, which were the only punches landed during the round. Houck decided to rough it up during the second round and Crouse responded immediately. While clinching Crouse found room to repeatedly use his right and uppercut into Houck's chin and nose. Houck's nose started to bleed and he also received a cut on the left cheek that started to bleed. Crouse began the third round by jabbing with a left and following with an overhand right. Houck's quick footwork thwarted this maneuver easily and it appeared that he may have been warned about this combination of Crouse's. The fourth round started with an effective triple jab by Houck, which resulted in Crouse momentarily losing his head and throwing wild punches. After Crouse settled down and gathered himself he snapped Houck's head back twice in rapid succession with a stinging left. Crouse then bulled Houck into a neutral corner and blasted him with blow after blow to both his head and body. Houck got out of the predicament by jabbing left to the face and following with a right cross. Houck's blows did minimal damage if any. Seconds before the bell signaled the end of the round Houck rocked Crouse with a right to his face. The fifth belonged to Crouse and the bleeding from Houck's nose and mouth had continued since the third round and by now seemed to bother him. Crouse wasted time as he continued to repeatedly throw ineffective right crosses that Houck easily avoided. Houck flashed brilliantly in the sixth. Knowing that he was behind he cut loose pell-mell.

Houck landed a right to Crouse's face and cut his lip, which immediately bled and worried him. Once again, Crouse lost his head and went wild. Houck took advantage of his condition and jabbed Crouse at will in the face. Crouse responded with a smile each time Houck connected but never attempted to counter punch.[76]

Leo received the newspaper-decision loss. Durlacher and Leo immediately requested a rematch before the end of 1911.

Jimmy Mason, Crouse's manager, agreed to the rematch, another six-rounder, on December 9 at the National A.C. in Philadelphia. Leo was anxious to prove that he was the better fighter and wanted his fans to know that the last contest was hardly a true test of his ability. Leo's relationship with his fans was a faithful one and he never made excuses for a loss or draw. Instead, he promised to improve the next time out, especially in a rematch with an opponent who had defeated him.

This last match of the season gave Leo an opportunity to improve over Crouse and shore up his fan support. Newspaper reports differed about the fight's outcome. The *Harrisburg Telegraph* stated confidently that the margin of difference was minimal but Leo easily outpointed Crouse and reversed the verdict from their November 15 meeting.[77] The *Boston Globe* panned Crouse's performance as compared to his last fight and claimed the best to be expected was a draw based on this account.

> In the first two rounds Houck constantly backed away from Crouse. During the third round Houck dropped that habit and started to lead. Crouse was overanxious and started to swing wildly. All of the swings missed their intended target. Crouse did manage to deliver some hard punches to Houck's stomach. At times Houck struggled and seemed to lag but soon recovered and came to the front and pasted Crouse's face with a left.
>
> Crouse concentrated on Houck's kidneys and belted him continuously with rights. Both fighters had a tendency to swing wildly during the latter rounds and had some limited success in landing their blows. Overall, the mill was fast paced and hard but it appeared as if neither boxer took any real chances.[78]

Some official sources list the newspaper-decision as a win for Leo, while others identify the outcome as a draw.

Overall, Leo had another outstanding season during 1911 and posted eleven wins, three losses, and two draws from a total of sixteen bouts. He remained at the very top of the current middleweight rankings and now looked forward to another overseas adventure—boxing in Europe during the beginning of 1912. Leo and Billy Papke were scheduled to sail for England on December 28 and then leave for Paris on January 9. Papke, only several weeks earlier, announced that he had retired and was through with boxing, but soon afterwards changed his mind and promptly signed for five fights at the Cirque de Paris, France's largest fight club.

While Leo was in Paris during 1911, he met and sparred with Georges Carpentier, the "Orchid Man," who was the current European welterweight champion. In 1912, Carpentier captured the European middleweight title and the following year claimed the European light heavyweight title. He went on to become the world light heavyweight champion in 1920 after knocking out Battling Levinsky in four rounds, and held the title until 1922.[79]

Leo taught Carpentier the finer points of his effective left jab during the 1911 trip and encouraged him to use the jab on Harry Lewis. Carpentier may have taken the lesson to heart and applied the left jab when he defeated Harry Lewis on December 13, 1911, at the Cirque de Paris. The *Harrisburg Telegraph* reported that Houck would fight Carpentier in France during the return trip in 1912.[80]

There were a multitude of French fans that loved Leo and eagerly anticipated his return. They looked forward to a match with their own national hero, Carpentier, who currently straddled the European welterweight championship summit. French knockout artist Marcel Moreau was also mentioned as a possible opponent. The fight plans for Leo's campaign in Paris were formidable but uncomplicated: defeat Carpentier, Moreau, and Papke in any order, and return home triumphantly with the world middleweight championship title.

7

Top of the Heap, 1912–1913

1912

The return trip to Europe was temporarily delayed. Durlacher and Leo signed a $600 offer to fight Jack Dillon, the "Hoosier Bearcat," on New Year's Day in a ten-rounder at the Auditorium in Indianapolis. A fight with Dillon at this moment was a risky proposition, especially on the eve of an important trip overseas, but the purse was ample and hard to resist. Dillon was the most dangerous middleweight around. He was feared and avoided by many heavyweights, his favorite quarry; but Leo's confidence in his pugilistic abilities was rock-solid and he realized that a win or draw with Dillon before leaving for Europe would increase his stock tenfold by the time he reached Paris.

There was an underlying reason that also may have prompted Leo to accept the short-notice fight. The *Pittsburgh Daily Post* published a direct challenge and offer by Dillon to fight any middleweight contender. He stated that he felt compelled to, once and for all, settle the current middleweight muddle and promised that he could dominate the middleweight division. His top four choices as opponents included Frank Klaus, Buck Crouse, Bob Moha, and Leo Houck. Whoever could step up first and sign was welcome to do so.[1] Bold public challenges like Dillon's always captured Leo's attention and, in fact, he took this one quite seriously after he read about his preferred status as an opponent.

The training conditions for Leo prior to the battle with Dillon were stark and uncomfortable, an ominous harbinger preceding an outcome that resulted in tumult, dashed plans, and a lengthy convalescence. The *Lancaster New Era* published Leo's own story about the fight on July 5, 1926, some fourteen years later, when he set the record straight.

> There are two technical knockouts to my boxing record, one at the hands of Jack Dillon, of Indianapolis, known as Jack the Giant Killer, for his ability to polish off opponents heavier than himself, and the other was Billy Murray, of San Francisco, who at the time I fought him in that city was managed by Jack Kearns, famous manager of Jack Dempsey, world heavyweight champion and now handling the affairs of the recently dethroned welterweight champion, Mickey Walker.
>
> This tale will be of the famous meetings between the Giant Killer and myself.
>
> Our first clash was on New Year's Day, 1912, at Indianapolis, Dillon's hometown. I arrived at Indianapolis with my manager, Lou Durlacher and Freddy Kelly, at that time a prominent lightweight, about four days before the bout. I'll never forget our first impression of that city. The mercury was about fifteen below zero and I thought we were in Alaska.
>
> We made our headquarters at the Hotel Edwards and the first thing we had to do was look up a gymnasium for Kelly and myself to work out. Kelly was on the same card meeting "Young Saylor."

After several hours' search, which covered a great part of the city, we finally located a place that was formerly used by a group of theatrical acrobats. It wasn't a desirable gym, but time was too short and we had to get down to training. I was carrying several pounds of excess weight, which I had to get rid of before weighing-in time on the day of the fight.

The three days of training which I put in that improvised gym were three days of torture. But every cloud has a silver lining and who should turn up to the surprise of everybody on the second day of training but my friends Harry Mohler and Harry Rieker, of Lancaster. Both were members of the Arion Club, which in those days was a great booster for sports for the younger generation. There was no heat in the gym but they stuck around to watch me work and I still wonder how they stood it, for even though I was working I was chilled through and through and I thought I'd never get thawed out.

The longer we stayed in Indianapolis it seemed the colder it got. Finally, the day of the fight rolled around. What a relief to know that I didn't have to work in that cold gym anymore and that I was down to the required 158 pounds.

Came the night of the fight, which was held in the Auditorium. The place was packed to the rafters for Dillon was a great favorite throughout the middle west and became a great favorite throughout the country. Lew Durlacher, Freddy Kelly, and Freddy Hoe, the last a promising young heavyweight from Indianapolis, were my seconds.

When the first bell sounded Dillon and I met in the center of the ring. There wasn't much fooling in those days and we went right to the business of fighting. The pace was terrific, with honors about even. The fans were on their feet from the start and they stayed that way until I was unable to respond for the eighth round.

During the second round we continued coming at a furious rate. Near the close of the session I felt a stinging pain in the lower part of my stomach. I did not take it seriously and continued to battle away until the round ended. I told Durlacher of the pain when I got back to my corner and it kept getting worse with each breath I took. He told me to go out and shake it off.

I went out for the third and for a time was able to hold my own but finally the pain became so great that I could not breathe properly and was just able to defend myself. Near the end of the round I couldn't even do that and was forced to take a sound thumping.

At the end of the round I told Durlacher again of the pain, but he told me to finish the ten rounds. I took his advice and tried to, but the best I could do from the fourth round until the end of the seventh was take a sound mauling. The pain was so great after the seventh that I was unable to respond for the eighth and Dillon was awarded the fight on a technical knockout. After the second round the fight was too one-sided to be interesting.

I went to my dressing room, barely able to walk, and was examined by a physician. He found that one of my lower ribs had been fractured. He put on a few strips of adhesive tape and told me to stay in bed for a few days, so I did.

After the fight I wired my mother and told her that I was not hurt badly, but she was not satisfied and sent my brother Ed, and Frank Gottselig to Indianapolis to find out the real trouble. I stayed in Indianapolis another week, but the pain was not getting any better, so I decided to return home and place myself under the care of a local physician.

Dr. Newton E. Bitzer was called on my arrival home. He also informed me that a rib was broken but instead of a few strips of tape he bandaged me in adhesive from my chest down to my hip. Let me tell you it was like being placed in a strait jacket. I wore the tape for a month and it was a bitter pill, for I was physically fit otherwise and wanted to move about.

That was a bad January 1, as the St. Joseph's Catholic Club basketball team, of which I was a member, was defeated by Lancaster High School, 14 to 9. There were also a few casualties in that game. Summing up it was a bad day for the Eighth Ward.

In an article titled "Leo Houck Did Not Go to Paris," the *Harrisburg Telegraph,* upon Leo's return home, reported, "He feels confident that he can defeat Dillon under favorable conditions and hopes to meet him again."[2]

Leo's injuries were more extensive than one broken rib. "An X-ray examination revealed a fracture of the lower-most rib on the left side and the complete detachment of the two lower floating ribs from their cartilages."[3] Doctor Albert P. Berg, who performed the examination, told Leo he would not be in condition to fight for approximately two months. Many years later, Leo told his entire family about his multiple fights with Dillon. He stated quite emphatically that Jack Dillon was by far the toughest fighter and hardest hitter he ever faced.[4]

Dillon had effectively ruined Leo's planned return trip to Europe early in January 1912. The fight with Dillon prior to leaving for Europe might have been a bad decision, an outright mistake, a slight miscalculation, or a result of Durlacher's questionable management.

Leo remained hugely popular in France and continued to receive offers even after the loss to Dillon. French fighters Marcel Moreau and Georges Carpentier, who was the European middleweight champion, both wanted bouts with Leo.[5] Even Al Lippe, Harry Lewis's manager, believed that many American boxers wore out their welcome at home by sticking to one place or locale. He advocated that boxers needed to travel and box in Europe, which would replenish their coffers and make them a fortune. If successful, the prestige gained overseas could garner them larger purses once they returned home.[6] Unfortunately, Leo never returned to Paris during 1912.[7]

There is no evidence to suggest that this missed opportunity was a bungled affair caused by mismanagement. Leo was mature and level-headed and knew that his contender status made him a pivotal boxer within the middleweight division. Other opportunities were on the horizon. Moreover, he was ranked as one of the top five middleweights in the nation and realized that he could choose to remain in the United States, continue to earn purses, eliminate other middleweight contenders, and quite possibly win the middleweight championship title on American soil. In other words, Leo seemed content to forego the larger purses offered in France, which allowed him to bypass the inconvenience of overseas travel and time spent away from home and family. More importantly, Leo had another reason to remain close to Cabbage-Hill. Her name was Anna Kirchner.

Within weeks after the Dillon fight, Leo had improved enough to referee a fight on January 25 at the Lancaster A.C. By February 27, Leo was back on the basketball court and played guard for his team, the St. Joseph's Catholic Club, against the York Y.M.C.A.

The newspapers continued to follow Leo's sporting activities outside of the ring. Without any additional explanation the *Evening Report* stated, "Robert E. McCusker, a well known sporting manager, has been engaged by Leo Houck, the Lancaster middleweight, as manager."[8] The Hauck family speculated that a rift existed between Leo and Durlacher, which precipitated this change in management twice within a five-and-a-half-month period. However, the reasons why remained vague and, for the most part, unsubstantiated.[9]

There is a saying: "Time heals all wounds." Fourteen years after the second Houck-Durlacher split, Leo submitted an article to the *Lancaster New Era* titled "Leo Houck Meets Up with Old-Time Manager." If any hard feelings had actually existed between Leo and Durlacher, time had effectively managed to erase any past unpleasantness, at least on Leo's behalf. In the article, Leo stated, "Durlacher handled my affairs in many of my important fights and I hold him in high regard."[10] This positive acknowledgment about Durlacher was a distinctive and fundamental hallmark of Leo's nature and ability to retain longtime friendships with both his peers and the numerous opponents he had defeated in the ring.

Three and a half months after the Dillon bout, Leo was slated to fight middleweight

Peck Miller, of Philadelphia, on April 12 at the Lancaster A.C. The fight with Miller was canceled and rescheduled for April 23.[11] Several days after the cancellation with Miller, Jack McGuigan, a Philadelphia matchmaker, contacted Bob McCusker, Leo's new manager, and offered a match with middleweight contender Bob Moha, aka the Caveman. Leo accepted Moha as a substitute but still considered Miller as the tougher boxer. He was a palpable threat and touted by the newspapers as an up-and-coming middleweight contender.

Leo had eight additional days to prepare for the Moha fight on April 20, at the National A.C. in Philadelphia. Moha was two inches shorter than Leo and was described by the *Pittsburgh Post-Gazette* as "the stump western fighter who is not much taller than the average lightweight."[12] The newspaper failed to report that Moha was also ranked as one of the top five contenders currently vying for the middleweight championship title. He had outpointed and won over Billy Papke, the current middleweight champion, on October 31, 1911.

The fans were keen to witness Leo's return to the squared circle after a painful and lengthy convalescence. They expected him to fight defensively and cover up his midsection at all times.

Leo was surprised by Moha's nonperformance during this important elimination fight. Fourteen years later, Leo offered his own recollection about the fight in the *Lancaster New Era* and corroborated by an unnamed Philadelphia newspaper in the same article.

> I had expected a very hard bout with Moha, but much to my surprise, and I presume to the hundreds of others who watched the fight that night, Moha proved easy for me. The following account in a Philadelphia newspaper the following day will testify:
>
> "Houck seemed to be able hit him when and where he pleased, whenever the 'phenom' would forget to clinch. Moha also violated the boxing rules on many occasions, by using the kidney punch and other infractions of the Quaker code. Moha throughout the entire contest seemed at a disadvantage, as he failed to block or exchange blows with any degree of accuracy, and at the end of the second chapter blood was streaming from his nose and mouth and he showed signs of deep distress."[13]

Leo received the newspaper-decision win.

Three days after the Moha bout, Leo prepared to fight Peck Miller in a six-round wind-up on April 23 at the Lancaster A.C. Miller was an up-and-comer in the middleweight division and described by the press as a strong opponent and legitimate threat to upend Leo. Advance publicity about an opponent never distracted Leo. The *Harrisburg Telegraph* reported, "Houck is of the opinion that he must get rid of all the claimants to reach the highest honors."[14]

The local press never published an account about the Tuesday night fight with Miller. Official records list a newspaper-decision win for Leo.

Two weeks later, Leo returned to Boston and faced Buck Crouse on May 7, in a twelve-rounder at the official opening of the Pilgrim A.A. This was the third time they fought and Crouse still figured prominently in the middleweight muddle. He had five consecutive wins from January 22 until April 18, 1912, leading up to this fight.[15]

Only minutes before the first gong, Johnny Mooney, the matchmaker in Boston, pulled a "switcheroo" and substituted a new referee, Martin Clougherty, without any explanation, discussion, or approval from the Houck camp.[16] This abrupt change of referees was highly uncommon. Leo, his manager, and seconds instinctively knew this last-minute substitution reeked. They suspected some sort of set-up or underhanded scheme.

In a special to the *Pittsburgh Daily Post*, the fight was bylined with an account titled "Houck Has All the Best."

> Houck took command and led from the very start. He finally woke up Crouse who sleepwalked through the first six rounds. Houck gained a substantial lead on points with his relentless jabbing and hooking. There was a considerable amount of in-fighting and Crouse took a flatfooted style, which suited Houck just fine. By the eighth round Crouse started to measure his man successfully and picked-off some of Houck's stinging lefts. Crouse also tried for Houck's recently repaired ribs and pounded them relentlessly looking for the spot where Dillon did his best work. Houck never winced or backed up and countered successfully with a series of short jabs and hooks. Crouse threw some fast lefts that produced a bruise above Houck's left eye. Crouse was devoid of any speed throughout the fight and was completely unsuccessful in keeping his opponent at bay. The steady onslaught of punches from Houck prevented Crouse from ever seriously engaging his opponent. The total number of points and victory clearly belonged to Houck.[17]

The substitute referee, Clougherty, did not pick the winner at the end of the fight. Instead, he sent each man back to his corner and then raised his hand and pointed it to Crouse's corner, awarding him the victory. The crowd was stunned and refused to leave the arena for over an hour afterwards hissing and booing the referee while they discussed the worst ring decision ever by a local referee. There was a unanimous opinion from the fans and Pilgrim A.A. club directors that Leo had easily won going away and rightfully deserved the honors.

The referee, Clougherty, made matters worse by admitting that "he had Houck in mind, but inadvertently pointed toward Crouse."[18] The *Altoona Tribune* reported that the referee talked with the Pilgrim A.A. directors and admitted he did err and meant to award the decision to Houck but became confused.[19] Crouse and his manager, Jimmy Mason, stated, "The decision was given to Crouse without hesitation as soon as the fight was over and that the referee never stated after the battle that he had made a mistake and intended to declare Houck the winner."[20]

The most plausible reason for these suspicious goings-on might have involved the large sums of money that were reported to have been wagered on Crouse, who was favored at ten to seven. Three Providence, Rhode Island, men were reported to have wagered $7,000 against $14,000 that Houck would win.[21] Gamblers who bet two bits or the high rollers who doubled-down with large sums of folding money waited nervously as the referee's decision was questioned and reviewed. The matchmaker for the National Club, John McGarvey, who held all the bets, declared that only ring decisions count and gave all the money to the Crouse supporters.[22]

A few hours after the fight, Leo was met at the railroad station by the Boston fans and seven directors of the Pilgrim A.C. Oddly enough, Clougherty, the referee, was also part of the gathering. They all felt obligated to make things better for Leo and decided to give him a warm ovation, a lucrative rematch offer the next week, and best of all, sent him home with the winner's end of the purse. Leo left the Boston rematch offer with Crouse on the table, but they did meet again during 1913.

The Houck camp was resolute in their efforts to eliminate any and all middleweight challengers. Leo used the next fifteen days to train for his match on May 23 with Jack Fitzgerald, aka the Fighting Harp, at the Lancaster A.C. The *Harrisburg Telegraph* touted Fitzgerald as a recognized middleweight aspirant and the "original fighting hope of Philadelphia."[23] Moreover, in a special to the *Harrisburg Telegraph*, the hype about Fitzgerald continued. He was billed as the only real middleweight contender within the division most likely to succeed—so much so, that a number of middleweight aspirants for the crown ignored any challenges from him. The newspaper's endorsement of Fitzgerald as a threat to Leo was manna from heaven for promoter Hensel of the Lancaster A.C. Special trains were required to transport fans from Philadelphia, Reading, Lebanon, Harrisburg, and York. The demand for seats exceeded any prior boxing show in Lancaster.[24]

The newspaper's hoopla over Fitzgerald was overblown and skewed. From December 24, 1910, until March 4, 1912, Fitzgerald had fought a total of sixteen fights and posted one win, two draws, and thirteen losses.[25] His upcoming fight was billed as an elimination bout, but looked more like a set-up.

The *Lebanon Daily News* published a brief story about Leo and his domination of the "The Fighting Harp."

> When Fitzgerald entered the ring the fans noticed that he had quite a bit of weight over Houck. Before the end of first round they also discovered that Fitzgerald lacked the wind to carry that excess. Houck fans were unusually blood thirsty during this bout and hollered at Houck repeatedly for a knockout over his sluggish opponent. Houck had his way from flag-fall to finish. Fitzgerald clinched repeatedly just to save himself. During the fourth round Houck almost put Fitzgerald to sleep. He held onto Houck for dear life until the round ended. The last two rounds also belonged to Houck. Fitzgerald, to his credit, took his medicine from Houck like a shot of castor oil and managed to make an effort throughout.[26]

With another newspaper-decision win under his belt, Leo now looked forward to a deserved layoff of seventeen days.

Leo's next bout, a six-rounder, was his second engagement with George Chip, whose manager, Jimmy Dime, sent Hensel a certified check to guarantee the presence of his fighter on June 13 at Rossmere Park in Lancaster. Boxing shows had steadily increased in popularity with the opposite sex throughout the United States. Hensel, who loved to fill the seats, recognized this latest development and advertised that special accommodations will be reserved for the ladies who attended the fight.[27]

Up until 1912, Chip hardly ever fought east of Pittsburgh. By this time, he was considered a legitimate threat within the middleweight division, but not yet mentioned or ranked as a top-ten contender.

A crowd of 3,000 spectators jammed Rossmere Park. Leo, the hometown favorite, never gestured outwardly in acknowledgment of his fans. In fact, he appeared totally oblivious to the cheering and commotion on the other side of the ropes. The anticipation over what was expected to be an exciting boxing match was tempered early on by Leo, who easily repulsed Chip's efforts.

The next day, in a special to the *Harrisburg Telegraph*, the fight was described in a short article titled "Leo Houck Had Another Easy Job."

> Houck did most of the leading throughout. Chip clinched and covered up repeatedly. Chip bulled Houck into the ropes but was unable to contain his opponent and land any blows. Houck used his stinging left jab, one of his favorite punches, which sapped the energy from his opponent. Chip was unable to avoid the punishment from Houck and looked doomed from the first round. Houck flashed brilliantly in the final round while Chip looked bleary and dazed. By the final round Houck had demoted Chip from contender to pretender.[28]

After the fight, Robert McCusker was deluged with offers for Leo to fight in Europe, as well as clubs throughout the United States. One offer included a bout with Frank Klaus in Paris, while another proposed that Leo participate in a middleweight elimination contest during the fall of 1912 in the United States.

All of the incoming offers were considered but put on hold for the time being. Leo was now twenty-four years old, in love, and planning to marry his childhood sweetheart, Anna Maria Kirchner, during the summer of 1912. Leo and Anna had been neighbors and friends since childhood. Her father, Ambrose Kirchner, and her mother, Elizabeth Kirchner, owned a thriving Cabbage-Hill grocery store located at 703 Manor Street, across from the silk mill.[29]

The Reverend Father Echterling married Anna and Leo on August 22 in St. Joseph's Catholic Church. John Kirchner, a brother of the bride, and Miss Miriam Houck, a sister of the bridegroom, attended the couple. Their honeymoon trip included a visit to Niagara Falls and a short excursion into Canada. They planned to return to Lancaster no later than September 10 so Leo could resume training for a September 19 engagement with Peck Miller.

The six-rounder with Miller, his second fight with Leo, was held at the Lancaster A.C. Miller had two consecutive wins over Joe Borrell on July 30 and again on September 2, prior to his bout with Leo.[30] In contrast, Leo had been on an extended layoff for almost three months.

The *Harrisburg Daily Independent* covered the fast-paced wind-up.

> From the first to the last gong Houck showed he was the master of Miller. Miller managed to stay the entire six rounds but clinched repeatedly and often held on hard. Houck used his favorite weapon, the left jab, and followed with a right uppercut. Miller attempted to stand flatfooted against Houck during the infighting and failed. Miller escaped the infighting and pushed Houck to the ropes several times. Houck broke loose every time and counter punched with a left jab-right uppercut combination. Houck easily outpointed Miller throughout.[31]

Leo received the newspaper-decision win over Peck Miller.

Eight days later, on September 27, Leo fought middleweight champion Billy Papke, the "Illinois Thunderbolt," at the Olympia A.C. Some newspapers incorrectly reported that Papke was the former middleweight champion. In fact, he was still the current middleweight champion. Papke initially claimed the middleweight title after Stanley Ketchel's death in 1910, but lost it on March 5, 1913, due to a foul on Frank Klaus in Paris. After that fight, "Klaus was acclaimed universally as the new middleweight champion."[32]

The build-up for this match reached a fever pitch. Boxing fans and the press expected nothing less than an all-out donnybrook that would end with either Leo or Papke sprawled flat on the mat and unable to respond after the nine-count.

This fight had one predominant "what-if" theory regarding the eventual outcome. Papke was supposed to fight Georges Carpentier, the European middleweight champion, in France after his fight with Leo. The newspapers reported that Papke's assurances to fight Carpentier were not ironclad. Only one condition, a win over Leo, could guarantee Papke's match with Carpentier. Moreover, a loss by Papke would automatically cinch Leo's undisputed preference to replace Papke in France. Leo had no interest in weighing in over his chances to replace Papke in France. Instead, he told the newspapers, "The Illinois Thunderbolt will go to France with a defeat marked against him."[33]

Leo was exceedingly confident that he could master Papke. Most boxers who faced Papke probably trained right up to the day before the fight, but not Leo. He wanted another diversion and agreed to umpire five baseball games during a conference championship in Lebanon County, which started three days before his bout with Papke.[34]

A total of 4,000 fans attended the fight. They had no idea that Papke had attempted some nasty shenanigans in his dressing room only minutes before the fight. He had a reputation as one of the toughest and most durable fighters of the day, but also one of the foulest to ever enter the ring.[35] Ed Hauck took his job as his brother's keeper very seriously, and decided to visit Papke's dressing room prior to the fight. He witnessed Papke punching the rough concrete walls of the dressing room with his gloves and noticed he had shredded them. The gloves, in that condition, would have cut Leo's face to ribbons. This scheme was a new low for Papke. Fortunately, Billy Rocap, the famous sportswriter, who had accompanied Leo to Paris in 1911, refereed that night.

After both fighters received their instructions in the ring, Ed advised Rocap to examine Papke's gloves. Only a cursory inspection was required. The jig was up. Rocap immediately ordered the removal of Papke's gloves and chucked them into the audience. The shredded gloves were replaced with a new pair. The "Illinois Thunderbolt" was incensed at the thought of being outsmarted.[36]

The *Lancaster Sunday News* published a story about the fight fifty years later titled, "50th Anniversary of a Memorable Fight," a brief but colorful version of this rowdy bout.

> The Lancaster boy started his famous left hand jabs to the jaw and had the champion bewildered.
> Duke Kelly, a lifelong friend and a famous second, had Papke enraged by his constant chatter. In those days the seconds were allowed to coach from their corners.
> In the third round, Papke leaned out of the ring and spit in the Duke's face. Leo then landed a terrific right uppercut and knocked Billy into the audience. After scrambling back into the ring the "Thunderbolt" deliberately jumped at Leo, using his head as a battering ram, opening his [Leo's] eye.
> In the last round Leo rushed from his corner and nearly upset Papke with a right hand uppercut to the jaw and battered Papke to the ropes with rights and lefts, which brought the crowd to its feet calling for a knockout.
> The onslaught continued until the bell, ending the fight.[37]

The fight belonged to Leo all the way and he received the newspaper-decision win. Papke was awarded the "raspberries" from the *Washington Post* after they described him as a small Chinese firecracker instead of the "Illinois Thunderbolt."[38]

Soon after the fight, Al Lippke, who was a silent partner in French boxing promotions and Papke's manager, matched his boxer with Carpentier for a bout in France. Sportswriters and fans thought that Leo deserved the Carpentier match. On the surface, it looked as if Lippke had bilked Leo out of an opportunity to fight Carpentier. The opposite was true. Lippke's signing Papke to fight Carpentier was just straight-up business.

All the post-fight rumpus and discussion about who should have rightfully fought Carpentier vanished within days. Leo felt satisfied and accomplished exactly what he had promised earlier when he said, "The Illinois Thunderbolt will go to France with a defeat marked against him."

Leo had only eleven days for the cut above his eye to heal, the result of Papke's head butt, before his next six-round wind-up fight on October 9 with Eddie McGoorty, from Oshkosh, Wisconsin, at the National A.C. in Philadelphia. McGoorty was a middleweight contender who earned an equal ranking with Frank Klaus, Billy Papke, Jack Dillon, and Mike Gibbons. From April 12, 1911, until September 23, 1912, McGoorty racked up fourteen consecutive wins, which included four knockouts and one technical knockout.[39]

The *Lancaster New Era* published Leo's appraisal of McGoorty, which included a brief synopsis by the Philadelphia press for this middleweight elimination fight.

> McGoorty had developed a great left hook. After he came to New York, he was cutting a wide swath into his opponents, via the haymaker route, with his left delivering the knockout drops. But Eddie was also a very clever boxer and hard to hit. The *Philadelphia Press* had the following to say of the fight:

> "Leo Houck, popular resident of Lancaster, handed a nice lacing to 'One Round' McGoorty. McGoorty only landed one of his famous left hooks, but the blow was too high to do any damage. The 'Oshkosh Battler' found that it was impossible to hit Houck with his punches. Leo started the blood flowing from McGoorty in the fifth, after a hearty exchange. In the last round Houck made victory more decisive by jabbing and hooking McGoorty all over the ring."[40]

Leo's newspaper-decision wins over both McGoorty and Papke changed the current middleweight contender rankings. Frank Klaus still remained at number one. Leo moved up and was now ranked equally at number two, along with Jack Dillon and Mike Gibbons. Middleweight contender Mike Gibbons from St. Paul, Minnesota, was barely mentioned in the eastern regional press, but was generally acknowledged as a top-ranked contender who was capable of winning all the marbles.[41] By this time, the top four boxers, Klaus, Houck, Dillon, and Gibbons, had either completely eliminated or subordinated the remaining middleweight contenders.

After the McGoorty fight, Leo had nineteen days to simply enjoy being a newlywed. He was in superb condition without any nagging injuries, and required only minimal training before his next fight against Jack Fitzgerald on October 28, at the Town Hall in Scranton. This was Leo's second meeting with Fitzgerald. Since their last meeting on May 23, Leo had fought four fights. During the same period Fitzgerald had fought only once and lost to Emmett "Kid" Wagner. Since December 1910, Fitzgerald's career had started to tank. This fight looked easy for Leo.

The *Scranton Truth* covered the wind-up, a fast-paced six-rounder that pleased the crowd and highlighted Fitzgerald's dogged perseverance against a superior boxer.

> Houck opened the first round with a left jab to his opponent's neck. Fitzgerald sparred and mixed it up with Houck. Both fighters punched, jabbed, and hooked at each other but few blows actually met their intended targets.
>
> Houck pasted Fitzgerald seconds after the second round started with a right to the jaw. Fitzgerald countered with a left and Houck side-stepped and the blow, which landed lightly on his arm. Fitzgerald was undaunted but swung weakly both left and right. Houck countered with a left and right to the body and threw three rapid-fire left jabs.
>
> By the third round Houck showed his championship skill by landing every punch he threw. Houck's left jab, one of the most effective punches in his repertoire, was shortened up and connected effectively to Fitzgerald's jaw. The effects slowed Fitzgerald down considerably and he clinched until the end of the round.
>
> During the fifth round Fitzgerald continued to hold onto Houck and clinch. Houck, a master at infighting, abandoned that style during this round fight and instead, displayed his ability to box. At times Fitzgerald tried unsuccessfully to rush Houck but overall, received a thorough beating.
>
> The sixth round opened with both boxers exchanging body blows. Houck threw lefts to the head and rights to the body. Fitzgerald clinched. After the breakaway Fitzgerald landed a punch onto Houck's stomach with little effect. Once again, Houck continued with lefts to the head and rights to the body while Fitzgerald tried to clinch. Houck poured it on until the end of the round and easily outpointed Fitzgerald who showed the fans that he was one game fighter.[42]

Leo received the newspaper-decision win over Jack Fitzgerald.

Since returning to the ring on April 12, Leo seemed unrivaled and was widely acknowledged as a stumbling block to any aspiring middleweight contender. The only fight that spoiled his perfect win record since April 12 was the fight with Buck Crouse when the referee mistakenly gave Crouse the controversial win.

Leo next turned his attention to Australian middleweight Dave Smith, who was completing an American tour that had started on September 2, 1912, and would end after his bout with Leo on November 8 at the Olympia A.C. in Philadelphia. Eddie McGoorty had surprised Smith with a first-round technical knockout during his first fight in the United States. After that loss, Smith won three consecutive fights. He had an impressive win over Battling Levinsky, who was now mentioned in the press as a serious contender for the middleweight championship.[43]

The *Scranton Truth* reported that Leo's success in this fight was attributed chiefly to his left-handed punches in an article titled "Left Jabs Win for Leo Houck."

> Dave Smith of Australia lost his six round bout to Leo Houck at the Olympia last night. Houck had the best of the argument in four of the six rounds, hitting the Australian three to one, and closing his left eye so effectually that it was with difficulty that he could see his adversary. Houck's stinging left hand punches did the work.
>
> In the early rounds Smith started off as though he were going to make short work of the Lancaster boy, but after the third round Houck stopped him and never gave him a chance to land excepting a few blows.
>
> In the fifth round Houck reached Smith with a left uppercut that raised him off his feet, and it looked as though Houck had caught his man asleep. Smith rallied, however, but he rushed into a clinch at the bell. At the close Houck was without a mark.[44]

Both the *Scranton Truth* and the *Allentown Leader* reported that Leo was the clear winner, but the *Pittsburgh Post-Gazette* called the fight a draw and never mentioned that Leo closed Smith's left eye with his repeated left jabs. The omission of that significant fact raised the question of which individual really had the closed eye.

Six-round bouts, as opposed to ten-, twelve-, or fifteen-round bouts, were often so fast that sportswriters occasionally reported different outcomes for the same fight. For whatever reasons, this fight produced a similar dilemma. The outcomes reporting a win and a draw are both listed in the official records.[45]

Two days before Leo's next bout on November 15, the *Harrisburg Telegraph* published a story that stated, "The impression prevails in Lancaster that Houck is not being taken care of properly by the sporting writers." Even Henry Hensel, matchmaker, promoter, and manager of the Lancaster A.C., felt the same way and believed that Leo never received the recognition he deserved from the sportswriters. "Bat" Masterson, Indian fighter, buffalo hunter, gunfighter *par excellence*, and renowned New York City sportswriter, dismissed this idea and suggested what Leo really needed was a big-time promoter who would turn him into a money-making empire.[46] Without question, the possibility existed for Leo to sign with a nationally recognized boxing promoter who possessed the Midas touch. That never happened.

Two days after the *Harrisburg Telegraph* story, Leo fought Larry Williams, a middleweight from Bridgeport, Connecticut, who was fighting primarily at the Broadway A.C. in Philadelphia during 1912. He agreed to substitute for Billy Adams, who canceled his engagement with Leo at the Lancaster A.C.

This was Williams's second year in professional boxing and second bout with a ranked middleweight contender. The first bout against middleweight contender Battling Levinsky, on April 4, 1912, resulted in a loss for Williams.

Leo knocked Williams down in the second and third rounds. In the fourth, Williams took a nine-count nap after Leo looped and landed a crushing hard right to his opponent's jaw.[47] This was Leo's first knockout since October 11, 1910, when he caused Tommy Quill to thud unceremoniously onto the chilly Bean Town canvas. A win by Williams would have put him squarely on the middleweight contender map. After the fight, a magnifying glass was required in order to discover exactly where Williams was located on this map.

The last fight of the season for Leo, a six-rounder against Emmett "Kid" Wagner, occurred on November 25 at the Douglas A.C. in Scranton. Wagner started his professional boxing career on New Year's Day in 1911. He already possessed a win over George Chip during 1912, and had faced but lost to both Battling Levinsky and Jack Dillon that same year. Wagner never shied away from any top-ranked middleweight contender, or heavyweight, who wanted a match.

Both the *Pittston Gazette* and *Altoona Tribune* reported that Leo had the best of Wagner. The *Wilkes-Barre Record* provided a vivid description of their hometown favorite, "Kid Wagner," who employed all his might in an effort to upset Leo.

> Worked up as they were at Town Hall on Monday night during the fast and furious fifth round of the six round go between Leo Houck of Lancaster and Kid Wagner of Wilkes-Barre, the big crowd howled until the bell rang. It was in this round that Wagner took on the appearance of a real dyed in the wool demon fighter. He acted as if it was his life he was fighting for and he tore into his more experienced opponent with both fists shooting out like piston rods on a fast engine.
>
> As he threw aside all fear of a sleep punch by Houck and landed on the Lancaster man's body the crowd shrieked. Many were standing upon chairs, waving hats, slapping one another on the shoulders and talking on in great shape. It was worth the price just to see this part of the excitement.[48]

Once again, the newspaper-decision outcomes differed. Official records list both a win for Leo and a draw.[49]

The French Boxing Federation and Leon Seis, one of their main proponents, announced late in November that they wanted to stage a world middleweight championship in Paris. Frank Klaus, Billy Papke, Jim Sullivan, Mariel Moreau, Eddie McGoorty, Mike Gibbons, Jimmy Clabby, and Leo Houck were all cordially invited to participate. Bob McCusker received an offer directly from Seis. He offered Leo two round-trip tickets to Paris and a guarantee of $14,000 for four consecutive contests with one condition—Seis would have the exclusive rights to name Leo's opponents.[50] Leo and McCusker grabbed the offer and promised to sail for Paris on January 6, 1913.[51]

It appeared that things could not get any better for Leo. He had dominated the current crop of middleweight contenders during the year, capped it with a deal to make a king's ransom in Paris, and started to play basketball in December with his team the P.R.R.Y.–Y.M.C.A.

1913

Most people welcome in the New Year as a brand-new opportunity to improve some facet of their lives or fulfill uncompleted resolutions from the previous year. Leo was no different. In the middle of December 1912, Leo had already made an advance New Year's resolution and vowed revenge against Jack Dillon. Leo told the *Scranton Republican* that he was ready to fight Dillon and stated, "In the last four months I have fought four of the best men in the world: Bob Moha, Eddie McGoorty, Dave Smith, and Billy Papke, and beat them all."[52] Leo's declaration for revenge might have disqualified the resolution as a constructive or positive one. However, that minor inconsistency hardly mattered to Leo. Every New Year's Day after 1912 until the end of Leo's career automatically summoned the unpleasant apparition of Jack Dillon, who fractured Leo's ribs that day in the fourth round.

Leo's first match of the year was a six-round wind-up against Detroit's Freddie Hicks on January 13 at the Lancaster A.C. Hicks had faced some classy boxers, but usually lost against that type. Leo put out the word that he had dropped his sympathetic feelings and needed to clean up the middleweight division in order to get what was coming to him.[53]

Promoter Hensel advertised the bout as the most expensive ever presented by the Lancaster A.C. The fans immediately recognized that announcement as one of his well-known schemes to generate a larger take at the gate, but Hensel always got away with it, and increased the price of admission.

The *Harrisburg Telegraph* described Hicks's awkward efforts to stay conscious during this lopsided fight.

> To avoid punishment Hicks dodged all of Houck's advances from the first to last round. Hicks tried to belt Houck but missed or was blocked every time. Houck smashed Hicks with a couple of blows before he clinched. Hicks knew he was in trouble and decided to cover up and protect himself from a possible knockout. In the fifth round Houck pasted Hicks's lip and cut it open. In the sixth round Houck provided a severe lacing to Hicks who ran around the ring. Houck dropped Hicks to the canvas on one knee with a left to the jaw but he popped up immediately. Hicks was groggy afterwards and sleepwalked for the remainder of the sixth. Hicks was unable to land a single blow throughout the entire fight.[54]

The *Reading Times* reported that Hicks's face was badly cut and that he suffered a closed eye at the finish.[55] In addition, the *York Daily* reported that Hicks was also cut behind the left ear.[56] Leo received the newspaper-decision win.

The fight with Hicks gave Leo a painless entry into the 1913 boxing season, but his second fight with Jack Dillon, a six-rounder on January 22 at the Olympia A.C. in Philadelphia, was another matter entirely. Almost thirteen months had passed since their first meeting. Both fighters now weighed more, but there was no forfeiture for exceeding the 158-pound middleweight limit.

Two circumstances surrounding this fight with Dillon were identical to the prior year. First, Leo had once again made plans for a return trip to France early in January, when he would box in a middleweight elimination contest. Second, he postponed the anticipated date of departure because he wanted to first fight Dillon first.

During 1912, Dillon practically owned the middleweight division, fighting a total of twenty-nine times and accumulating twenty-six wins. Two fights smudged Dillon's record that year, his back-to-back losses against Frank Klaus, who was still ranked as the number-one middleweight contender.[57]

Lancaster fans waited impatiently for Leo's day of retribution against Dillon. The bout created so much local interest that promoter Hensel had to arrange for a special train to travel from Lancaster to Philadelphia. Advance ticket sales were brisk and expected to reach 250 by the day of the fight. Fans from Harrisburg were also invited to take advantage of this special $2.50 round-trip deal.[58]

Several regional newspapers covered the bout, but the *Allentown Leader* was exceptionally critical and panned the fight by describing it as one of the most disappointing that had been seen in Philadelphia that winter.

> Neither of the men displayed any knowledge of boxing, and it was a case of lead and clinch during almost every second of the first three rounds. For a full minute at a time the men would hold each other in a death-like grip and do a slow waltz around the ring, covering nearly every foot of the big square enclosure. For the first three rounds neither man landed half a dozen clean punches.
> In the fourth round there was a little more action, Dillon forcing the fighting. His work was the

cleaner, but there was little to his punches and they did no particular harm to the Lancaster man till the last round when Houck looked pretty well tired out. He was bleeding at the mouth, but suffered no serious injury. Houck seemed slower than usual, his constantly increasing weight appearing to have taken all the sap and steam out of him.[59]

In a special to the *Harrisburg Telegraph*, Leo was blamed for easing up on Dillon when he had a clear opportunity for a knockout.[60] In contrast, the *Harrisburg Daily Independent* reported that during the last three rounds, both boxers fought hard and each attempted to land a blow that would end the contest.[61] The *Allentown Leader*, *Harrisburg Daily Independent*, and *Harrisburg Telegraph* all reported that the battle ended as a draw. Official records list the fight as both a newspaper-decision loss and a draw for Leo.

Before his next match, Leo expected a bit of downtime, but Hensel asked Leo if he would box a couple of exhibition rounds with the featured heavyweight Luther McCarthy on February 6 at the Lancaster A.C. Leo agreed straightaway. McCarthy was a "Great White Hope," who was twenty years old, weighed 215 pounds, had an 81-inch reach, and was picked to defeat the current heavyweight champion Jack Johnson.[62]

What happened next was totally unexpected. On the night of the fight, Leo jumped into the ring and started to look all around for McCarthy, who appeared to be missing. McCarthy's manager, Billy McCarney, told Hensel that he would not permit his fighter to go against Leo and demanded a substitute fighter. McCarney got his way, and Al Norton boxed the exhibition match with McCarthy.[63]

"A Philly sportswriter stated that after Houck defeated Papke that Leo would be the man to defeat Jack Johnson if he were twenty pounds heavier. Perhaps this is what the shrewd McCarney was thinking about when he refused to have Leo box McCarthy."[64]

Two days later, Leo did some nimble dodging of his own as he drove down the basketball court and scored five field goals for the St. Joseph's basketball team during their win over the Hershey Y.M.C.A.[65] After the basketball game, Leo realized he had only one day to prepare for his fight against Al Rogers from Buffalo, New York, at the Lincoln A.C. on February 10 in Altoona, Pennsylvania.

Rogers fought chiefly in New York and California. He started the 1913 boxing season with two losses, against Buck Crouse on January 13 and Jack Dillon on January 18, prior to his third fight of the season, which was against Leo.[66]

The *Altoona Tribune* and *Reading Times* reported an easy win for Leo. In an article titled "Houck Had Easy Win," the latter reported, "Rogers is only a strong fellow and he knew little about the clever side of the game. Houck took no chances and just feinted him into openings and then slammed him with short punches."[67] Conversely, the *Wilkes-Barre Record* reported a draw, but gave Leo a shade advantage on form and points. Official records have recorded the fight as both a newspaper-decision draw and a win for Leo.

Leo's next bout, against George Chip in Pittsburgh, was canceled due to Leo's injured right hand. The *Scranton Truth* reported that Leo broke his right hand, which forced him to postpone his journey to Europe. The newspaper stated that the injury would cost him in the neighborhood of $2,000.[68] That figure may have been an estimate of purse money lost in the United States while rehabilitating his hand. In reality, the missed trip to Europe, where Leo would have engaged in four boxing matches, amounted to $14,000 in lost purse money. The return trip to Europe was canceled for the foreseeable future.

On March 8 Leo tested his broken right hand. He played with the St. Joseph's basketball team, who appeared as a special attraction during an ongoing tournament championship involving two teams from Harrisburg.[69]

7. Top of the Heap, 1912–1913

Close to the end of March, Leo reacted angrily to several newspaper reports critiquing his recent performances in the ring.

> Houck is sore because of newspaper criticisms on his work in his last three engagements. His besetting sin is letting up on his opponents when the latter seems to be weakening, and this generous policy on the part of the Lancaster middleweight cost him the decision once or twice recently, when opponents thus spared by Houck finished strong and had Houck at a disadvantage later in the bouts. Slamming his opponents hard from the first ring of the bell will be the order from now on.[70]

Leo's hand had healed satisfactorily by March 27. He was eager to erase the recent criticism from the press and intended to belt out Dick Gilbert, of Jacksonville, Florida, in a six-rounder at the Lancaster A.C. Gilbert was described by the press as the middleweight and light-heavyweight champion of the South. Gilbert had four fights with Battling Levinsky during 1912 and lost to him three times in a row.[71]

A small contingent of Pennsylvania legislators wanted to draft a bill to license boxing and establish a boxing commission. They attended the Houck-Gilbert fight on a fact-finding mission and wanted to determine if boxing matches should remain as six-round events or possibly be expanded to ten rounds. Public opinion was divided. Some believed that a six-round fight was satisfactory, while others favored an increase to ten rounds, since many fighters never got started until four or five rounds had been fought.[72]

In a special to the *Harrisburg Telegraph*, Leo was described as being in the pink of condition for his comeback fight.

> Houck dominated Gilbert completely throughout the fight. Gilbert attempted to bull Houck into the ropes while swinging wildly and did manage to land some blows. Houck countered and used his infighting tactics to deliver crushing blows to Gilbert's midsection and ribs. By the third round Houck relied primarily on his left jab and had Gilbert almost out.[73]

Leo's comeback fight, a clear victory, earned him another newspaper-decision win.

Leo and Gilbert's performance that evening provided support for the idea that fights of six rounds provided ample time for well-conditioned boxers to prove themselves. But the legislators in attendance reached a different consensus upon their return to Harrisburg, the state capital, and proposed the legalization of ten-round fights and the establishment of a boxing commission in the Perry Boxing Bill.[74]

After the Gilbert bout, Leo had a forty-day layoff. He stayed in condition by playing basketball with the St. Joseph's Team of Lancaster.

During Leo's layoff, the *Pittsburgh Post-Gazette* reported that Frank Klaus was due to arrive back in the United States from Paris on April 15. Klaus claimed there were no more middleweights to fight in Europe. Soon after his arrival his manager, George Engle, gave Eddie McGoorty first call against Klaus.[75] McGoorty was the safer choice for Klaus, who wanted to avoid a tangle with Leo or Mike Gibbons, who were both currently ranked second in the middleweight division. Klaus had beaten Dillon twice during 1912, and avoided Mike Gibbons, who easily out-boxed but lost to McGoorty during 1912 when he was unable to land any blows against his opponent. Gibbons was a defensive boxer who could make a seasoned boxer like Klaus look foolish.

New York sportswriter Bat Masterson claimed that Leo Houck was the most logical candidate for the middleweight honors.[76] That assertion by Masterson was a correct deduction. Klaus had two wins over Leo during 1911 but knew he was a much-improved boxer by 1913 and decided to avoid him too.

By the end of April, Leo's constitution had changed noticeably. His weight had continued to increase slightly in spite of all his recent activity on the basketball court. In the past, Leo had had no problems with his weight and could easily reduce to 154 or 158 pounds for a middleweight fight. Leo fought his next fight as a 162-pound light heavyweight, a ten-rounder against George "K.O" Brown from Chicago, on May 7 at the St. Nicholas A.C. in New York.

The *Allentown Democrat* reported that Brown, "Chicago's Star Middleweight," failed to twinkle in an article titled "Houck's Uppercuts Too Much for Knockout Boy."

> Houck fought a careful, heady bout, taking few chances and studiously keeping clear of Brown's deadly right. It was fairly even up to the seventh round, both fighters strong for the body, but with little result.
>
> It was Houck's right uppercut that won for him. He connected with this punch a dozen times in the last rounds and had the Windy City lad swinging wildly. Brown fought desperately at the finish but his blows failed to find their mark.[77]

Since the beginning of 1913, Leo had improved his capability to overwhelm an opponent with a combination left jab and right uppercut. Those two punches, especially the right uppercut, sometimes lifted his opponents off their feet. This combination of punches eventually took their toll on Brown and earned Leo another newspaper-decision win.

A twenty-two-day layoff after the Brown match suited Leo. He continued training and playing basketball, and looked forward to playing baseball during the summer. Hensel, on the other hand, had no such distractions, and worked all of the days arranging the details for Leo's next fight, a long-anticipated rematch with Buck Crouse, on May 29 at Rossmere Ball Park. The fight preparations included the erection of two rings, one outside at the Rossmere Ball Park and the other inside at the Lancaster A.C. just in case of rain or cold temperatures. The ballpark could accommodate a whopping 3,000 spectators. Hensel prayed to the "Boxing Gods" for fair weather and a massive gate.

During his layoff, Leo continued to train with Henry Hauber, a Philadelphia heavyweight.[78] Hauber was a recent addition to Leo's team, but not the only one. The *Harrisburg Daily Independent* made a reference to Jack McGuigan, a Philadelphia fight manager and matchmaker, who accepted the terms for the Crouse match on Leo's behalf.[79] This change in management, like the shakeups before, was abrupt and unexpected. Bat Masterson had suggested earlier that all Leo really needed in the fight game was a big-time manager. Maybe this declaration from Masterson influenced Leo and prompted him to fire McCusker and hire McGuigan.

McGuigan was a step up and not an unusual or unfamiliar choice for Leo, who had close relationships with many Philadelphia boxers and managers. McGuigan managed Johnny Kilbane, featherweight champion from 1912 to 1923. He was also closely associated with Johnny Loftus, the legendary trainer and conditioner of many champion fighters including Jim Corbett, Jim Jefferies, and Stanley Ketchel. These are only a smattering of the many fistic greats he trained. Loftus joined the Houck camp as Leo's trainer during the latter part of 1913.

Without a doubt Leo had plenty to think about when it came to Crouse, who had established an incredible record from January 22, 1912, until May 19, 1913. During this time he fought seventeen bouts, which included sixteen wins, and a loss to Jack Dillon.[80] The most recent win over Blink McCloskey on May 19 was a knockout. Crouse's manager, Jimmy Mason, stated he was positive that Crouse would have little trouble beating any middleweight claimant.[81] The latter part of Mason's statement about "any middleweight claimant" was a broad generalization from a manager in denial. Perhaps Mason had

Before the end of the 1913 boxing season, Leo suddenly fired his manager, Robert McCusker, and hired Jack McGuigan, a prominent Philadelphia manager, along with Johnny Loftus, one of the most highly respected trainers and conditioners of the period. Seated from left to right are: Jack McGuigan and Johnny Loftus. Standing from left to right are: Johnny Kilbane, Leo F. Houck, and Sam Robideau (courtesy LancasterHistory.org, Lancaster, Pennsylvania, John Hauck Collection, MG-63, JH-02-06-35).

forgotten that Leo was eventually awarded the winner's purse after his match with Crouse on May 7, when the referee bungled the decision at the end of the tenth round and mistakenly awarded the win to Crouse.

Unfortunately, the big gate expected at the Rossmere Ball Park never materialized due to inclement weather. The fight was moved indoors to the Lancaster A.C. However, Hensel was still a very fortunate man. His star boxer, Leo, could have fought more often in the larger and more profitable venues available in Philadelphia, only a short train ride eastward, but instead fought principally in Lancaster. Moreover, as Lancaster's premier sports figure, Leo might have received advice from his managers to ask Hensel for an extra inducement, like a small percentage of the gate, to remain and fight in Lancaster whenever possible. There is no evidence available to support that Leo ever received a percentage of the gate during his career, and chances are he never did. Their personal and business relationships were uncomplicated and friendly, and remained so until Hensel's death in 1915. The Crouse bout was no different from the other fights held at the Lancaster A.C., and Leo once again helped Hensel fill the seats for another Thursday night boxing show.

The *Harrisburg Telegraph* reported the fight in an article titled "Buck Crouse Easy for Lancaster Boxer."

> During the opening rounds both boxers clinched frequently, failed to open-up, or land any significant blows. The crowd showed its displeasure after four rounds of monotony.
>
> By the fifth round Houck blasted his opponent. He used his left jab repeatedly and hooked right. Crouse felt the blows and by the end of the round looked weary.
>
> Crouse and Hock both flashed in the sixth round. Houck was relentless in his use of the left jab and caught Crouse under the jaw with a left that lifted him off his feet. Crouse clearly showed the effects of Houck's final drives.[82]

In contrast, the *Pittsburgh Daily Post* reported that Leo lost the fight and was battered up, while Crouse showed the better form and exited the fight without a scratch.[83] Official records list the fight's outcome as both a newspaper-decision win and a newspaper-decision loss for Leo.

During the next three months, Leo donned his baseball jersey and pitched for the Lancaster Aeries from the Eagles Club.[84] He also found time to play with the Southwark Field Club.[85]

Early in September, Leo diverted his attention from baseball to boxing and prepared for a six-round bout with Tommy Bergin, aka the Lewiston Bearcat, on September 6 at the National A.C. in Philadelphia. Bergin, from Lewiston, Maine, was in his last year of professional boxing during 1913, and had only two wins from a total of fifteen bouts that year.[86]

This fight was a tune-up for Leo, who was now a full-fledged light heavyweight at 165 pounds.[87] Leo carried more weight and was a great deal taller than Bergin. Those two facts, combined with Leo's ring experience, put Bergin's chances of winning at about 50 to 1.

The *Harrisburg Telegraph* reported, "Houck had an easy time with Bergin. He hit him at will and was hardly hit himself. Bergin tried hard, but the Red Rose lad knew too much for him."[88] Leo received the newspaper-decision win.

Hensel negotiated over three months to arrange Leo's next match, and finally secured a signed contract from Jack Dillon to fight Leo on October 2 at the Rocky Springs Park in Lancaster. This was a major deal for Hensel, who knew that the park had seating for approximately 3,000 spectators. No one covered all the angles better than Hensel, especially when it involved making more money. He noticed an opportunity to sell an additional 150 premium ringside seats directly on the stage where the boxing ring was located, and was immediately rewarded with a demand from the well-heeled.

Dillon was shrewd and did not post a forfeit for weight or rescheduling if necessary. He was known as "The Giant Killer" and liked to retain a weight well above 158 pounds for when he fought opponents in the heavyweight division. Leo was unconcerned about Dillon's weight and decided to reduce to 158 pounds, the middleweight limit.

For the next four weeks Leo maintained a rigorous training regimen and also started football practice with the St. Joseph's C.C. football team.[89]

Dillon, on the other hand, late in September unexpectedly called off the October 2 battle and asked for a week delay. He talked Hensel into an October 9 meeting and posted a forfeit to that effect.[90] For some reason, Dillon wanted the additional week to train, which hardly made sense. His conditioning was flawless and his last two wins had been by knockouts. Naturally, public opinion regarding the delay was shaped around the idea that Dillon was afraid of Leo. Dillon might have been wary of Leo, but hardly afraid of him. Dillon had a long campaign during 1913 and may have needed the additional week to recover from a recent or nagging injury. In any event, he and a full contingent of sparring partners set up camp in Columbia, directly across the Susquehanna River from Lancaster.

In a "Special to the Telegraph," the fight was described as a great exhibition that lacked a decisive finish in an article subtitled "Large Crowd Witnessed a Great Battle, but They Longed for a Finish."

> Dillon outweighed Houck fully by ten pounds. The Lancaster man was the aggressor throughout, Dillon's tactics appearing to allow Houck to wear himself out, but at the conclusion both men were fresh.
> The consensus of opinion was that if either man had anything on the other it was a shade in Houck's favor. A lot of blows were struck, but none did any particular damage. Houck's favorite attack was his famous left jab to the jaw and he frequently rocked Dillon's head.
> Dillon played throughout for Houck's ribs, but failed to land many telling blows. Dillon's superior weight counted and he twice pulled Houck to the mat in clinches.
> The first and fourth rounds were Houck's on good margin, the second, third, fifth, and sixth even breaks.
> The warmest fighting was in the fifth round, when the men broke from a clinch and went at each other for a knockout, the only stage of the fight when both threw caution aside and took big chances. It was a game battle throughout.
> Everybody who ever saw Leo Houck in a battle knows that he does the right thing at the right time, but his many admirers are tired of seeing him in six-round fights and posing as a strong contender for middleweight honors, and are anxious to hear that he has taken up more serious work.[91]

On October 10, the *Harrisburg Telegraph*, the *Pittston Gazette*, and the *Scranton Republican*, all reported the fight outcome as a clear draw. Official records identify the outcome as both a newspaper-decision win and a draw for Leo.

The blast from the newspaper about "more serious work" from Leo was a "cheap shot," which suggested that he should engage only in fights longer than six rounds. Astute fans of the pugilistic game, on the whole, generally subscribed to the idea that high-caliber fighters like Leo and Dillon often needed the additional rounds to determine a finished fight. The Perry Boxing Bill, which proposed the legalization of ten-round fights in Pennsylvania to alleviate this type of dilemma, never made it out of committee, slipped into obscurity, and disappeared.

Something extraordinary happened approximately one month before Leo's next scheduled bout with George Chip on November 15 at the National A.C. in Philadelphia. Chip scored a technical knockout over middleweight champion Frank Klaus on October 11 at Old City Hall in Philadelphia, and claimed the middleweight crown. "Frank said it was all a mistake and Chip gave him another chance. The second time Chip did the trick in five rounds."[92] After three years, the middleweight muddle was over, at least for the time being.

This sudden turn of events in the middleweight division was particularly fortuitous for Leo, who had been scheduled to fight Chip before he won the title from Klaus. Never was Leo positioned more favorably in his career to repeat his performance of 1912, when he defeated Chip handily the first time.

In their article titled "Houck Beat Chip," the *Wilkes-Barre Record* reported that both boxers weighed in at under 158 pounds and appeared to be evenly matched.

> Early in the first round Houck scored a knockdown and sent Chip to the canvas with a right to the jaw. Chip's jaw is made of granite. The blow would have easily knocked out an ordinary man. Chip rushed Houck throughout the fight and drove him from corner to corner while he scored numerous blows to Houck's head and body. Chip has a tendency to swing wildly and most of the punches did little or no damage to his opponent. Chip had a tendency to run directly into Houck's devastating left, which threatened to unhinge Chip's head.[93]

The *Scranton Republican* reported that Chip was better suited to the ten-round overland route, and lacked the ability to win over a clever boxer in a short-round contest.[94] The *Reading Times* and the *Pittsburgh Daily Post* both reported that Houck delivered a decisive win over Chip.

Chip showed up the next day in Scranton without a scratch and joined the training camp of his buddy and fellow boxer Tommy Conners, who was preparing for a bout with Jimmy Tighe. Chip told the *Scranton Truth* that he was off his balance when Leo knocked him down during the first round. He also mentioned that during their mix-up on the ropes he was on the outside and was pitched forward when Leo stepped backwards, which released the tension on the ropes. Chip explained further that his sudden unbalanced movement forward gave Leo the opportunity to clip him on the chin and knock him down. Some newspapers conveniently forgot to mention that Chip immediately bounced back up like a rubber ball.[95]

Later on the *Allentown Leader* reported that Chip claimed he could do better in a longer bout against Leo and wanted another contest. Leo let it be known that he was prepared to accommodate the "Pittsburgher's" wishes.[96] The win over Chip was a splendid moment for Leo. He had outpointed the new middleweight champion and was awarded the newspaper-decision win.

Three days after the fight, Leo claimed the middleweight title and offered to defend the title by challenging any fighter who believed he had a real claim to the championship. Jack McGuigan, Leo's manager, announced that he would take immediate steps to claim the title for him. He elaborated further and stated, "Houck's wonderful ring record proves him to be what I claim for him, a champion. Houck will now get that which he is rightfully entitled to."[97]

McGuigan's endorsement of Leo as the new middleweight champion was genuine and straightforward, but technically incorrect. He entered a public protest over Chip's claim to the middleweight title in a letter submitted to the *Pittsburgh Post-Gazette*, and challenged Chip to a rematch so Leo could prove that he was indeed the master of Chip.[98]

McGuigan absolutely needed a rematch for his boxer. He understood the one unyielding rule of thumb that applied to the acquisition of an uncontested championship title. Any boxer engaged in a no-decision bout, where the referee has no power to render a decision at the end of the bout, had to score a knockout or a technical knockout over the current champion in order to rightfully claim the crown.

After defeating Chip, Leo, the new middleweight champion, found himself on top of the pugilistic world. It seemed that things could not possibly get any better for him. Nevertheless, things did get better, much better, and in fact, blessed. On November 29, Mary E. Hauck, Leo and Anna's first child, was born.

Leo had twenty days off to enjoy his new role as a father before his next bout on December 20 with Joe Borrell at the National A.C. in Philadelphia. Johnny Loftus, Leo's new trainer, was well known for his ability to successfully train a boxer up to the day of the fight, and made certain that Leo continued to show up at the gym to train. Loftus disregarded the fans' perceptions that Borrell had little chance against Leo, who entered the fight as the favorite. During the period from May 9 to December 1, 1913, Borrell reeled off ten consecutive wins, including a technical knockout on October 13 against Harry Lewis.[99] The National A.C. was packed with approximately 4,500 spectators for Leo's last match of the season.

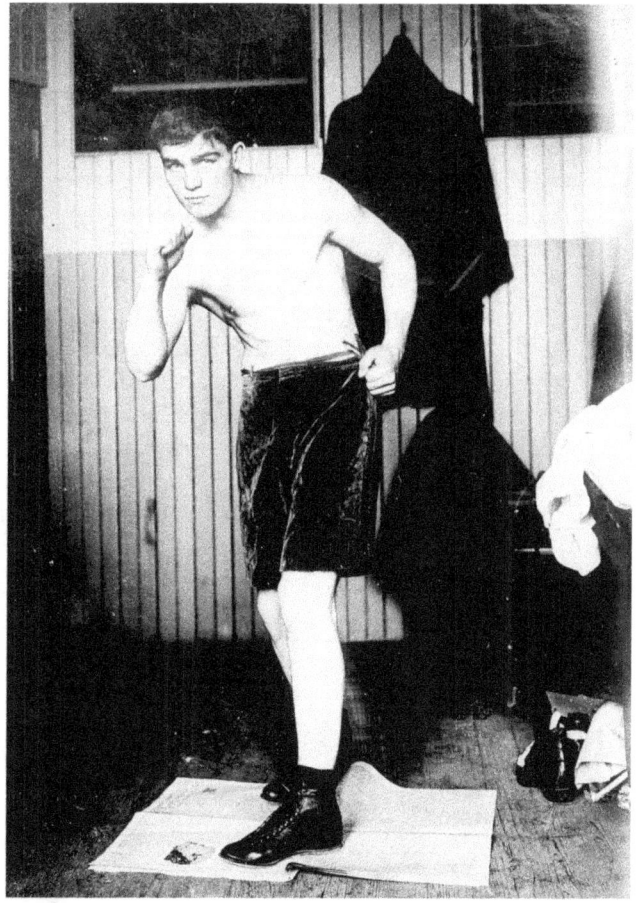

Top of the heap: At the conclusion of a successful 1913 boxing season, Leo F. Houck had positioned himself rightly to challenge George Chip, the current middleweight champion, for his title (courtesy Library of Congress, LC-B2-2980-15).

The *Allentown Democrat* reported the fight in an article titled "Leo Houck Easily Defeats Borrell."

> The rival middleweights were not out of their corners more than a minute, when Houck shot his straight left to Borrell's jaw, and the Kensington man dropped flat on his back. He took a count of nine, and the crowd felt sure that Leo had landed a sure knockout. Borrell got up groggy, but finished out the round by doing some clinching. Houck's hard left cut Borrell's mouth, and caused the blood to flow in the remaining rounds.
>
> Houck almost sent Borrell down again in the second, but the latter clinched when he was in danger and then rallied a trifle.

> The first three rounds were Houck's. He did the most aggressive fighting and landed the cleaner blows. Borrell appeared very cautious after the first round but opened up in the fourth and was entitled to the honors. He had Leo holding on several times. The last two rounds were even, but Borrell put up a sensational stand in the sixth that worried Houck a lot.[100]

Leo received some criticism from the *Wilkes-Barre Record* after he failed to finish Borrell in the first round and eliminate him as a serious middleweight contender.[101] However, the fight was so decisive a win for Leo that fight promoters canceled Borrell's next bout with Jack McCarron. They believed that Borrell would not be up to snuff as a top drawing card after being whipped by Leo, a top contender.[102]

By the end of the 1913, Leo was on top of the middleweight division. He had eliminated middleweight contenders Buck Crouse and Jack Dillon and had scored a newspaper-decision win over Chip, the middleweight champion. Two important pieces of unfinished business still remained before Leo could declare himself the boss of the middleweights. First, McGuigan needed to secure a signed contract with Chip that would guarantee a rematch with Leo. Secondly, Leo needed to knock out Chip during the rematch in order to rightfully claim the middleweight crown.

8

Baseball, the Blahs and Catchweight Battles, 1914–1915–1916

1914

Leo's first fight of the season was a six-round contest with Joe Borrell on January 17 at the National A.C. in Philadelphia. He had remained idle since his first meeting with Leo on December 20, 1913. Borrell planed to fight in England and France early in 1914 and good performances against Leo, George Chip, and Tommy Hopkins before leaving would make an impression on the boxing fans abroad.

Everyone who traveled from Harrisburg or Lancaster to watch the fight in Philadelphia may as well have stayed home. The *Harrisburg Telegraph* blasted both fighters and included the referee for good measure when they explained the lousy contest.

> Truthfully speaking, the match was not even a good boxing contest. Both fighters clinched frequently and violated the rules prohibiting clinching. Neither man was hurt. On view of the fact that Houck is announced as going after honors in the West, friends of the Lancaster lad are of the opinion that he will have to do some real fighting if he hopes to make good.
>
> The referee was censured Saturday night for not insisting on close observance from the ring. Borrell earned the decision Saturday night because he landed the majority of the blows.[1]

The fight, no matter how dull, provided a newspaper-decision win for Borrell.

Two eastern cities, Pittsburgh and Youngstown, Ohio, each vied for the opportunity to host Leo's second fight of the season, a rematch with George Chip. Pittsburgh, the "Smoky City," had offered the better money. McGuigan gave the promoters in Youngstown a chance to sweeten the purse before he finalized a proposed contract with Pittsburgh. Youngstown upped its offer and won the contract after Pittsburgh declined to counteroffer.

Jimmy Dime, acting for Chip, contacted McGuigan and had the Youngstown Boxing Club obtain Leo's signature for a twelve-round bout at the Grand Opera House on February 20. The articles of agreement stated that both boxers weigh in at 158 pounds and post a $100 forfeit ten days before the fight, for the agreed-upon weight limit.[2]

The length of the fight was Jimmy Dime's idea. He had developed a theory about the necessity of longer fights for his boxer. Dime suggested that Chip could dole out more punishment to a boxer already weakened from the sixth to tenth rounds, if he made it that far, and therefore win more decisively during the final rounds of a longer fight.

Dime disclosed exactly how Chip would launch his fight strategy against Leo. After the first tap of the gong, Chip would immediately begin punching Leo in the stomach and continue punching until he weakened.[3] The repeated punches to Leo's stomach during the early rounds would soften him up sufficiently and provide Chip with an opportunity to find an opening for a possible knockout when Leo dropped his guard during the latter rounds. This strategy was successfully field-tested beforehand by Chip, who had applied Dime's instructions in a recent win over Tommy Gavin.

Everything looked rosy for the upcoming Houck-Chip rematch. Then it happened. During the Chip-Borrell fight on January 26 at the Olympia A.C. in Philadelphia, Chip broke his right hand. Jimmy Dime announced that Chip's physician told him not to think about boxing for several weeks.[4] The Houck-Chip rematch was postponed until March 12.

Unexpected contingencies that required a "Plan B" were McGuigan's specialty. He quickly found another spot for Leo in Daly City, California, a twenty-rounder against middleweight Billy Murray. Of course, Murray was largely an unknown on the East Coast, but was nothing short of a complete sensation in California. During a period that ranged from February 2, 1912, until January 1, 1914, Murray had fought forty-five times and amassed an impressive record of forty-one wins and four draws.[5]

McGuigan never believed that Murray was a threat and advised Leo to take the fight and pick up some easy money. Moreover, McGuigan extended himself even further and told the press, "It will be soft for Leo."[6]

Murray's manager, Jack Kearns, had big plans for his fighter.[7] His strategy, if successful, could establish Murray as a serious middleweight contender. The short-term plan was contingent on several conditions. First, Murray needed to eliminate Leo and then Jimmy Clabby. After that, Kearns needed to persuade Jimmy Dime, George Chip's manager, to bring his fighter to California for a middleweight championship contest with Murray. Finally, the money had to be right. Dime was previously offered and refused a $2,000 guarantee to have Chip fight Clabby in California. He said, "We can get twice that much in Milwaukee or New York."[8]

It rained almost every day after Leo arrived in California, which ruined his road workouts. During the nine days leading up to the fight, the press examined Leo like a bug under a microscope while they observed him working out at Millet's training camp in California. During the public workouts and sparring sessions, Leo was dubbed by the press as "Silent Leo" and was described as reticent and reserved. The *Courier* reported that his conversations from the press were limited to a "Good morning" or "Good evening" or the occasional head bob in the affirmative, depending on the question.[9] The press meticulously described his stance, how he delivered powerful blows without drawing back his elbows, and his tendency not to crowd his sparring partners simply for the entertainment of the crowd.

On the day of the fight all the smart money, more than $8,000, was wagered on Leo. By the time he entered the ring the odds on him were 10 to 6.[10] Maybe McGuigan was right. This fight would be easy for Leo.

Everyone who read the sporting news the next day anticipated an exciting round-by-round description of the fight. Instead, all of the ring action was replaced with controversy and hearsay that focused primarily on the outcome of the contest. Several newspaper bylines were titled, "Is Leo Houck the Victim of Fakirs?," "Charge Fake in Frisco Scrap," and "Was Houck Given a Raw Deal in Frisco?" They all suggested that a dirty deal might have gone down during the fourteenth round. The fight had progressed fairly evenly up until then. One newspaper reported that Leo remained unemotional under punishment, was never in trouble, and let his opponent lead. He was counting on Murray to fight himself out.[11]

Leo was reported to be on his toes and battling during the fourteenth round when the referee, Jim Griffin, stepped in between the fighters, halted the bout, and held up Murray's hand. Leo protested and said to the referee, "What is the matter? I am going great and will beat this fellow." After their one-sided exchange, the referee quickly jumped from the ring.[12]

The fight was a frame-up all the way and the wise guys cleaned up. Frank Mantell, one of Leo's former opponents, was clipped for several hundred dollars, while boxer Eddie Hanlon, aka Cute Eddie, lost $1,000. Later, all reports failed to show anything to justify the referee's stopping the bout. Action photographs clearly depicted Leo as an alert fighter, on his toes, in no distress, and waiting to resume the fight. Murray received a newspaper-decision technical knock out for the debacle.[13]

Before Leo left California, he found out that George Chip had recently reinjured his broken right hand during a workout. Their upcoming match scheduled for March 12 was now postponed until April 21.[14] Leo took advantage of the nearly two-month layoff. He had more than ample time to train for the bout with Chip and forget the "Fiasco in Frisco."

Chip may have needed a soft spot to make sure his right hand had healed satisfactorily before his scheduled bout with Leo. Chip's manager settled on Al McCoy, a so-so middleweight and southpaw from New York. This was a ten-round set-up for Chip on April 7, at the Broadway S.C. in Brooklyn. One small detail was omitted. Someone forgot to tell McCoy he was the pushover.

Less than two minutes into the first round, McCoy landed a left-handed uppercut onto the tip of Chip's chin, which dropped him onto his back and bounced his head violently on the deck. Chip could not respond to the ten-count and was carried back to his corner, where he remained in a dazed condition for several minutes after McCoy had left the ring.[15]

The mind-boggling win by McCoy abruptly halted Leo's arduous three-year campaign in which he had methodically eliminated all the middleweight contenders on his way toward a title shot. He was forced to contemplate the cruel irony of being usurped and denied a title shot by a boxer who barely moved the needle on the middleweight scale. Nevertheless, Leo had long since grown accustomed to the twists of fate, injuries, and nonnegotiable terms dictated within the ranks of the "Cauliflower Industry."[16]

The recently dethroned Chip, now on the comeback trail, met Leo again on April 21 in Youngstown. Leo informed the eastern critics that he would defeat Chip by slipping over a haymaker on him. In addition, he told the press, "The technical knockout by Murray in California was bogus and nothing more than a total frame-up."[17] The next day, McGuigan piled onto Leo's statement and told the press, "I know Houck can beat the man Chip if he only gets going right. He is in the best of condition and if we lose we won't have anything to say."[18]

On April 22, the *New Castle Herald* reported an in-depth, round-by-round description of the fight in an article titled "George Chip and Leo Houck Fight Cleverly to Twelve Round Draw."

Round 1: It was plain to all that the style of the fighters was vastly different. Houck seemed to play for Chip's face while Chip played for Houck's wind and body all the time. Houck landed several stiff lefts to the face. Both were wary and when a blow was struck a clinch followed immediately.

Round 2: Houck missed several jabs to Chip's face. Chip plays right to Houck's body, landing three jolts. Chip missed a wicked right and then landed one of the same kind. Chip lands short right. Houck covered up well, and the blows seemed not to effect him. However, this round belonged to Chip.

Round 3: Chip proves better at infighting. Houck slips to the floor in rush and Chip allows him to get up bringing applause. Chip makes rushes to Houck's corner. Houck lands right to the face. Both play to wind in clinching.

Round 4: Chip lands short right and then two lefts to face. Houck lands to the face twice with hard rights. Chip misses vicious left swing. He then landed left. Both boys mix it in the center of the ring at tap of gong.

Round 5: Chip lands left to face then both play to body. Chip lands left. Houck lands a stinging right. Houck lands vicious left that tears open left eye of Chip drawing first blood. Both boys mix as gong sounds.

Round 6: Houck and Chip exchange rights to face. Houck lands a right cross and then a short left to the face. Chip seems to be bothered by the amount of blood streaming from face where eye was cut.

Round 7: The boys exchanged stinging lefts but no harm was done in this round, being as even as could be.

Round 8: Infighting was in evidence and Chip had the best of this. Houck missed vicious swings. Chip forces Houck and then misses strong swing. Houck grabs the advantage and lands hard right. It was an even round.

Round 9: The boys exchanged well-timed left jabs. Chip then landed a right cross and left jab. Then came another stinging left that seemed to bother Houck but he covered up so well that Chip could do no more damage.

Round 10: Chip landed three stinging lefts in succession. Houck came back with a hard left and followed this one with a left jab. Chip at the close of the round landed five short left jabs to Houck's face and neck. Chip made his best showing in this round.

Round 11: Houck landed left and right but Chip got in several good body blows before clinching. This round was a fair exchange and was even.

Round 12: Both boys tried hard to connect with stinging blows in this round and both landed hard lefts. However, both were too wary and the fight ended with the lads in the center of the ring in a clinch.

Regional newspapers reported three differing outcomes. Leo was awarded a newspaper-decision win, a loss, and a draw. Official records list the fight as a newspaper-decision win and loss for Leo.

After the fight, Leo immediately sought a middleweight title challenge against McCoy, who stubbornly rejected all offers.[19] One could hardly blame McCoy for not wanting to face Leo. Fighting a superior middleweight contender like Leo entailed too much risk for McCoy. From hereon, McCoy selected his future opponents very carefully.

McGuigan's "Plan A," securing a fight with McCoy, failed. However, McGuigan always had a "Plan B" for Leo and recommended that he grab a prior offer to fight five bouts in Australia and earn $7,000. A prolonged journey to Australia a hemisphere away was totally out of the question for Leo, especially right on the heels of the recent trip to California with the miserable training camp and rain nine straight days leading up to the debacle with Billy Murray. Without hesitation, Leo nixed "Plan B" and settled on his own "Plan C," a four-month layoff when he played baseball for the Lancaster Actives, the Steelton A.C., and the Hanover Club.

Extended layoffs for Leo usually required no explanation and were typically the

8. Baseball, the Blahs and Catchweight Battles, 1914–1915–1916

Throughout Leo's boxing career he always found time between bouts and during extended layoffs to practice baseball, his lifelong passion. Leo is sitting at right. He played baseball almost exclusively during 1914, his shortest and most disappointing boxing season. He might have been attempting to switch to a career in professional baseball during that same season (courtesy LancasterHistory.org, Lancaster, Pennsylvania, John Hauck Collection, MG-63, JH-03-10-35).

result of injuries suffered in the ring like a broken bone in his hand or fractured ribs, which needed time to heal and often required rehabilitation. He had been fighting steadily for the last twelve years, especially the last three, when he established himself as a premier middleweight contender. Leo deserved a break from the rigors of the boxing game. Most likely, Al McCoy's outright refusal to fight Leo plainly frustrated him and influenced his decision to take a lengthy time-out and concentrate exclusively on playing baseball.

Moreover, baseball represented much more than a passing interest to Leo. The sport was a lifelong passion from childhood onward. He continued to develop his abilities in baseball as he matured, and demonstrated those talents when he competed professionally with the Tri-State League. The four-month period spent playing baseball while on a layoff might have been Leo's own personal acid test to determine if he possessed enough talent to switch careers and play baseball professionally.

Leo's son, Edward Hauck, provided his own personal recollections about his father, which underscore Leo's love of baseball.

Personally, my impression over the years is that baseball was his sport. Why do I think this? As a kid, Leo played and managed baseball. Local sports pages attest to his talent. At Penn State he was accepted and worked as a baseball coach. He took my brother, Leo, and me to Philadelphia Athletics and Phillies games. He was a fan of radio sports announcer Stan Lomax and tuned in evenings at 7 to catch the latest scores. He coached a couple of guys who made it to the big leagues; he knew and introduced us to a couple of managers after games in Philly, like Bill McKechnie, who managed Cincinnati; and another time to the manager of Detroit. Oh, yes, a regular evening assignment was a two block errand to the corner store to pick up the late edition of the *Philadelphia Ledger*, which carried all the big league baseball scores. This is not to say we were shielded from boxing. We attended many Penn State boxing matches. When he refereed at local or nearby professional cards, we tagged along.[20]

During Leo's layoff the press forgot that he was still a leading middleweight contender during 1914. One newspaper, the *Pittston Gazette*, created a brand-new middleweight muddle. They started the confusion by failing to acknowledge that Al McCoy was the new rightful owner of the middleweight crown. Instead, they supported George Chip, who was knocked out by McCoy. Jimmy Clabby, Eddie McGoorty, and Billy Murray were also identified as part of the new top-ranked contender crowd. The latter was the most outlandish inclusion on the list.

By this time, sportswriters had generally acknowledged the fact that the Houck-Murray fight was a frame-up and that Murray's much-publicized campaign afterwards in the east fizzled after two consecutive losses to Al McCoy in New York. Moreover, the paper continued to peddle the news that Murray had a legitimate technical knockout over Houck, and also maintained that Leo was now eliminated as a top-ranked contender, and lumped him in with the third-tier contenders who were regarded as the least likely to eliminate the aforementioned "beauties."[21] One reported fact was accurate: Jimmy Clabby deserved to be ranked as a number-one contender. William H. Rocap, sporting editor for the *Philadelphia Ledger*, declared, "There was no reason to scour the country for a boxer to fill the late Stanley Ketchel's shoes. Jimmy Clabby has saved them the trouble."[22]

By the middle of August, Leo started to train for his upcoming fight with Tommy Gavigan, a twelve-rounder at Wright Field, in Youngstown. Gavigan had lost his last five bouts and had only fought twice during 1914.[23] The newspapers reported that Gavigan was a boxing teacher who liked the finer points of boxing but disliked the slugging and bang-slam of the boxing game.[24]

The fight, which looked easy for Leo, turned into a shambles during the eleventh round. The next day, after the dust settled, the newspapers reported several different outcomes for the fight—Houck wins on a knockout; Houck loses on a foul; Houck assaults referee; and police stop bout in the eleventh round.

During the eleventh round, Gavigan claimed a foul and stopped to dispute the infraction with the referee. Leo continued to fight and threw a right to Gavigan's jaw and knocked him out. It appeared that Gavigan had ignored the referee's pre-fight instructions to protect himself at all times.[25] The *Pittsburgh Daily Post* reported a different version of the fight, stating that Leo hit the referee, Garvey, on the jaw after Gavigan claimed a foul, which prompted Police Captain McNichols to jump into the ring and stop the bout.[26]

The *New Castle Herald* provided a commentary from M.J. McHale, sports editor of the *Youngstown Telegram*, which seemed to debunk the misreporting of several other regional newspapers, and set the record straight.

> In reference to the Houck-Gavigan contest, I will say that Houck scored a clean knockout. The referee stopped the bout and not the police, although the former had to hurry to beat the blue coats to it. Even after stopping it the referee started the count and reached seven when Gavigan's seconds rushed in and took their man to his corner. It was sometime before Gavigan was himself. It would be a gross injustice to Houck to deprive him of the credit due him on such a flimsy excuse. Gavigan was

Leo played basketball with several teams in Lancaster, Pennsylvania. The "L" on their uniforms may have identified the Lancaster Red Roses basketball team. Leo is third from left. He frequently experienced injuries while participating in other sports during the boxing season. On one occasion, Leo suffered a leg injury when he collided with another player while playing basketball. Within days, he returned to the ring and fought his opponent while wearing a splint on his leg (courtesy LancasterHistory.org, Lancaster, Pennsylvania, John Hauck Collection, MG-63, JH-03-11-02).

knocked out in the eleventh round. The Cleveland boy put up a splendid fight as long as he could, but was beaten by Houck and in my opinion will have to retire for good.

The events of the contest were sorted out quickly and Leo received a technical knockout win over Gavigan.

After the Gavigan fight, Leo had another extended layoff of two months. Once again, the long period of inactivity between fights cannot be explained. The decision to fight only six times during the year might have been entirely Leo's. Local newspapers provide no information during 1914 to support an idea that management problems or quarrels existed between Leo and McGuigan. The lengthy hiatus must remain a mystery until new facts emerge.

Leo used the two-month period to play basketball with the St. Joseph's Five and scrimmaged every day with the college teams in Lancaster.

During this time frame, Leo also trained for a November 7 bout, a six-rounder at the National A.C. in Philadelphia against Jacob K. Woodward, aka Young Ahearn, who was also known as the "Brooklyn Dancing Master."

Ahearn had recently returned from a ten-month campaign in Europe, where he boxed in both France and England. During that period, which extended from January 3 until October 31, 1914, he posted ten consecutive wins, including three knockouts and one technical knockout.[27] Ahearn was the "real deal" and had the right to say so. In addition, he also had draws with Jack Dillon and Jimmy Clabby, plus a non-decision win over Al McCoy, the current middleweight champion. His record and the caliber of opponents whom he fought against established him as a legitimate top-ranked middleweight contender.

The *Pittsburgh Daily Post* reported that Ahearn handed Houck a severe beating.

> The New Yorker hooked, jabbed, and uppercutted Houck at will and from any old angle at all. Houck never had a chance.
> The third round was a nightmare for him. Ahearn started out by ripping a few lefts to the face and then switched his attack to the body. He landed many smashing punches on the ribs that had Houck hanging on and running away trying to cover up.[28]

The *York Daily* reported that Houck was slow in the ring and afraid to take any chances.[29] In addition, the *Scranton Republican* reported that Houck was out of condition.[30] The fight was unquestionably a newspaper-decision loss for Leo.

Two days later, Leo fought Emmett "Kid" Wagner, a light-heavyweight from Wilkes-Barre, in a six-rounder at the Lancaster A.C. Their previous contest during 1912 had resulted in a draw.

The *Scranton Republican* reported that Wagner had been on the decline after Mike Gibbons knocked him out on October 30, 1913, and claimed the "Kid" could barely walk for several weeks afterwards.[31] The story about Wagner's decline after the Gibbons knockout was a smoke screen. Only two weeks after the Gibbons fight, Wagner went on a seven-bout winning streak that included two consecutive knockouts leading up to his contest with Leo.[32]

Leo had a lot to prove to his fans. The *Scranton Republican* reported that Wagner fought at a weight disadvantage.[33] The *Wilkes-Barre Record*, which reported that Leo had fifteen pounds on the Wilkes-Barre middleweight, corroborated the weight difference between the fighters.[34] By this time, Leo was fighting at over 165 pounds as a light heavyweight.

The *Pittsburgh Post-Gazette* provided the best account of this fast-paced match.

> In the opening round the Lancaster man was slow. Houck landing a few left jabs and getting in return several punches in the wind, but none of the punches counted much and honors were even. Wagner opened the second round with a rush, at one stage of the game beating Leo to the ropes. Houck appeared to wake up in the third and went after his man strong, and all the honors were his by a small margin.
> In the fourth Houck pounded Wagner all over the ring. Wagner went at Houck hard in the fifth, but his steam soon gave out and he contented himself with frequent clinches to protect himself. Both men tried hard for a knockout in the final round and took big chances. Leo's superior strength enabled him to pound Wagner hard, and the round and fight were Houck's by a small margin.[35]

The regional newspapers were divided regarding the outcome of the bout and called it a draw, a win for Leo, and a win on-points for Wagner. Official records all list the fight as a newspaper-decision win for Leo.

Overall, the year provided only a modicum of success for Leo. On the surface, it appeared as if he might have seriously considered a career switch to professional baseball, but Leo's future in boxing remained intact and was encouraging. He continued to be a top-ranked middleweight contender, but weight gains later in the season had moved him up in class to a light heavyweight.

On a personal note, the end of the year was a joyous time and cause for celebration for the Houcks. One day after Christmas, Leo and his wife Anna were blessed with the birth of their second daughter, Margaret.

1915

Mary Houck, Leo's mother, loved to attend her son's fights at the Lancaster A.C. and cheer him onward. She was only forty-nine years old when on February 11, 1915, she succumbed to heart problems and dropsy.[36] Her husband, Edward, had predeceased her by eleven years, dying at age fifty. They were both German immigrants who had successfully assimilated into American society, and soon became naturalized citizens who worked tirelessly every day of the week in order to provide a home for their children in the predominantly Catholic working-class neighborhood of Cabbage-Hill.

Of importance is the fact that, while during this year Leo fought mostly as a light heavyweight, he was not disqualified from fighting middleweights too, a common occurrence practiced by some boxers in the early 1900s.

Leo opened the boxing season at the Lancaster A.C. on March 22 in a six-rounder against Jack Toland, who was substituted for the ailing Johnny Howard. Toland, a middleweight from Philadelphia, had only seven wins after thirty-one matches at the time he faced Leo.[37] It took a great deal of courage for Toland to step into the ring with Leo.

The brief summary of the fight reported by the *Harrisburg Telegraph* may have taken longer to write than witness. The Philadelphian was very much outclassed, but he was plucky to the finish. Honors were even in the first round, but in the second Houck put it all over Jack. Early in the third round a stiff left to the jaw sent him to the mat for the count and a little later a right to the jaw proved a knockout drop.[38]

Five days later, Leo fought George Ashe, a light heavyweight from Philadelphia, in a ten-rounder at the Irving A.C. in Brooklyn. Ashe, who was six years younger than Leo, fought primarily in New York and Philadelphia. His most recent fight on March 8, against Battling Levinsky, now fighting as a light heavyweight, had resulted in a loss.[39]

The newspaper coverage of the fight was scant. The *Scranton Republican* reported that Leo won the bout but was "floored early in the go."[40] The newspaper-decision win was awarded to Leo.

On a moment's notice, Al Grayber, a middleweight, traveled all night from Pittsburgh to Philadelphia after he agreed to replace "K.O. Harry Baker," who was slated to fight Leo in a six-rounder on March 30, at the Fairmont A.C. Leo drew a formidable replacement who had an effective sleeper punch and a superior record when compared to Baker's.

The *Evening Ledger* reported that Grayber kept Leo busy, bloodied his nose in the fourth, and opened up an old cut under his eye in the fifth.[41] The *Pittsburgh Daily Post* reported that Grayber threatened throughout the fight and managed to throw an overhand right that landed on Leo's jaw, which stopped Leo momentarily.[42] The *Lebanon Daily News* countered the other papers' bias about Grayber's efforts by pointing out that Leo won all the way and consistently forced the fight by landing hard and clean jabs.[43] Leo was awarded the newspaper-decision win.

Leo's next bout was a peculiar match up. He traveled all the way to Atlanta, Georgia, to fight George "KO" Brown in a ten-round bout on April 8 at the Bijou Theater in Atlanta. The selection of Brown as an opponent appeared to be a haphazard management decision, which would accomplish zilch to advance Leo either in the middleweight or light heavyweight class, if he won. Most likely, Charlie Rieker, the new president of the Lancaster A.C., and manager Jack Milley, were attempting to temporarily handle Leo's affairs since Jack McGuigan's departure, and figured that the match made sense.

The *Atlanta Constitution* made a big fuss over Brown by citing the fact that he had fought numerous top-ranked middleweight contenders like Jack Dillon, Eddie McGoorty, Jimmy Clabby, Hugo Kelly, Frank Claus, George Chip, and Sailor Petroskey without experiencing a knockdown.[44] The statement was an entertaining April Fool's joke, since it appeared in the paper on the first day of that month. Brown had fought all of the aforementioned boxers but lost all of his fights with these opponents. He did manage to distinguish himself in another way during his career by losing to Jack Dillon a total of eight times.[45]

Britt Craig, of the *Atlanta Constitution*, provided the commentary about the fight in his story titled "Leo Houck Gets Decision Over George 'KO' Brown."

> The fight went the full ten rounds. Houck at all times had a shade, the best of the affair. To an outsider it looked as though Brown's wicked punishment of the heart and kidneys was meat to Houck. Whatever his weak spots are, Houck doesn't carry them around in his heart, stomach, or kidneys.
>
> Although there was much dissention [sic] during the early rounds because of Brown's penchant for driving Houck to the ropes and forcing him there for the infighting and because of Brown's apparent love for clinches, the large audience of fans warmed up in enthusiasm from the fifth round to the tenth. Houck was a wide favorite with the crowd and his ability to absorb unlimited punishment won his fight.[46]

Leo was awarded the newspaper-decision win against Brown.

The ten-round rematch with Young Ahearn on April 22 at the Irving A.C. in Brooklyn was Leo's fourth consecutive road trip where he bounced back and forth between New York and Philadelphia, with one curious side trip to Atlanta. New York promoters discovered that Leo was a great drawing card in Gotham and promised him more work there, going the ten-round route.

Ahearn was also promised more work. A decisive victory over Leo could earn him a clash in Madison Square Garden against top-ranked contender Mike Gibbons.[47] That prospect loomed large for Ahearn, who wanted to settle a score with Gibbons after being knocked out by him in June 1913.

Leo entered this fight at 170 pounds while Ahearn fought at 156 pounds, two pounds below the middleweight maximum of 158 pounds. There was no monetary forfeit on either side regarding a set weight limit.

The *Evening News* provided a concise but one-sided account about Ahearn's handling of Leo.

> There was never a minute during the early stages of the bout that Ahearn was not Houck's master. Several times he staggered the Lancaster fighter with hard rights to the jaw and invariably made him clinch at infighting. In the first inning Houck began forcing matters and started to fight at close quarters with both hands. Ahearn was just as willing to mix it as Houck and soon had the latter clinching from the effects of heavy body blows.
>
> Ahearn tried hard to win by a knockout in the final round and several times drove Houck across the ring. However, he was unable to floor him and when the bell sounded to end the bout both fighters were in a lively mix-up in the center of the ring.[48]

Leo received a newspaper-decision loss for the fight. However, not all of the New York newspapers awarded Ahearn the decision. The *Mail* reported, "The Lancaster boy won."[49]

Mike Gibbons may have heard some inside buzz about the fight or read the *Mail* story about Leo's performance against Ahearn. The *Scranton Republican* reported that Gibbons praised Leo's work in the fight and offered him a May 26 contest in New York, instead of Ahearn.[50]

Two days after the Houck-Ahearn contest, the *Scranton Republican* reported that Lew Durlacher was now back on board as Leo's manager.[51] Leo might have felt that Jack McGuigan, his former manager, was already mismanaging him early on during 1914. Leo was scheduled to fight George Chip on March 12, 1914, but Chip had broken his hand in a bout prior to their scheduled contest. Jimmy Dime, Chip's manager, had talked McGuigan into a postponement of almost five weeks. Three weeks later, Dime had arranged a tune-up bout for Chip to fight Al McCoy on April 7. In retrospect, an argument could be made that McGuigan had temporarily lost his focus on Leo and had carelessly agreed to the five-week postponement. McGuigan had never considered the possibility that Dime might squeeze in another fight for his boxer during that period.

The postponement of five weeks spelled disaster for Leo after he lost his place in line to fight Chip first. McCoy fought Chip first, knocked him out, and returned straight away to New York as the new middleweight champion. McGuigan failed to think ahead by negotiating a shorter postponement and, more importantly, solidify the agreements of contract by insisting that Leo fight Chip first. These oversights resulted in a squandered opportunity and an irreversible blunder that most likely had prompted Leo's decision to fire McGuigan.

Durlacher immediately took charge of Leo's affairs and matched him with Frank Mantell in a twelve-rounder on May 19 at the Rhode Island A.C. in Providence. The fight was their third and last engagement. Mantel's skills had diminished considerably as a middleweight since their last meeting in New York during 1911, but he was still competitive and had posted two wins out of a total of six bouts that season, before meeting Leo.[52] The fight was a well-timed tune-up for Leo, only six days before his next scheduled bout against Mike Gibbons.

The *Scranton Republican* provided two measly sentences describing the bout. "Houck won all the way except in the fourth round, when Mantell held him even. Houck boxed rings around his rival and several times jarred him with hard right hand punches to the jaw."[53] The fight was a newspaper-decision win for Leo.

After the fight, Leo left Providence and traveled to New York for his next scheduled bout. He started training at the Polo Club and sparred with Jim Coffey, a six-foot-three-inch heavyweight from New York who had a career knockout rate of fifty-four percent. Mike Gibbons, Leo's opponent, trained at the St. Nicholas Rink, where they were scheduled to fight on May 26, in a ten-round contest.[54] Leo agreed to fight Gibbons at 158 pounds and posted a forfeit to that effect. He currently weighed around 170 pounds and needed to reduce by at least two pounds a day for the next six days.

The significance of this fight was obvious to both Durlacher and Leo. They knew Leo could preserve his top-ranked status as a middleweight contender with a win or draw against Gibbons. Moreover, a win could go a long way in helping to alleviate the bitter ending of Leo's 1913 season and the "Fiasco in Frisco" during his short and disjointed campaign of 1914.

Gibbons was, hands-down, the number-one middleweight contender in America.

Alexander Johnson described him as a "marvelous hitter, a beautiful boxer, but not a hard hitter."[55] The latter part of the statement by Johnson was inaccurate. In fact, Gibbons was a hard hitter with a lifetime career knockout record of twenty-nine percent.

On the night of the fight, Leo had reduced to 165 pounds while Gibbons weighed 151 pounds. Gibbons refused to claim the weight forfeit.[56]

The *Harrisburg Daily Independent* provided a detailed account of the fight in their story titled "Houck Body Punished in Bout with Gibbons."

> Mike Gibbons, the master boxer, met a tough customer at the St. Nicholas A.C. last night in Leo Houck, of Lancaster, who outweighed him fourteen pounds. Despite the fact that Mike nearly cut the Quaker to pieces the Lancaster man was tearing in at the finish and in the ninth round by sheer weight and aggressiveness landed several hard punches and had Gibbons doing his best to even up the round.
>
> In the sixth round Houck landed a low blow, but it did not hurt and was overlooked. While the men were banging away for dear life in the tenth another low blow caught Gibbons and doubled him up. He recovered in time to finish with a display of speed and accuracy that had his opponent dazzled.
>
> There were more clean hits crowded into the first round than are generally to be seen in the whole encounter and all were landed by Gibbons. In less than thirty seconds a light right opened an old cut under Houck's eye and the crimsons poured forth so that both men were covered with gore at the finish of the round. Gibbons used every kind of punch in this session and threw off Houck's leads with the greatest ease. Houck took plenty of punishment in the second, but let up as soon as he found he had his opponent at his mercy. The fight nearly ended before the bell, when Gibbons missed with a wicked left hook.
>
> The same clever work on the part of Gibbons with little actual results continued in the third, but in the fourth Mike let up again by sending in a few body punches and driving Houck to the ropes. The Lancaster man was entitled to an even break, the best he got all the way through except perhaps the ninth round when he surprised both Gibbons and the crowd by carrying the fight to his man. From the fourth to the ninth round there was the usual display of speed and science by Gibbons who used every means of avoiding punches with entire success.[57]

The fight's outcome was a newspaper-decision loss for Leo.

The *Harrisburg Telegraph* called Leo a punching bag for Gibbons and maintained that he could have easily knocked out Leo anytime during the fight, but wanted to save him for another fight. Their reporter claimed that whenever Leo was in distress Gibbons would deliberately turn his back on Leo and walk to the center of the ring.[58] The preeminent sportswriter of the day, Damyon Runyon, saw the fight unfold a different way and believed, "There were signs indicating that Mike was striving for a knockout through the fight but Houck gave the so-called champ a struggle in his own peculiar way and was industriously toiling onward at the finish."[59]

Leo had a ten-day break after his fight with Gibbons, which ended a demanding tour of six consecutive fights on the road.

Leo's next bout against Young Ahearn was their third and final ten-round contest. They fought on June 7 at the Capitol District A.C. in Albany, New York. Young Ahearn had remained idle for forty-six days since his last meeting with Leo on April 22. Conversely, Leo had fought in three ten-round contests and one twelve-rounder during the same number of days.

During the ten days leading up to the fight, Leo regained the seven pounds he had shed before the Gibbons fight. His fighting weight now consistently hovered around 172 pounds. Ahearn weighed in at 154 pounds, four pounds under the middleweight limit. The fighters met before a crowd of 5,000 fans who believed that Ahearn could cinch a future bout with Mike Gibbons with a decisive victory over Leo.[60]

The *Allentown Democrat* reported that Ahearn decisively defeated Leo, had him on the verge of a knockout several times, and simply outclassed him.[61] Ahearn's style was described as artistic by the *New Castle Herald* and corroborated the *Allentown Democrat's* report that Leo was outclassed. Winning easily on points without the advantage of a knockdown, KO, or TKO against a middleweight contender like Leo hardly validated the contention that he was outclassed. However, one fact was clearly evident. Leo, who usually figured out an opponent's style by his second or third meeting with that same opponent, was totally bamboozled by Ahearn.

The constant road trips and ten-round bouts ceased temporarily for Leo after the Ahearn fight. The number and frequency of bouts for early 1900s boxers like Leo were physically punishing, and demanded that the underpinnings of any fighter's success hinged on an absolute physical toughness, coupled with a well-practiced stoical philosophy. The forty-nine-day lull before his next bout left Leo plenty of time to rest, train, and play baseball.

After the layoff, Leo faced Charlie Grande, aka Sailor Grande, a middleweight from San Francisco, in a six-round match on July 26 at the Lancaster A.C. Grande started his professional boxing career during 1912 and by June 14, 1915, already had a win over George Chip, a former middleweight champion. Grande was an up-and-comer, but at this point lacked the scope and range of Leo's generalship in the squared circle.

The *Reading Times* provided a brief report about the six-round wind-up at the Lancaster A.C. "Leo Houck and Sailor Grande boxed six hurricane rounds before the Lancaster Athletic Club, and at the end it was a toss up as to the winner, though Grande tried hard to score. Houck did most of the leading and used his left jab, while Grande kept boring in and was battling all the time using both hands."[62] The *Scranton Republican* reported the fight about even with the popular opinion slightly in favor of Leo.[63] Official records list the fight as a draw.

Two weeks after the Grande fight, Leo returned to New York and fought Bert Kenny, aka Wild Bert Kenney, in a ten-round contest on September 10 at the New Polo A.C. Kenny was a light heavyweight who had started his professional boxing career only a year earlier and was, by all accounts, an unseasoned boxer and a peculiar choice for an opponent. The purse offered must have been the overriding inducement for Leo to fight Kenny. Durlacher's fiscal management seemed sound, but his direction in guiding Leo was now adrift and lacked the planning necessary for a serious campaign. This was an immense departure from the years 1910 to 1913, when Durlacher skillfully guided Leo from a lightweight to a top-ranked middleweight contender.

Regional newspapers gave no detailed account or outcome about this fight. However, the *Courier-News* in New Jersey reported that Kenny outpointed Leo in the wind-up. Official records all list the fight as a newspaper-decision win for Leo.[64]

Four days after the Kenny bout, on September 14, Leo fought Herman Miller, aka Young Herman Miller, in a ten-rounder at Conestoga Park in Lancaster. Miller, a middleweight from Baltimore, was advertised as the "Southern Middleweight Champ" by the *York Daily*.[65] The title "Southern Middleweight Champ" sounded impressive, but the southern territory was actually a regional area whose perimeter was a bit uncertain and hard to identify. The best guess is that it might have included any county south of Lancaster County and the Mason-Dixon Line but ending at Baltimore, where Miller did most of his fighting. His fight record from 1911 through 1914 included nineteen wins, five draws, and two losses, from a total of twenty-six bouts.[66]

Two thousand fans crowded into Conestoga Park for the fight. Most believed that Miller, who never faced Leo's type, would be lucky to survive the entire ten rounds.

The *York Daily* reported that Miller threw in the sponge after six rounds.

> Miller fought gamely in the opening and second rounds but went to pieces in the third when Houck by clever in-fighting rushed him to the ropes and rained blow after blow to his stomach. In this round Miller began to weaken and called the referee's attention to the fact that Houck was fouling on the breaks.
>
> Houck, however, took advantage of the opportunity and landed a hard blow to Miller's jaw that staggered the "Southern Champ." When the gong sounded Miller could hardly find his corner. The fourth round was about even, although the Red Rose City lad did all the leading. Miller at times landed terrific blows on Houck's head but they failed to take effect. In the fifth Houck toyed with Miller and again directed his attack at the stomach. The sixth mill was all Houck's as he landed whenever and wherever he wished. Miller went down under the strain for the count of eight and when he arose Houck rushed and landed both right and lefts to the head that again sent Barrett's protégé to the floor. This time he did not attempt to rise and the bell saved him from a knockout. Joe Barrett threw in the sponge after he was satisfied that Miller could not last the limit.[67]

Official records list the outcome of the fight as both a knockout and technical knockout for Leo.

The win over Miller was a well-timed tune-up for Leo's next bout two weeks later on September 30, against Johnny Howard in a six-rounder at the Rocky Springs Theater in Lancaster. Howard, a middleweight from Bayonne, New Jersey, was a legitimate middleweight contender. In a "Special to the *Telegraph*," Howard was said to have had two draws with Jack Dillon and one with Mike Gibbons.[68] The statement was completely bogus. All three contests resulted in losses for Howard.

The *Wilkes-Barre Times Leader* gave the first four rounds to Leo based on his continual jabbing and excellent infighting, and commented that both fighters were going strong at the finish.[69] Leo was reported to have passed on numerous opportunities to knock out Howard.[70] The observation about Leo not taking chances to knock out an opponent appeared now and again in the press throughout his career. Leo never responded or commented publicly about any newspaper's conjecture that he rendered sympathy to an opponent whenever it suited him. The fight's outcome was another newspaper-decision win for Leo.

During the interim, while Leo was on an extended layoff, the Bethany Boys Club football team lined up against the St. Joseph's C.C. team on October 16. Coach Hill of the St. Joseph's team ran his Red Rose City eleven, which included Leo at fullback position, through a secret signal practice the evening before.[71]

Official records are at odds regarding the acknowledgment of Leo's next bout on November 11, a three-rounder against Bill "Wild Bill" Fleming at Falcon Hall in Meriden, Connecticut. The *Meriden Journal*'s sports page advertised a four-round bout between a Tommie Houck of New Haven, Connecticut, against Bill Fleming.[72] Tommie Houck fought on November 11 against a different opponent named Teddy Fabryck at Casino Hall in Bridgeport, Connecticut.[73] The newspapers in the tri-county region of Lancaster, Harrisburg, and York failed to mention or advertise the upcoming bout between Leo and Fleming.

The November 11 match between Fleming and Leo at Falcon Hall might have served as a tune-up for Leo three days before his contest with Al Rogers. Fleming was an accomplished middleweight who had a win over Al McCoy, the middleweight champion, on December 1, 1914. With that fact in mind, the match could have made some sense, or appeared somewhat credible, in order for Leo to find out if his conditioning was solid upon returning to the ring after a forty-five-day layoff. However, it had seemed unusual that the fight was ignored and never mentioned by the press in Lancaster and the surrounding communities, beforehand or afterwards. In addition, Leo's manager could have simply arranged a tune-up bout for him locally with an opponent from Philadelphia. Some official records list the three-round fight as a draw, while other records fail to recognize the fight at all.

During the football season, Leo continued to train and spar with Al Mason, a boxer from Lancaster who had fought a career total of seven times from October 10, 1915, until November 20, 1916.[74] They both trained together in preparation for their bouts at Frohsinn Hall on November 15 in Altoona, Pennsylvania, where Leo fought middleweight Al Rogers in the wind-up after Mason had battled Art Stigall in the semi-wind-up.

Leo's opponent, Al Rogers, from Buffalo, New York, had an impressive win three days earlier over Young Ahearn, a boxer who had totally bewildered Leo during their three clashes.

The fight was Altoona's inaugural boxing show. Over 400 spectators showed up for the "boxing carnival," which included four bouts arranged and promoted by Mort Henderson, a popular local wrestler.[75]

The *Altoona Tribune* reported that Rogers and Houck received a standing ovation as they entered the ring.

At the tap of the bell they started to feel each other out. They went together and most of the mixing was in the clinches. The crowd called for fighting and in the next round things warmed up considerably and the bout gave indications of being a good one. Rogers started to rush things but was a trifle wild in his leading, Houck getting inside most of his blows and dealing out short arm jolts to the body and head. Houck had the best of the round.

The third round opened with both going the way the fans liked. Houck was the more cautious while Rogers waded into him in an effort to put him away. For his trouble he got the worst of the round and when it ended was slightly groggy.

Rogers came back in the fourth round and made Houck fight. The fifth round was the round of the fight. Houck at this stage of the bout showed his cleverness. He got inside of Rogers' leads and generally with a head and body blow. He next played jabs on Rogers' head and had him groggy and swinging at random. Rogers was rushing into Houck swinging wildly but covering well. Houck tried to land a body blow but failed and couldn't connect with a knockout.

The sixth opened up with both men going at it hammer and tongs, but Rogers lacked generalship while Houck met his leads with short arm jabs to the head and body and strong jabs to the jaw. The latter blows had a telling effect on Rogers and only for covering he might have been put away. It was Houck's bout by long odds and with more at stake he would surely come through a winner.[76]

The *New Castle News* reported, "Houck showed superiority in every round and might have scored a knockout had the fight gone longer."[77] The fight's outcome garnered Leo his ninth win of the season.

Only one day after the Rogers bout on November 16, Leo fought Sailor Grande in a six-rounder at the Douglas A.C. in Philadelphia. A one-day break between fights would push the physical boundaries of any conditioned fighter, but fortunately, Leo had handled Rogers easily the previous evening and came away from the contest unscathed. Grande had his own aspirations and knew a win over Leo would help pave the way toward a future match with Jack Dillon, the current light heavyweight champion. However, Grande needed to first eliminate Leo and then George Chip before securing a match with Dillon.[78]

The *Allentown Leader* reported the fight drew only a small crowd and belonged to Grande all the way. The bout was hard and rough, Grande consistently beating Houck about the body. In the fourth round Grande landed a right-hand swing to the side of Houck's head and opened up a cut that bled freely.[79]

Leo could have complained that the one-day interval between fights had left no time for him to recuperate and contributed to his being less watchful in the ring. Instead, he remained silent, took the loss in stride, and accepted the newspaper-decision loss.

The end of the boxing season for Leo was only six days away. It concluded with a six-round bout against Willie Baker, a New York City middleweight, on November 22 at the Olympia A.C. in Philadelphia. Baker fought a total of eleven bouts during his professional career that lasted from May 4, 1911, until June 20, 1916.[80]

Leo had little to worry about regarding Baker and decided to play football the day before the fight. He scored two touchdowns for his club, the St. Joseph's C.C., against the visiting Bethany B.C. from York.[81]

The *Pittsburgh Daily Post* made an observation about Leo's sub-par condition at the end of the season and noted that he now weighed in at 174 pounds, was below form, and had difficulty against Baker, whose limited ring experience barely qualified him as a journeyman fighter.[82] The *Allentown Leader* reported that the bout was slow with an abundance of clinching and wrestling. In addition, the spectators showed their disapproval by hooting at both fighters during the bout, as well as when they exited the ring.[83] The fight was an extremely untypical performance from Leo, who always attempted to please the audience with his best efforts, and it looked particularly terrible because Leo struggled against an easy set-up like Baker. Leo barely received the newspaper-decision win.

The end of the boxing season seemed anticlimactic for Leo, and overall did little to advance or distinguish him as a serious light heavyweight contender. He finished the year by playing basketball in the Tri-County League for the Ephrata Springs basketball team.

By and large, Leo's schedule and the caliber of fighters he had faced did improve briefly under Durlacher's management after he returned. Durlacher knew that Al McCoy, the current middleweight champion, had continued to dash all efforts by Leo's camp to arrange a contest between them as early as 1913. A shot at the middleweight championship for Leo during 1915 was simply out of the question while McCoy held the title. That still left another viable option: Leo could fight and eliminate the current crop of light heavyweight contenders in order to cinch a match with Jack Dillon, the light heavyweight champion. Probably the most outstanding questions about Durlacher's management style were his lack of a cohesive fight strategy, lack of commitment, or both, in order to secure Leo a match with Jack Dillon during 1915. Whatever the reason, the opportunities for Leo to participate in a title bout were steadily dwindling. Boxing seasons typically start with a reasonable amount of excitement, anticipation, and momentum; but this season had faltered after June, and ended flatly two days before Thanksgiving, totally devoid of any bid for a light heavyweight title fight.

1916

Leo had rejoined the St. Joseph's basketball team as their captain in January, after he had finished playing for the Ephrata Springs basketball team. His "Olympian"-like abilities and the boundless energy required to engage in multiple sports during the boxing season never seemed to flag. Those effortless segues from one sport to another were often mentioned by the press, but were never recognized or described as an unrivaled accomplishment, especially when compared to his boxing contemporaries from the early 1900s.

However, basketball, baseball, and football did not pay Leo's bills. A new boxing season was about to commence, and Leo had to switch his focus to the first fight of the season, a six-rounder, on February 14 at the Lancaster A.C. with Billy Berger, a middleweight from Pittsburgh.

The fight was Berger's final professional bout. By all accounts, it looked as if Berger had already considered retirement during 1915, when he fought only three times. Berger and Leo had both fought many common opponents like George Chip, Jack Dillon, Buck Crouse, Bob Moha, and Frank Klaus. Unfortunately, Berger never became a middleweight contender during his career, but did have a notable win over George Chip and two draws with Buck Crouse.[84]

The fight was a tune-up for Leo, but Berger's fans in Lancaster and Harrisburg hardly minded. They remained devoted to this fighter who had plenty of steam left in his punches.

In a "Special to the *Harrisburg Telegraph*," Berger was described as game and willing but simply outclassed by Leo, who left the ring without a mark at the conclusion of six rounds.[85]

Ten days after the fight with Berger, the *Altoona Tribune* published an open letter from Duke Kelly of Philadelphia, on Leo's behalf. This was the first mention publicly of yet another management switch for Leo. The announcement was hardly a surprise, considering Leo's disappointing 1915 season after reuniting with his former manager Lew Durlacher.

Leo Houck, the eastern Pennsylvania boy, who is extremely popular among

Leo abruptly fired Lew Durlacher, his manager during 1915, and replaced him with Duke Kelly (standing above next to Leo). Leo fired numerous managers throughout his career but always did so quietly and without any personal public disclosure in order to avoid rumor and controversy. Inadequate management may have been a contributing factor to Leo's failure to achieve a championship title fight during his career. In addition, Leo's continuous participation in other sports throughout every boxing season may have also produced a level of inattentiveness that caused him to lose focus on boxing, his principal vocation (courtesy LancasterHistory.org, Lancaster, Pennsylvania, John Houck Collection, MG-63, JH-03-05-30).

Altoona boxing fans, is seeking bouts with any middleweight in the country, bar none, according to his manager, Duke Kelly, of Philadelphia. Kelly wrote to the *Tribune* sporting editor yesterday as follows:

"Just a line in behalf of Leo Houck who is back in the game after a lay-off on account of an injured hand. He is in good condition and eager to meet any middleweight in the country. He would especially like to box in Altoona again, to demonstrate to his friends that he is OK. I noticed that Miller and 'K.O. Baker' boxed in Altoona. Houck stopped Miller in Lancaster and if Miller wants more of his game Houck will gladly stop him again. This goes also for 'K.O. Baker.' Thanking you in advance, I am yours in sport.

"Duke Kelly

"1714 Vine St.

"Philadelphia"[86]

Within five days of the publication of Duke Kelly's public challenge, Willie Baker, a middleweight from Philadelphia, stepped up and agreed to fight Leo on February 29 at the Coliseum Hall in York, Pennsylvania.

Unfortunately, Baker had to scratch from the fight after injuring his hand during training. "Battling Brandt," a heavyweight from Chicago who weighed 215 pounds, substituted for Baker.[87] The "Midwestern Goliath" outweighed Leo by approximately forty pounds. Brandt had knocked out "Bull Kessler" in Philadelphia only four days prior to his match with Leo.

The *York Daily* provided a detailed account titled "Leo Houck Beat Chicago Giant."

The big boy from Chicago earned an even break in the first round by forcing his opponent and by landing in the clinches. Brandt is the biggest man that ever entered a local ring and Houck deserves the credit for the victory. On several occasions Brandt swung vigorously at Houck, who managed to keep clear.

In the second round Houck was the aggressor jabbing Brandt in the face and playing tattoo on his stomach. This kind of punishment did not effect the big fellow in the least as he was always ready to take more. Brandt rushed Houck to the ropes many times in the second session and the pair nearly fell to the floor on one occasion.

Houck was again the aggressor in the third round sending hard rights and lefts to the region of the stomach but the "heavy" was too strong and would shove his opponent to the ropes. Brandt only landed one hard punch during the round and that was of little consequence.

Houck kept right after the big man in the fourth and by two left hooks to the jaw and a right to Brandt's nose the claret started flowing. Brandt in a clinch landed hard on Houck's neck, the Lancaster boy having his head lowered. The punch was landed when Brandt was off his feet. The two boys clinched often in this round and the infighting was spirited.

The fifth and sixth rounds were all Houck's. He landed time after time with both hands on the heavyweight but he did not succeed in putting him away. The crowd hissed Brandt when he held and shoved the Lancaster boy around the ring.[88]

Leo was awarded the newspaper-decision win based on points scored.

Six years had elapsed since Leo last fought in Reading as a welterweight. Advance ticket sales were brisk for his next bout, a six-rounder, against middleweight Eddie Revoire on March 7 at the Reading A.C. Revoire, from Philadelphia, was a favorite of the local matchmakers, who thought he was a worthy adversary for Leo in the evening's wind-up.

The *Reading Times* reported that Leo weighed in at around 165 pounds and wanted to add on ten more pounds so he could fight the "heavies," since there would be more money in it for him. Revoire, who was ten pounds lighter than Leo, said that he'd "fight him if he weighed a ton."[89]

Only one day before the Houck-Revoire battle, the *Pittsburgh Daily Post* published a brief story titled "Whaddye Mean, State Title?" The paper had advertised a fifteen-round fight between Joe Borrell and Jack McCarron for the Pennsylvania Middleweight Championship, but also disclaimed the validity of the bout as a true championship fight since George Chip, Buck Crouse, and Leo Houck never had the opportunity to participate in any elimination fights leading up to this over-hyped match.

The next day, over 1200 fans crowded into the auditorium for the Houck-Revoire fight. In between the preliminary bouts leading up to the wind-up, a local author, Elwood McCloskey, sold his books and recited John L. Sullivan poems to keep the crowd thoroughly entertained.[90]

The *Reading Times* covered this exciting match, which reinforced the durability and versatility of boxers from this era to battle each other competitively, regardless of a weight advantage or disadvantage.

> It was announced that Houck tipped the scales at 165 pounds and Revoire at 155, although the latter looked just as heavy as the Lancaster boy when they stripped for action. They fought carefully for the first two rounds, doing much infighting, while the leading was about even. Neither did any damage in the first round, but in the second Revoire cut loose and had the best of the milling. Houck landed a left to the jaw and rocked Revoire's head in the third. Houck did a lot of leading with his left in the fourth but was outfought by Revoire in the infighting, which was more furious.
>
> The fifth was the fastest round of the fight, Revoire forcing and exciting his seconds to call for him to keep it up and get a knockout. The Philadelphian landed to Leo's jaw repeatedly and opened a scar on his chin. Houck came back with stiff jabbing as the round ended.
>
> In the last round Revoire did most of the leading and landed hard lefts to the head. A left uppercut to the jaw was one of the best blows landed, but Houck suffered little damage. Both men were apparently fresh when the bell sounded.[91]

Official records list the outcome of the fight as both a newspaper-decision loss for Leo and a draw.

Only six days after the Revoire-Houck fight, a light heavyweight from Shenandoah, Pennsylvania, named "K.O. Sullivan" fought Leo in a six-rounder at the Lancaster A.C., which had recently changed quarters to the Family Theater on Orange Street.[92]

Sullivan had surprised fight fans early on during his second year of professional boxing when he had had a draw with Eddie Revoire at the Capitol City A.C. in Ardmore, Maryland, and then followed up soon afterwards on October 10, 1915, with a win on points over Al McCoy, who was the middleweight champion from April 7, 1914, until November 4, 1917.[93]

Sullivan's accomplishments in the ring during 1915 were impressive, but Leo quickly showed Sullivan who was the real ring boss. The *Harrisburg Telegraph* reported that Leo tore into his opponent and gave him nothing short of a severe lacing in the second round when he threw a right that connected with Sullivan's jaw and dropped him to the canvas for a count of six. From the second to the sixth round, Sullivan survived by hanging on to his opponent.[94] The fight for Leo was easy and earned him the newspaper-decision win.

Leo had sixteen days to rest and train until his next bout, a six-rounder, on March 29 against Jack Reck at the Keystone Athletic Cub in the Orpheum Theater in Harrisburg. Reck was a light heavyweight from Philadelphia who learned how to box while serving in the United States Marine Corps. He had practiced the art of the "sweet science" as often as possible while stationed at League Island in Philadelphia.[95] He had fought only one time during the season prior to this match and entered the fight fresh after a month-long layoff.[96] The *Harrisburg Telegraph* reported that Houck easily walked away with four of the six rounds.[97]

In addition, The *Harrisburg Daily Independent* added a smidgen more detail about the fight. Leo would bore in time after time and send his left through Reck's guard, making it count about fifty per cent of the time. Reck's dukes went wild in an effort to land an uppercut. Houck put up a better fight in four of the six rounds. The fourth round was the Philadelphian's by a good margin and the first was even. The fight's outcome was a newspaper-decision win for Leo.

One week after the Reck bout, Leo fought a six-rounder on April 7 against "Young" Herman Miller in York. Seven months prior to this bout, Leo had scored a technical knockout over Miller during their first engagement at Conestoga Park in Lancaster.

Local and regional newspapers had failed to publish any advertisements promoting the bout or coverage about the fight afterwards. Leo received a newspaper-decision win over Miller based on points scored.

Several days after the fight with Miller, Leo refused to fight his next opponent, Ralph Erne, a middleweight from Philadelphia, on short notice. He received a postponement until April 25, when they both met at the Coliseum Hall in York. Leo had finished his training with Jule Ritchie in Lancaster the day before the fight, while Erne concluded his training by sparring a few short rounds with Johnny Gill at his camp.[98] Erne expected to win in a walk while his manager had predicted that Leo would experience a premature ending to the wind-up event. Time and time again, wannabe middleweight contenders like Erne underestimated Leo and believed they could easily eliminate him and advance within the division. The record had showed that Erne never had a win over Leo's type, which included Jack Dillon, Jimmy Clabby, and Buck Crouse.[99]

The *York Daily* stated that both fighters entered the ring at 164 pounds, appeared to be conditioned to the minute, and used everything they knew in a crowd-pleasing slugfest.

> The first round was even while the next five belonged to Houck who battered Erne at will. Houck inflicted severe punishment to Erne's face. The claret started to flow from Erne's nose in the second round and continued flowing to the end. Erne used Houck's shoulders and arms for a handkerchief and had more blood on his opponent than he had on himself.
>
> In the fourth and sixth rounds Houck shot many blows to Erne's stomach, which compelled the Philadelphian to raise his knees for protection. These blows weakened the Quaker and had the bout gone another round Houck would have scored a knockout. In the initial round both Houck and his opponent made missteps and almost fell from the ring, which does not have the regulation platform outside the ropes. In the fifth round Houck landed a dozen or more vicious blows to Erne's face, but the latter held on in an almost helpless condition.[100]

Leo seldom engaged in any public pre-fight hype, but never forgot an opponent's boastfulness or promises regarding his future health and well-being in the ring. He had remembered Erne's claim that the fight would be easy, which turned out the opposite and earned Erne a most unsympathetic beating, which might have been the trigger that sent him into boxing obscurity five fights later, when his career ended. The newspaper-decision win for Leo was probably not as noteworthy as the message he had telegraphed to any aspiring or current middleweight contender. Leo was still a formidable opponent and potential stumbling block to any fighter intent on eliminating him on their own journey toward capturing the middleweight crown.

Only two days after the fight, Henry Hensel, manager of the Lancaster A.C., retired due to ill health and died shortly afterwards. Leo had become familiar with Hensel's every methodology when promoting fights and his cleverness in advertising even the most ho-hum fight card as the next biggest event in pugilism. Hensel had watched Leo's boxing career blossom from the two-round fights as a teenager right up to his regular spot in the wind-up as a top middleweight contender. Leo had trusted Hensel implicitly during their friendship. The relationship and trust had been reciprocal. Hensel had known that he could always count on Leo, his star boxer, to help pack the house and stuff the coffers.

Hensel's death created a void at the Lancaster A.C. Charles A. Rieker, a Lancaster resident and businessman, took over the reins as the new president of the Lancaster A.C., while Jack Milley, Leo's first trainer, served as the manager.[101]

Several days after Hensel passed away, Leo had signed on to play baseball with the Black Fronts of Lancaster.[102] On May 6 the Black Fronts played their first games of the season in a large tournament held in Reading, when a number of semi-professional teams competed against amateur teams.[103]

By the end of the first week in May, Leo had started a six-month layoff. However, he had one brief interruption during the layoff and was committed to meet Jack Reck on May 15 in a six-round wind-up at the Lancaster A.C. Reck, the Fighting Marine, had been idle since April 29, his first engagement with Leo.

Henry H. Hensel was a reporter for the *Lancaster Intelligencer Journal* for thirty-nine years. In addition, he was the manager of the Lancaster A.C. He also promoted the boxing shows held at the Lancaster A.C. Hensel was exceedingly proficient in generating publicity about ongoing rivalries and upcoming rematches between opponents from Lancaster and Philadelphia. His star attraction, Leo F. Houck, who typically fought the wind-up, always packed the Lancaster A.C. (courtesy LancasterHistory.org, Lancaster, Pennsylvania, John Houck Collection, MG-63, JH-03-02-42).

On the day of the fight, the *Wilkes-Barre Times Leader* published a story about Leo, written by Joe "Buck" Kelly. The article was a short synopsis of Leo's career, but started on a rather sour note when Kelly claimed in his first few sentences, "Leo has slipped and is about done."[104] Reporters seldom, if ever, took disparaging broadsides at Leo. He still had a lot of ring mileage left in his legs and continued to prove it successfully for the next six years. Kelly had made an erroneous assertion about Leo being all in. In a roundabout way, Kelly had hinted at another underlying issue which involved the caliber of opponents Leo had faced since the beginning of the 1916 boxing season, and his lack of attention to a genuine campaign for the light heavyweight title.

Later that same day, after Kelly's article had hit the newsstands, Leo proved that he was far from "about done" when he won over Reck and earned the newspaper-decision win based on points.

Despite Joe "Buck" Kelly's assertions that Leo was washed up, Leo's popularity as a boxer never diminished throughout his entire career, especially at the regional and state levels. His reputation as a boxer provided him with the opportunity to fight close to home and earn sizeable purses without any lengthy or inconvenient road trips. At this juncture, Leo almost always fought the wind-up and might have received an average purse of between $400 and $500 per bout. He fought a total of fifteen bouts during 1915, making his total earnings for the year over ten times that of the average worker, who earned approximately $687 per year, according to the 1915 census.[105]

Early in October, Leo decided to return to the ring, having agreed to fight Al Grayber, a middleweight from Pittsburgh, in a six-rounder during November, at the Power Auditorium in Pittsburgh. The fight was postponed until December 9 after Leo injured his knee in a collision on November 20 while playing basketball for the Big Five of Lancaster.[106] Many of Leo's friends tried to persuade him to drop the other sporting activities that sometimes resulted in injuries and urged him to concentrate solely on boxing.[107]

Red Mason, Grayber's manager, had believed that a fight against a veteran boxer like Leo was a mandatory requirement for Grayber's pugilistic education and particularly important if he expected to move up in class.[108] Mason's strategy for his boxer reinforced the idea that Leo was still a force to be reckoned with in the middleweight ranks.

One day before the fight, the *Pittsburgh Daily Post* reported that Grayber had told some of his friends that he was determined to win the fight or else quit the ring.[109] After the fight, Grayber did quit boxing, but returned to the ring on January 10, 1919, two years later.

Jim Jab covered the lively battle for the *Pittsburgh Press*.

> Coming up from behind, A. Grayber, local slammer, broke down a nice lead held by Leo Houck, of Lancaster, in a dandy six-round bout at the Power House A.C. Grayer, however, failed to stay on even terms and Houck, in the last round, by a dint of a fine left, earned enough of a margin to entitle him to a slight shade.
>
> For three innings Houck took the tricks by the use of a rapid left mitt that baffled Grayber. Then the home boy began to shoot his left in unison and had the veteran harried. Round four and five were in Grayber's favor and Houck seemed tired at the gong. Starting the sixth friends of the Greater Pittsburgher expected him to pull away for a victory. Here Houck recuperated and was going the best at the finish. Grayber's rough stuff didn't please all fans and some booed him. It was a hard battle and both men did neat work at stages. Houck was most punished.[110]

Leo earned the newspaper-decision win. Official fight records list the fight as a draw.

Two days after Christmas, Leo fought his final bout of the season against Fay Keiser in a ten-rounder in Cumberland, Maryland. During 1915, Keiser had fought and won over a young Harry Greb early on in his career. Greb later turned out to be one of the most superlative boxers and champions in pugilistic history. The pre-fight publicity by the *Harrisburg Telegraph* was negligible but contained one interesting note stating, "After the holidays it is Houck's idea to get into the best possible condition and resume his ring work."[111] Official records all list the Houck-Keiser fight as a win for Leo. However, the *Everlast Boxing Record 1924* identifies the fight as a draw.

The end of the 1916 boxing season had one conspicuous similarity that linked it to the 1915 season. Leo had boxed another season and avoided a serious campaign focused on a drive toward the light heavyweight championship. He had committed to fighting as a light heavyweight, but seemed uninterested in eliminating other light heavyweights in order to move up in the division. Leo had settled for fighting at catchweights in the

8. Baseball, the Blahs and Catchweight Battles, 1914–1915–1916

middleweight division and matching against second-tier light heavyweights.[112] During the year, the local and regional newspapers never bothered to suggest or mention a possible title bout between Leo and the light heavyweight champion. Duke Kelly, Leo's manager, might have attempted to negotiate a title bout but was unable to reach an agreement. By the next season, Duke Kelly had redeemed himself when he finally positioned Leo advantageously in his chase for the most elusive goal of his career.

9

Light Heavyweight Sensation, 1917–1918

1917

The day before his first bout of the season, Leo had played guard for the Lancaster Red Roses against the York basketball team. His opening fight on January 21 was a six-round rematch with Eddie Revoire at Frankie Erne's Gymnasium in Lancaster. Eleven months earlier, Revoire and Leo had provided their fans with a great contest in Reading.

The *Harrisburg Telegraph* published a one-sentence report about the outcome of their second fight by stating, "In this fight with Eddie Revoire the Lancaster boy showed he was far from 'all in' and was entitled to the verdict at the end of six fast rounds."[1]

The next day, Leo continued his winning streak by assisting his team, the Lancaster Red Roses, with a pair of field goals during their victory over the York basketball team. Less than a week later, Leo signed on to play basketball with the Lancaster Professionals.

Leo had a two-month layoff after his first bout and played basketball exclusively during the months of February and March.

On March 30, Leo returned to the ring for a six-rounder against Dummy Ketchel from Baltimore, at the Lancaster A.C. Ketchel's aka of Dummy was not a self-deprecating or humorous slight that referred to an obvious lack of intelligence, but referred to his inability to speak. Ketchel had carved out a professional boxing career that lasted nine years despite an impediment that could easily have resulted in a very different life, one minimized by discrimination and the absence of equal opportunities.[2] One factor in Ketchel's favor was the fact that Leo had his left leg in splints, the result of a prior injury while playing basketball, which handicapped his movement in the ring. In addition, Ketchel weighed more and that slight advantage also contributed to his ability to finish the fight on his feet. Ketchel had waltzed into a buzz saw. The *Allentown Leader* reported that Leo had beaten Ketchel badly in every round but "was unable to stop the tough mute."[3]

Seven days after the Ketchel bout, on April 6, Leo fought Tommy Burke in a six-rounder at the Fulton Opera House in Lancaster. This was the first boxing show held at the opera house and the large attendance would have delighted the recently departed boxing promoter, Henry Hensel. The bout was another tune-up arranged by Duke Kelly, Leo's manager, in preparation for an upcoming contest with Battling Levinsky. During 1917 Tommy Burke would fight four times and quit boxing on June 8. He would return

9. Light Heavyweight Sensation, 1917–1918

to the ring on July 30, 1920, fight nine more times, and then retire from boxing permanently.[4] The *Harrisburg Telegraph* reported the outcome of the short and sweet fight by stating, "The local boy showed his superiority the entire six rounds, his opponent landing but few clean blows the whole distance and was tired at the finish."[5] Official records list the newspaper-decision as a win for Leo.

Leo had a thirty-day layoff after the Burke fight before he fought Jackie Clark, a middleweight from Allentown, on May 7 at the Lancaster A.C. Clark had fought a total of thirty times during 1916 and won twenty-three of the bouts. One of the bouts resulted in a no-decision win on September 28, 1916, over Al McCoy, the middleweight champion.[6] Clark had class and had looked poised to win the middleweight title. He had proved his mettle only four days before the contest with Leo, by battling Harry Greb to a draw after a twenty-round marathon on May 3 in Cumberland Park, Maryland.[7]

In a "Special to the *Allentown Leader*," a tough Clark was described as the hands-down winner. "Jackie Clark defeated Leo Houck in six rounds here last night by a comfortable margin. Houck refused to do any leading and when Clark led he would rush into a clinch. In the last session Clark staggered Houck in his own corner with a volley of swings to the head and jaw."[8]

The next day, the *Scranton Republican* had the fight closer and credited Clark with a slim margin of victory over Leo.[9] What had appeared to be a newspaper-decision win for Clark ended up in the official records as a newspaper-decision win for Leo.

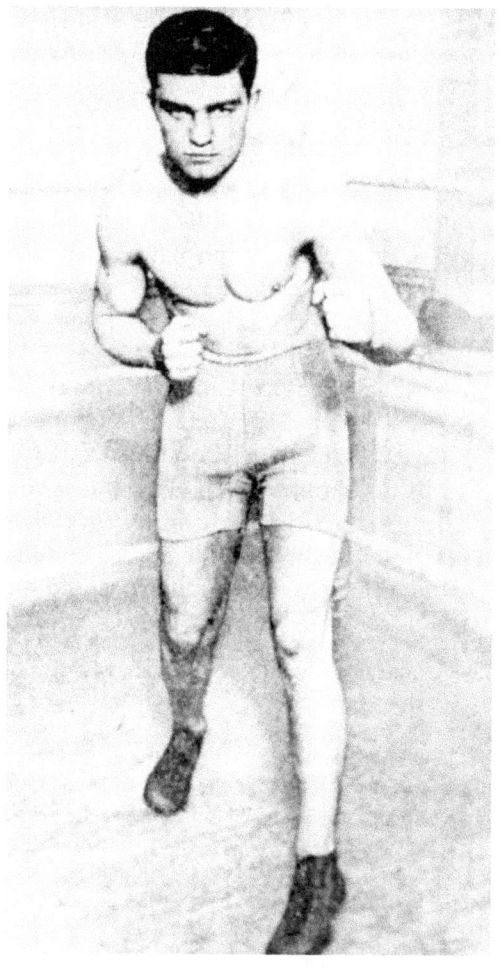

Publicity photograph of Leo F. Houck (undated). His approximate age may have been thirty years. A very similar photograph of Leo in the same pose was featured on the cover of *The Veteran Boxer*, Summer Issue, Ring Number 1, 1945 (courtesy LancasterHistory.org, Lancaster, Pennsylvania, John Houck Collection, MG-63, JH-02-06-44).

Joe Barrett, matchmaker and promoter for the York A.C., scored a major coup when he successfully arranged a six-round contest on May 16 between the new light heavyweight champion, Battling Levinsky, and Leo at the York Opera House.[10] Battling Levinsky had pummeled Jack Dillon, the light heavyweight champion, severely in Boston on October 24, 1916, and won the title. Levinsky was a paragon of durability and persistence. He had successfully transitioned from a middleweight contender into a light heavyweight champion during 1916, when he fought a total of thirty-three bouts. Dan Morgan, Levinsky's manager, had also started making plans to advance his fighter into the heavyweight class with a challenge against Jess Willard, the heavyweight champion.

The *York Daily* reported that Houck had "started training immediately, and should he lose will have trouble pulling down the easy money he has been receiving the last couple of years."[11] Owing to the importance of the bout, Dan Morgan, Levinsky's manager, and Charlie Rieker, who represented Houck, both posted a forfeit of $150 each for a non-appearance of the principals."[12]

Leo's fans had witnessed him defeat almost every opponent he had faced during the last two years, but readily acknowledged that none of them were close to Levinsky's championship caliber. Some of Leo's staunch devotees were confident that he could win, while others doubted his ability to beat Levinsky.

This fight was Leo and Levinsky's fourth meeting. They had last boxed each other during 1911, when Leo defeated Levinsky three times during the same year. Time had not been able to erode a sticking grievance that Levinsky had continued to nurture over the last six years. The origin of the gripe was Levinsky's belief that the local papers always gave Leo, their homeboy, the win. Levinsky had promised to give Leo a proper drubbing this time around by showing him who the best man was.[13]

In their story, "Levinsky Toys with Leo Houck," the *York Daily* noted that Levinsky had thoroughly bewildered Leo and had refused to allow him to clinch by shoving him into the ropes, which almost caused him to fall several times.

> Both fighters entered the ring in top notch condition and the "Battler" started at the opening bell to inflict his punishment. Levinsky, who is said to be the cleverest and quickest big man in the ring, clearly demonstrated that there is some truth in this assertion as he did not give his opponent a moment's rest but rushed him all the time, and in the first and second rounds Houck did not get in a telling blow.
>
> Toward the end of the fifth round the "Battler" tried to inflict a knockout blow and had Houck in an almost helpless condition when the bell rang. Levinsky drove telling punches into Houck's stomach in every round, especially in the third when he sent at least eight to the midsection that had the Lancaster boy doubled up with pain. Houck was game until the final bell and, although he did little fighting himself, he showed that he can still take punishment.[14]

Leo's newspaper-decision loss to Levinsky was a passing dark cloud that had silhouetted a silver lining hiding behind it. The next day, Nancy C. Hauck, Leo and Anna's third daughter, was born.

Six days after Nancy's birth, Leo fought "See Saw Kelly" in a six-rounder on May 22, at the Lancaster A.C. See Saw was a major step backward after Leo's bout against light heavyweight champion Levinsky. Since November 30, 1914, Kelly had posted only eight wins after fighting twenty-three times.[15] The *York Daily* had predicted earlier that Leo would not be able to continue pulling down the easy money if he lost to Levinsky. Out-of-town newspapers like the *York Daily* had dismissed Leo's perennial appeal with his local fans. Still, they would always show up, even if Leo boxed three midgets at once in the wind-up. Leo belted out See Saw in the third round. Kelly's teeter-totter remained idle for two years afterwards. See Saw eventually returned to the ring in 1919 but retired in 1920 after three more fights.

For the next three months, Leo played outfield for the Eighth Ward Club of Lancaster. Zipp Hagg, a local pugilist from Reading and pitcher for the Reading Independents, had promised to work his head off during the season to show up Leo.[16]

During the first week of September, the *York Daily* advertised Leo's next six-round bout with "Young" Herman Miller at the Coliseum Hall in York. "Young Miller" and Johnny O'Donell, a fight promoter from Philadelphia and Miller's trainer, had joined forces as entrepreneurs in the establishment of the new American A.C., and had secured the backing of several local businesses to stage their first boxing show at the Coliseum. The mayor of York, E.S. Hugertugier, had endorsed the promotion and consented to the staging of two boxing shows a month.[17]

Only two days before the bout, Miller fought five rounds with each of his sparring partners, Bud Sipe and Benny Noland. Leo had defeated Miller in their last bout in 1916. Miller's fans had remembered their fighter was ill during his last bout with Leo and were confident that he would get quite a surprise this time around.[18]

One day before the contest, the *York Daily* reported that Miller believed he was in the pink of condition for the bout and vehemently disputed the fight fans' certainty that he would be "meat" for Houck, as in their former mill.[19]

Miller and his manager, O'Donell, even provided a musical diversion, the first time ever, by hiring an orchestra to play music during the boxing show. Unfortunately, the budding entrepreneurs suffered a setback due to a poor attendance during their initial promotion. The old adage, "The show must go on," applies universally to entertainment events of all sorts. Miller jumped into the ring and agreed to fight Leo for nothing in order to please the anemic assemblage.[20]

The *York Daily* reported that the fans who had attended the fight witnessed one of the best bouts ever staged in York, when Miller and Houck went for blood every minute of every round.

> The first two rounds were even while the third and fourth went to Miller. Houck gained a shade in the fifth and sixth by his strong infighting. In the fourth the referee was forced to warn Houck for foul tactics.
>
> Both boys started "feeling out" in the opener, and after a minute of slow fighting Miller started the "fireworks" with his famous left jab. Houck clinched and played a tune on the local boy's kidneys. Both boys were slashing hay-makers when the bell rang.
>
> Houck started off in the second round with three punches but Miller evened matters when he rushed the Lancasterian around the ring and scored with both left and rights to the face. Miller did most of the leading while Houck clinched and succeeded getting his favorite stabs in the local boy's stomach.
>
> Miller rushed at Houck in the third and landed on Leo's nose that started the claret flowing. Houck managed to coax Miller into a clinch and heeled the local boy several times with his left glove, which the referee detected and promptly called Houck's attention. Miller was strong at the finish and rushed Houck around the ring, but was unable to land.
>
> The fourth was faster than any of the previous rounds and the local boy was on top of his opponent most of the time. Miller made Houck miss many hard swings in this round and kept out of the clinches.
>
> Houck came back in the fifth round and managed to get Miller in the clinches. Miller seemed to be in top-notch condition and was able to stand the blows with ease. The fighters were so interested in their work in this round they failed to stop when the bell rang. The referee being forced to jump between them.
>
> The sixth round was a repetition of the previous one with the last minute of fighting the fastest ever witnessed in this city. Miller took his part in the clinches in this session and met Houck half way with his favorite brand of infighting. The small crowd present at the fight termed the bout as the best ever witnessed in this city.[21]

The *York Daily* reported the fight as a draw. However, official records list the fight as both a win for Leo and a draw.

Twelve days after the Miller-Houck battle, Leo refereed a contest in Lancaster between lightweight champion Johnny Wolgast and Jack Brady, who had substituted for

Joe Stefanic. Before the second round ended, "Referee Leo Houck stopped the fight to save Brady, who was merely a punching bag."[22] Refereeing on occasion had kept Leo close to boxing in between fights, had provided additional income, and allowed him to keep an eye on the local hotbed of pugilistic talent continually developing in Lancaster.

Three weeks later, Leo returned to Frank Erne's Gymnasium in Lancaster on October 22, for a six-round contest against Jack McCarron, a middleweight from Allentown. McCarron had a stellar fight record and was one of the most consistent winners and contenders in the middleweight division. He had an impressive win over Mike Gibbons in 1912. During 1913, McCarron had made it to the big time at Madison Square Garden in New York City, when he lost to Gibbons in a rematch. In addition, McCarron had a win over former middleweight champion George Chip, and a draw with middleweight champion Al McCoy.[23]

McCarron and Leo fought at catchweights but never even bothered to weigh in before the contest. The upcoming contest received little prefight publicity or local coverage afterwards. The *Harrisburg Telegraph* described the fight as a clinch-fest and gave Leo the second, third, and sixth rounds.[24] Ray Bronson, McCarron's manager, telegraphed the *Allentown Democrat* immediately after the fight and claimed that his fighter had earned a draw.[25] Bronson was quick on the draw but missed his shot. All official records list the newspaper-decision as a win for Leo.

Three days later, the "Frisco Fat Boy," Willie Meehan, fought Leo in a six-rounder at the Cambric Club in Philadelphia. Johnny Hauck, Leo's youngest brother, described Meehan as fat, but went on to add, "Despite his fat he was a well-trained athlete, had powerful arms, and strong legs, as well as a world of endurance. He would be wilder than the big fellows because they never knew what he was going to do."[26] Meehan fought the soon-to-be heavyweight champion, Jack Dempsey, to a draw on August 10, 1917. Only nine days before Leo's contest with Meehan, the "Frisco Fat Boy" had clobbered and won over the recently displaced light heavyweight champion, Jack Dillon. Johnny Cambria, a promoter for the Cambria A.C., had told Meehan that he wanted him for the club and that he would feed him Leo Houck, an opponent he should have little trouble defeating.[27] Once again, the pesky fairy tale about Leo being "all in" continued to persist, and in this case the "Frisco Fat Boy" gobbled up Cambria's convincing chatter and readily agreed to fight Leo.

The *Pittsburgh Daily Post* reported that the "Frisco Fat Boy" who lumbered into the ring at 190 pounds was lucky to have held Leo to a draw. Meehan's willingness to give the crowd value for its admission helped the entertainment, but he lacked his usual fighting speed. He repeatedly left openings that Houck was quick to take advantage of, and Meehan absorbed many jolts and jabs. Meehan's offensive work, even though it did little damage, enabled him to quit even.[28] All official records list the fight as a newspaper-decision win for Leo.

After the fight, Johnny Hauck had just removed the gloves from his brother's hands when suddenly Meehan came into the dressing room smiling and nursing a bleeding ear. He had removed his glove to shake hands and congratulate his opponent and then said, "Leo they told me you were all in. Well if you are, I would have hated to fight you when you were in your prime."[29] Leo's win over Meehan was remarkably noteworthy considering his extraordinary ring record.

Duke Kelly, Leo's manager, was soundly asleep at the wheel after the bout. He failed to understand that the win over Meehan had just qualified Leo as a legitimate heavyweight contender. Kelly's inaction and uninspired management style after the Meehan-Houck bout torpedoed any prospect of a contest between Leo and Jack Dempsey.

Meehan did a great deal better than Leo. One year later on September 14, 1918, at the Civic Auditorium in San Francisco, Meehan won the decision over heavyweight Jack Dempsey. Ten months after this bout on July 4, 1919, Dempsey defeated Jess Willard to win the world heavyweight championship.

Eighteen days after the fight with Meehan, Leo signed an agreement to fight Buck Crouse in a six-round wind-up on November 19 at Frankie Erne's Gymnasium in Lancaster. Erne, a professional boxer and boxing instructor, had recently become known as the manager of the "biggest little club" in the United States. His connections with boxers from all over the country had enabled him to provide top-level boxing shows for 600 spectators every two weeks.[30]

Crouse was having a terrible season during 1917. He had fought five times and lost five times before his scheduled bout with Leo. Somehow Crouse had reckoned that a win over Leo would give him another shot at middleweight Harry Greb, who had beat Crouse on a technical knockout four and a half months earlier. After his last fight of the 1917 season, Crouse retired for two years before returning to the ring on January 9, 1920.[31] The Houck-Crouse bout on November 19, 1917, was their fifth and last contest. Houck entered the fight at 166 pounds and Crouse at 164.[32]

The local newspaper reports about the outcome of the fight were evenly divided. The *Harrisburg Telegraph* reported that Crouse was too fast for Leo, who held on by clinching whenever possible and would have suffered a knockout if he would only have stood up and fought like a real fighter.[33] The *New Castle Era* provided a more balanced report and stated, "Leo was a terror on the inside throughout but during the fourth round Crouse had dropped Houck with a right to the jaw."[34] Official records list the outcome of the fight as both a win and a loss for Leo.

Leo returned to playing football during the next twenty days and participated in his first game on December 1, a grudge match between two bitter rivals from Cabbage-Hill, the St. Joseph's C.C., Leo's team, and the Eighth Ward Elevens. Both teams had members who were boxers who had also opposed each other from time to time in the boxing ring.[35]

Football in December also meant that the end of the boxing season was near. Leo had come on very strongly during his last four fights, especially his last two bouts against Willie Meehan and Buck Crouse. Leo next fought KO Willie Loughlin, a middleweight from Bethlehem, Pennsylvania, in a six-rounder on December 1 in Lancaster. Laughlin had fought twenty-five times during 1917 and had a forty percent knockout record for the year.[36] Knockout artists like Loughlin, and many before him, had failed to deliver a successful sleeper punch against Leo, who was now in his fifteenth year of boxing.

The *Allentown Leader* reported that Leo outweighed Loughlin by at least sixteen pounds and held his opponent at bay for four rounds. During the final two rounds Loughlin punished Leo with slamming body punches, which earned him the victory by a small margin.[37] Other local newspapers differed and reported the outcome of the fight as a win for Leo. All official records list the fight as a win on points for Leo.

On Christmas Day, Leo celebrated the holiday in both a traditional and an untraditional manner. Like most Christians, Leo observed the time-honored customs of the occasion and spent the early part of the day attending church and later gathering with his family at home. The untraditional part of the day included fighting light heavyweight George Ashe from Philadelphia in a six-rounder at Frankie Erne's Gymnasium that evening. Twenty days prior to the bout, Ashe, who had fought only ten times during 1917, was softened up in a loss to the future middleweight champion Harry Greb, who fought an amazing thirty-seven bouts the same year.[38] Both Leo and Ashe had committed to bringing home their Christmas bonuses the hard way. Neither boxer bothered to weigh in before crossing the ropes.[39]

The *Evening News* covered the fight and reported, "The 'Philly Lad' was a fast one," but Houck was able to control the fight, outpoint his rival during each round, and ended the contest by winning on the margins based on his superb infighting.[40] All official records list the outcome as win for Leo.

The 1917 boxing season was a success for Leo. During the year he had faced more of his type in the light heavyweight class, and had made a significant showing in the heavyweight class when he thoroughly waxed Willie Meehan. The loss against "Battling Levinsky," the light heavyweight champion, had marred Leo's season, but only slightly. The six-round fight was still the legal standard in Pennsylvania and might have contributed somewhat to Leo's inability to beat Levinsky. The more rigorous ten-round fights commonly practiced in New York were certainly a more preferable venue for a championship bout where two equally matched boxers like Leo and Levinsky could stretch out, test their stamina, and zero in on offensive and counterpunching techniques.

Probably the largest oversight during the season might have belonged to Duke Kelly, Leo's manager, who failed to take advantage of Leo's win over Meehan or perusing a potential agreement for Leo to fight Jack Dempsey. Although it was well intentioned, influence from both Charlie Rieker and Jack Milley at the Lancaster A.C., regarding the selection of Leo's opponents, might have also been a contributory factor to the lack of a well thought-out fight strategy during the season. However, that premise is unsupported by any concrete evidence. In fact, both Rieker and Milley might have been out of the picture for some time, chiefly because Leo had ended the latter part of the season fighting the wind-up at Frankie Erne's gymnasium, and not at the Family Theater managed by both Rieker and Milley.

1918

The last time Leo had fought on New Year's Day was six years earlier in Indianapolis, when Jack Dillon had fractured his ribs. Leo's opponent on New Year's Day of 1918 was Chuck Wiggins, aka the Hoosier Playboy, from Indiana, like Dillon. Wiggins had fought eleven fights during 1917 and had posted ten wins, which included two KOs and two TKOs.[41] The six-round contest with Leo was Wiggins's first fight in Pennsylvania. What appeared to be a competitive pairing turned into a routine tune-up for Leo. The *Pittsburgh Post-Gazette* reported, "Leo Houck with an advantage of weight, badly defeated Chuck Wiggins of Indianapolis."[42]

The twenty-one-day break after the Wiggins bout allowed Leo to play basketball with the powerful St. Joseph's C.C. On January 26 the St. Joseph's club thoroughly overwhelmed the newly formed Ben Hur basketball team from Steelton, Pennsylvania, by the score of 41–14.[43]

Twenty-six days after the St. Joseph's-Ben Hur game, Leo fought Jack McCarron in a six-round wind-up on February 22 at the Cambria A.C. in Philadelphia. Leo had won their first match during 1917. McCarron seemed more focused on an upcoming rematch against Mike O'Dowd, the middleweight champion, than on Leo. O'Dowd had won the middleweight title on November 14, 1917, after beating Al McCoy. Ten days later, O'Dowd defended his title and beat the Allentown middleweight, McCarron, at the National A.C. in Philadelphia.[44] McCarron told the *Allentown Leader* that despite the loss he remained confident in his ability to defeat O'Dowd during their rematch.[45]

Regional and local newspapers continued to rank both Leo and McCarron among the top middleweight contenders in Pennsylvania. However, by this time Harry Greb, an extraordinary middleweight from Pittsburgh and future middleweight champion, had already surpassed both Leo and McCarron in the rankings, and had been generally acknowledged by the press as the top middleweight in Pennsylvania.

The *Pittsburgh Daily Post* reported the McCarron-Houck fight as a "rough draw."

Frank Erne boxed professionally from 1910 to 1922. During that thirteen-year period he fought 18 times, which included 6 wins, 8 losses, 3 draws, and 1 no-decision bout. He owned Frank Erne's Gymnasium and Physical Culture Club in Lancaster, Pennsylvania, and also promoted many of Leo's fights. From 1918 until the end of his boxing career, Leo's bouts were typically held in Frank Erne's gymnasium (courtesy LancasterHistory.org, Lancaster, Pennsylvania, John Hauck Collection, MG-63, JH-01-02-73).

> The bout was rough and devoid of clever boxing.
> Attempts by each boxer to toss the other a wrestler's hold rather than with the gloves kept Referee Holland busy trying to tear them apart in the clinches and had the crowd hooting and jeering the men. There was entirely too much clinching and rough stuff to suit the crowd.
> McCarron tried a few straight jabs, but when these failed he roughed it and when Houck could not land with a right hand swing, he, too, indulged in the rough fighting.
> Some of the hot-headed spectators wanted to get an armful of snowballs and bombard the boxers while they were in the ring, but a cordon of the public prevented this.[46]

The *Allentown Leader* added an important detail omitted by the *Pittsburgh Daily Post*. McCarron had opened up an old cut over Leo's right eye in the second round, which continued to bleed until the end of the contest. In addition, the paper reported that Houck was fresh at the finish but clearly bested.[47] Official records list the newspaper-decision as a loss and a win for Leo.

Ten days after the fight, Leo fought the Hoosier Playboy, Chuck Wiggins, in a six-round rematch on March 4, at Frankie Erne's Gymnasium. Wiggins had been idle for two months after his first meeting with Leo. That fight had been a lousy contest that had disappointed the Philadelphia fans. The rematch with Wiggins proved to be just another set-up for Leo prior to his next contest with Johnny Wilson, a New York City southpaw and middleweight contender.

The *Allentown Leader* included some particularly bland filler about the fight in the sporting news the next day.

> In the windup at the Erne Club last evening, Leo Houck had little difficulty defeating "Chuck" Wiggins of Indianapolis. After the first round, which was even, Leo's superiority was apparent throughout, as he scored heavily at close quarters. There were no knockdowns, and it looked as though Wiggins was just there to stay the limit.[48]

All official records list the outcome of the fight as a newspaper-decision win for Leo.

Five days after the fight, Duke Kelly told the *Harrisburg Telegraph* that he was busy arranging a series of potential bouts for Leo, and had an offer for him to fight Tommy Gibbons, the brother of boxer Mike Gibbons, or another rematch with former middleweight champion George Chip, in Scranton. One drawback that could have prevented a Gibbons or Chip matchup was the condition of Leo's nose. In his fight with Jack McCarron in February, the Allentown middleweight hit Leo with a glancing blow on the nose. McCarron's glove had somehow infected Leo's nose. In the fight against Chuck Wiggins in March, Leo had managed to protect his nose, which was still healing and vulnerable to further injury.[49]

Three days after Duke Kelly's announcement, Leo traveled to Chelsea, Massachusetts, for a twelve-round contest on March 11 with Johnny Wilson at the Douglas A.C. Six years had elapsed since Leo's last visit to Massachusetts. Wilson, whose real name was Giovanni Pancia, was a middleweight contender who used his southpaw stance to good advantage and has been described in the book *Great Fighters and Boxers* as being quite a clever boxer for a left-handed fighter.[50] The slanted compliment about Wilson was hilarious and plainly identified the remaining pool of left-handed boxers as inept flatfooted athletes. The *Boston Post* loved their "Johnny Boy" and claimed, "Wilson has not worked in Boston for some time, for the one and single reason that all of his own weight who are worth paying any attention have refused to box him. They are looking for something soft, that old 'something for nothing' idea, and Wilson is not soft."[51]

Wilson was the overwhelming favorite over Leo. The *Pittsburgh Daily Post* reported that Wilson also lived up to his reputation as a clever left-hander by puzzling his opponent in the early going, but Leo soon discovered Wilson's vulnerabilities and targeted them accordingly. "Houck displayed signs of life in the second round when he scored hard to Wilson's body. The latter plainly showed the effects of the blows and the fans wondered why Houck failed to follow up his advantage."[52] All official records list the outcome of the fight as a win for Leo. Years later, the *Intelligencer Journal* reported that Johnny Wilson believed Leo was the greatest fighter he had ever met.[53]

On April 6, Duke Kelly, Leo's manager, submitted a letter to Tom J. Brislin, the Sporting Editor for the *Scranton Republican*.

Just a few lines in regard to Leo Houck, who at the present time is boxing in great form. In the last few months he has met and defeated such men as Kayo Loughlin, Herman Miller, George Ashe, Willie Meehan, and Jack McCarron and has just returned from Boston, where he beat Johnny Wilson. The Boston club thought so much of the latter bout that the men have been rematched for April 15. Houck is also scheduled to box Joe Borrell in Philadelphia on April 12, and Clay Turner at Lancaster on April 22. Turner is the boy who defeated Gunboat Smith in Wilkes-Barre Monday night.

I would like to show Houck in Scranton, as he always made good when he appeared there. He is satisfied to box Tom Gibbons, Jack McCarron, or Jack Dillon. Thanking you in advance for publishing this letter, I beg to remain, Yours in sport.

Duke Kelly
Manager, Leo Houck[54]

Nine days after Duke Kelly's letter to the *Scranton Republican*, Leo fought a twelve-round rematch against Johnny Wilson on April 15 at the Douglas A.C. in Chelsea. The *Boston Post* described the twelve-round match in the paltriest type of journalistic prose. "In spite of a handicap of more than 20 pounds Johnny Wilson reversed a decision which Leo Houck, of Lancaster, Pennsylvania, had earned in an earlier bout, when the Charlestown lad was awarded the honors in a feature bout at the Douglas A.C. last night."[55] The *Reading Times* published a special leased wire from Chelsea that had reported Wilson having had the better of every round.[56] All official records list the outcome of the fight as a loss for Leo.

On the evening of April 10, the articles of agreement were signed for a six-round fight between Leo and Clay Brannon, aka Chief Turner, on April 23 at Frank Erne's Gymnasium in Lancaster. Turner, a six-foot light heavyweight, was supposed to be a full-blooded Native American who was originally from Madison, Wisconsin. During the 1917 boxing season, Turner fought and won all sixteen of his matches. His knockout rate had catapulted to thirty-seven percent for the year.[57] Turner fought an incredibly difficult opponent, Tommy Gibbons, only five days before his match against Leo. Gibbons's record of thirty-two fights from September 5, 1911, until March 22, 1918, included thirty wins and only two draws."[58]

The *Evening News* lauded Leo's performance in the fight with an article titled "Leo Houck Displays Skill of Former Days."

> Fighting like the Houck of the days when he whipped Lewis over the twenty round route in Paris, a few years back, Leo Houck last night defeated the light heavyweight Chief Turner, in four of six rounds. Turner, a favorite, opened the scrap with hard lefts to the face repeating often and continued to take the offensive for the opening two rounds. Houck came back in the remaining four rounds with a flurry and fought the "Chief" off his feet. In the final chapter the Indian was bleeding profusely from the mouth and covering.[59]

Turner had expected a rebound and a win over Leo after the loss to Gibbons. Instead, Chief Turner discovered the hard way that Leo, an aging thirty-year-old light heavyweight, was going just as well as Gibbons, or better. All official records list the newspaper-decision as a win for Leo.

Duke Kelly issued another public challenge on behalf of Leo eleven days after his win over Clay Turner. The *Wilkes-Barre Times Leader* printed the letter and titled the article "Duke Kelly Says Tom Gibbons Is Afraid of Houck."

Philadelphia, Pa. May 4
Mr. "Effie" Welsh

Dear Sir:

> Kindly publish these few lines in regards to Leo Houck, the man Tom Gibbons was afraid to fight in Baltimore. Sam Harris the promoter tried to get Gibbons to box Houck there, but when Houck laced Chief Turner in Lancaster last week found some excuse. Now I hear the promoters up there are trying to match some opponent with Turner. What is the matter with Leo Houck, he'll be ready to show the fans that he has the goods and that it was no fluke he beat Turner in Lancaster, and this goes for Gibbons too. Houck is ready to meet any middleweight in the country and he bars none.
>
> Yours truly,
> Duke Kelly[60]

Kelly's brief letter-writing campaign ended unsuccessfully. Tommy Gibbons, the focus of Kelly's earlier invitation and later scorn, had been considered an important stepping stone for Leo. A win over Gibbons would have established Leo as a contender in both the middleweight and light heavyweight ranks. However, calling Leo a middleweight at this juncture was technically incorrect. He had been fighting at catchweights in the middleweight division and more correctly fit the weight profile of a light heavyweight.

The day after Kelly's letter to the *Wilkes-Barre Leader*, Leo played basketball with the Eighth Ward team against the St. Joseph's team from York. He continued to maintain his conditioning by playing basketball for approximately one month before his next fight, a six-rounder, on May 27 against heavyweight Gunboat Smith at an outdoors pavilion in Lancaster managed by Frankie Erne.

Gunboat Smith, a lumbering six-foot two-inch behemoth, had a terrible 1918 boxing season. He fought a total of nine times and posted only one win and a draw.[61] Jack Dempsey ended Gunboat's 1918 season with a knockout in the second round.

The *Evening News* reported that Houck had won every round of the fight, constantly led, and scored with every wallop.[62] The *Pittsburgh Daily Post* mirrored the *Evening News* story, but added one great detail by mentioning that Leo had knocked Gunboat through the ropes with a strong right-hand punch to the jaw.[63] Other regional newspapers reported the fight as a draw. Official records list the outcome of the fight as a win and a draw for Leo.

After the fight with Gunboat Smith, a lengthy layoff of thirty-four days occurred prior to Leo's next fight against Jeff Smith on Independence Day, in Lancaster. Interviews conducted with Leo's sons, Edward and Joseph, explained why Leo fought only four more times during 1918.[64] World War I was the primary reason.

The effects of World War I also impacted the Eighth Ward A.C. in Lancaster. On July 28, the Eight Ward A.C. was "shot to pieces" by the war, and eight of the original team members had shipped out to join the colors in Europe.[65] Leo joined the defense effort as a civilian employee at the Sun Shipbuilding Company in Chester, Pennsylvania.[66] Edward Hauck, Leo's son, recollected that Leo was part of a riveting crew and handled the red-hot rivets before they were installed in the ship's hull plating.[67] Leo returned home to Lancaster for the weekends after his work week ended. He also continued to box and fought Jeff Smith, aka the Bayonne Globetrotter, on July 4 in a six-rounder at Frank Erne's Gymnasium in Lancaster. Smith, a ranked middleweight contender without doubt, deserved the sobriquet "Globetrotter." He had fought extensively in France, Australia, England, Canada, and Mexico. Probably one of Smith's greatest victories was a win on Independence Day in 1919 over the hard-to-hit "St. Paul Phantom," Mike Gibbons.[68]

The Smith-Houck fight fulfilled all the conditions required for a classic Independence Day battle. Cities and towns throughout America typically celebrate July 4 with parades, festivities, picnics, and of course, sporting events. For whatever reasons, the local press had completely overlooked the fight and reports describing the fight the following day are lacking. Official records list the outcome of the contest as both a win and a loss for Leo.

Leo continued to throw punches, red-hot rivets, and baseballs throughout the summer of 1918. Somehow, he also found time to manage a "Kid-League" in Lancaster called the "Ironsides." The "Kid-Leagues" routinely drew crowds of 1,500 to 2,000 fans.[69] In addition, before the Eighth Ward A.C. had broken up on July 28, Leo played in a baseball game against the American Chain team and hit the only home run of the game.[70]

After each weekend, Leo returned to his job on a four-man riveting team at Sun Shipbuilding. The Sun Shipbuilding Association wasted no time in arranging an all-star twilight boxing show after they discovered that Leo Houck was now on their payroll. The company arranged a special double wind-up on July 18 and matched Leo against heavyweight Tim Logan in a three-round exhibition bout at the Sun Ship Athletic Field.[71] Matchmakers believed that Logan, who wanted to call himself the champion heavyweight of the Delaware River shipyards, needed to win against a boxer like Leo in order to gain the bragging rights. Earlier in the year Logan had fought a ten-round exhibition bout with Jess Willard, the heavyweight champion from 1915 until 1919, which ended in a draw.[72]

Over two thousand fight fans attended the twilight boxing and wrestling show held at the Sun Ship Field.[73] All of the fights were three-round affairs. The *Delaware County Daily Times* wasted little newsprint on reporting the details of the second feature of the double wind-up. They merely stated that the Logan-Houck fight ended in a draw.[74]

Twelve days later, the Sun Shipbuilding Association staged another wrestling and boxing show, which was held in the Chester Armory. This time around, matchmakers E.J. McShane and Dick LeTourneau arranged seven bouts including a triple wind-up. Middleweight Pete Malone, of the Chester Ship Yard, fought Leo in the final wind-up for the championship of the Delaware River shipyards. The last time Malone had fought professionally was on October 12, 1916, when Joe Bradley knocked him out at the Broadway A.C. in Philadelphia.[75] William H. Rocap, Leo's old friend and sports editor for the *Public Ledger*, refereed the bouts.[76]

The four-round contest produced an easy win for Leo and also secured him the title "Maritime Boxing Champion of the Delaware Shipyards." Leo continued to work at Sun Shipbuilding until the end of the year.

Leo ended the 1918 boxing season with a bout against Battling Levinsky on Christmas Day, in a six-rounder at Frank Erne's gymnasium in Lancaster. Levinsky, the light heavyweight champion, fought a total of eight non-title bouts during 1918. He had been rattled soundly on October 6 when the future heavyweight champion Jack Dempsey knocked him out in the third round.[77]

Frank Erne had the best drawing card in years in Lancaster and the *Harrisburg Telegraph* reported, "It drew a multitude to the ringside."[78]

The *Reading Times* reported the fight as a fast-paced contest dominated largely by the overly clever Levinsky. "Battling Levinsky defeated Leo Houck here today in a fast six-rounds. A clean knockdown in the fourth round that followed when the 'Battler' landed a left swing to the point of Houck's jaw, gave him the decision. Levinsky carried off the honors in the third and fourth rounds. Houck came back strong and won the fifth. The rest were even. Houck used a left jab all through the fight with good results."[79] Leo had been fooled into dropping his guard in the fourth, and paid for it by having to take a six-count after the knockdown. The last time Leo was anywhere close to a knockout was during 1909 when Kid Locke of Philadelphia had delivered a right to the tip of Leo's jaw, which put him into a wobbly zombie-like state for the remainder of the round.

After the fight, the *Harrisburg Telegraph* reported a cynical bellowing from Leo's fans who were beginning to think, "Leo Houck should announce his retirement, like many another good man in his day."[80] The *Harrisburg Telegraph* had a propensity for "theater in the boxing news" and incorrectly reported the anticipated demise of a superior fighter slightly past his prime.

The most interesting revelation during the 1918 boxing season was Battling Levinsky's domination over Leo. Levinsky had grown up and gobbled up the entire light heavyweight division. Five years prior, Leo held sway over Levinsky. Still, both fighters possessed an equal ability to win over opponents in the light heavyweight and heavyweight classes. Levinsky, like other boxers in the light heavyweight and middleweight divisions, was never able to claim the one record that Leo owned outright. Leo had never been knocked out.

Leo remained unfazed by the loss to Levinsky at the end of the season. Instead, he automatically switched to playing another sport and started to sharpen up his court skills for an upcoming game against the Reading Walnuts basketball team. During the next year, Leo experienced some unpleasant encounters in the ring: three fights against the pesky Human Windmill and one battle with the Midwestern Phantom.

10

Greb and Gibbons Give Leo Fits, 1919

Leo's opening fight of the season was a doozy. He fought middleweight contender Harry Greb in a twelve-rounder at the Armory A.A. in Boston. Greb was known as the Pittsburgh Windmill due to his devastating ability to swing both of his arms simultaneously like a windmill, punching and effectively landing blows on his opponents from all angles. No other fighters during the early 1900s or afterwards were able to replicate Greb's unorthodox boxing style, or rival his achievements in the ring. Even today, Harry Greb continues to be perennially ranked as one of the top ten middleweight boxers in pugilistic history. Greb's record for 1918 included twenty wins and two draws.[1]

In a "Special to the *News Journal*" from Boston, the byline story titled "Lancaster Boy Outpointed When He Fails to Follow Advantages—Greb Disappoints Boston Fans," never gets to the bottom of either fighter's supposed shortcomings or excuses for a somewhat dull contest.

> Houck fought on the defensive for practically all the fight. He gave a wonderful exhibition of blocking, the fast delivery of Greb failing to reach the part intended for it to reach.
>
> Greb was a huge disappointment to the members of the club. They expected to see a man of championship caliber perform when the Smoky City Battler appeared here but were greatly disappointed by his poor work.
>
> Greb worked crudely, and was wild as a hawk. Only his blows to the body reached their mark, and but once did he cut loose. That was in the seventh round when he rained several jabs to Houck's short ribs. The punches were so light, however, that the Lancaster boxer failed to show any ill effects from them.
>
> Houck was the best in the first round. He landed a left to the body in the opening round that fairly took the wind out of Greb. Apparently the Lancaster boxer did not realize his advantage, for he failed to follow the blow. Greb was noticeably slowed by the blow. Houck remained on the defensive, in spite of the opportunity offered him.
>
> In the third round Houck sneaked a right hook to Greb's jaw after a break and followed it with a left hook to the body that jarred Greb. The latter came back strong. In the fourth Greb dodged well, succeeded in landing a well-timed right over Houck's heart and followed with a left to the jaw.
>
> From then until the end of the fight the bout was uneventful. Greb did all the leading and was awarded the referee's decision at the end of the fight.[2]

In another "Special Dispatch" from Boston to the *New Era*, a probable explanation had surfaced explaining Leo's defensive posture throughout most of the bout. Leo had punched Greb squarely on the jaw early in the fight, and afterwards he complained that the punch hurt his thumb.³ The injury to Leo's thumb convinced both the critics and the fight fans that a do-over was in order, and subsequently a rematch was scheduled for March 6.

Six days after the Greb fight, Leo fought Andrew Kopinski, aka Battling Kopin, in a six-rounder at Frank Erne's Gymnasium in Lancaster. Duke Kelly, Leo's manager, made the agreement to fight Kopin, a middleweight on a losing streak since June 21, in order to keep Leo busy in the ring before traveling to Canada for a brief campaign. Kopin surely had guts. He fought Harry Greb twice in a row and had been knocked out both times.⁴ The fight with Leo was a total set-up. Leo realigned Kopin's glass jaw when he knocked him out early during the third round.⁵

Four days after the contest with Kopin, a curious story appeared in the *Harrisburg Telegraph* titled "If Dempsey Meets Houck." The newspaper had developed a fondness for taking cheap shots at Leo during 1918 and had labeled him as being "all in." In this case, Dempsey was reported to have been in Reading during this period and sprained his ankle but left shortly afterwards from Harrisburg. The newspaper insisted, "Dempsey will not be bothered by decimating Leo Houck, of Lancaster, if that native son insists on going in the ring with the demon."⁶ A sum of $1,000 was advertised as an inducement for Dempsey to stay three rounds with Leo. The newspaper's made-up challenge from Leo to box Dempsey would have been the sporting news headline of the day if it had been true, but no evidence exists to support the *Harrisburg Telegraph*'s sensationalized fantasy. Most likely, the story had probably been written by a broken-down and disillusioned sportswriter who disliked Leo, lost money betting on him, or both.

Another set-up bout needed to be fulfilled before Leo traveled to Canada. Bob Grant of the United States Navy fought Leo during a boxing tournament on February 2, at Frank Erne's Gymnasium in Lancaster. Forty seconds into the first round, Leo belted Grant in the solar plexus, which dropped him onto the canvas in an inert crumpled heap. He was carried out of the ring by his seconds. Leo was awarded the win by a KO.

Duke Kelly arranged a ten-round match for Leo against Roddy MacDonald, a middleweight from Canada, on February 20 in Halifax, Nova Scotia. A win over MacDonald would kick off a short campaign in Montreal and several other Canadian cities.⁷ MacDonald fought primarily in Canada, with a few boxing forays into the United States. MacDonald started his career during 1913, the same year that Leo had achieved a number-one ranking as the top middleweight contender in the United States. The match with MacDonald and the planned campaign afterwards in Canada seemed like misdirection on the part of Duke Kelly, Leo's manager. On the other hand, Leo's career as a boxer was undoubtedly limited to only a few more seasons, and Kelly might have reckoned that Canada offered easier opponents and even easier money.

Regional coverage of the fight in Canada was minimal. In a "Special Dispatch" from Halifax, the *Philadelphia Inquirer* reported, "Houck won all the way, giving MacDonald a bad beating."⁸ The outcome of the fight as reported by the newspaper had been sent directly from Canada, but most official records list the fight as a draw with one record giving the win to Leo.⁹

Four days later, Michael Fleming, aka the Zulu Kid, visited Lancaster for a six-rounder against Leo at Frank Erne's Gymnasium. The Zulu Kid was a light heavyweight who had been struggling in the ring since July 21, 1917. Leading up to his contest with Leo, the Kid fought fifteen times and had only two wins and a draw to his credit.¹⁰ Local and regional newspapers did not bother to advertise or cover the fight. The newspaper-decision was another win for Leo.

The boxing critics and fight fans had been waiting patiently for Leo's next fight, a much-anticipated rematch with Harry Greb on March 6 at the Fulton Opera House in Lancaster. Leo's fans were convinced an injured thumb had handicapped their hero during their first contest. Later, Greb had claimed that he was not at his best during their first meeting. Every fighter who had stepped through the ropes to fight Greb during 1919 lost. Greb fought an average of four bouts per week that season, and ended the year with an amazing total of forty-five bouts.[11]

For whatever reason, before Leo and Greb's second fight on March 6, Dr. Bitzer, the club physician, bandaged Leo's sore thumb and X-rayed the damaged digit in order to determine the extent of the injury. Leo's thumb had been injured initially on January 14 during his first fight with Greb.[12]

> Greb started right off the reel with his fast work, keeping Leo at long range by his dancing tactics and avoiding any close contact with Leo, who was held off by his speed, but his blows lacked force and he did not land effectively in the opening session.
>
> The Pittsburgher pursued the same tactics in the second session, his object being apparent in keeping Houck at a safe distance to prevent the body punches. When he came too fast Houck covered and escaped any damage, as many of Harry's blows landed on gloves and arms. In the third and fourth rounds Greb did his best work of the bout and took the honors. He shifted shots left and right over but Houck was ready for action in the fifth and got to Greb in such a manner that showed why the Smoky City battler used speed and long range fighting in preference to swapping at short distance. The final round found both battlers going along at the same gait with about an even break at the final bell in this session.[13]

Without a doubt, Leo had demonstrated his talent at defense while Greb had countered effectively on offense by taking the lead. During the fight, the spectators noticed that Leo seldom used his left hand and clinched frequently to save himself. Leo's inability to establish a successful offense during the contest might have been attributed to his injured thumb. The Pittsburgh Windmill had won on points, but overall the contest was a wash, with neither boxer receiving any discernable damage or achieving ring superiority by the final bell. Another rematch, their last meeting, was scheduled for April 25.

Eight days later, the Cambria A.C. in Philadelphia hosted heavyweight Jack Clifford and Leo in a six-round contest. The fight was Clifford's second professional bout. His manager should have had his head examined for agreeing to arrange a bout with a seasoned boxer like Leo.

The next day, in an article titled "Houck Beats Clifford," Leo received all the kudos, but Clifford also deserved some recognition as one tough gamer.

> The bout was rough from beginning to end there being a lot of holding and wrestling in each period. Houck, with a well directed right hand punch to the jaw dropped the Brooklyn man in the first round, but Jack was soon on his feet again. Then Leo with a steady stream of left hand punches to the face hammered Clifford till Jack was weary and tired in the last two rounds. In the fifth and again in the sixth Houck, with his back on the ropes, sidestepped Clifford's rushes and Jack almost pitched head forward out of the ring.[14]

Clifford managed to land one blow during the third round. When Referee Holland separated both fighters during a clinch, Clifford swung wildly at Leo, missed, and planted his glove directly onto the tip of Holland's nose, causing it to bleed.[15]

After an eleven-day break, Leo fought Mike Gibbons, the St. Paul Phantom, in an eight-rounder at the Coliseum in St. Louis, Missouri. The last time the two fighters met had been four years ago during 1915, in New York at the St. Nicholas Arena, when Gibbons outpointed Leo. The *Scranton Republican* reported that Gibbons had been selecting easy marks and has-been fighters during the 1919 season. Leo, along with Gibbons's other opponents like George Chip, Billy Kramer, and Len Rowlands, had been described as third-raters by the newspaper.[16] The drivel reported by the newspaper missed the mark as far as Gibbons was concerned. He understood that an inside mix-up with Leo during this match needed to be avoided at all costs. Leo liked to in-fight and slam an opponent hard on his side, in the stomach, and in the heart. Gibbons knew that his opponent could end his season prematurely by separating his ribs from the cartilage that held them together.

Approximately 6,000 fans attended the fight. The receipts for the match totaled $4,400, with Gibbons receiving $1,500 and Leo $750.[17] In this one fight, Leo earned almost two and one-half times the average worker's 1919 salary of $312.[18]

The *Pittsburgh Daily Post* reported that the fight was won on points by Gibbons, who outboxed Leo in every round. Leo drew the ire of the fans, who hissed and booed at his constant clinching while Gibbons struggled to get away.[19] There was a reason for the constant clinching—Leo's injured thumb.

Three days after the Gibbons fight, Leo fought Larry Williams, a light heavyweight from Bridgeport, Connecticut, in a six-rounder at the Orpheum Theater in Harrisburg. The last time the two fighters had met was November 15, 1912, when Leo knocked out Williams in the fourth round.

Sam Driver, Williams's manager, possessed a very inventive imagination. In a letter to the sporting editor of the *Harrisburg Telegraph*, Driver claimed that his fighter was the only boxer in the East who had a win over Willie Meehan.[20] In fact, the fight against Meehan resulted in a loss for Williams. Moreover, Driver piled it higher and deeper by stating, "Larry Williams today is one of the best light heavyweights in the country and has won every bout he fought this year."[21] On the contrary, Williams had fought five times during 1919 before he faced Leo and had posted only one win on January 27 against Clay Turner.[22]

The *Harrisburg Telegraph* reported that the fight was a fast-moving, hard-punching contest, but failed to satisfy the fans, who hissed loudly throughout.

> It may have been the continually in-fighting of Leo Houck which caused the uproar. But this was his cue, for Larry Williams had it on him in weight and reach and height, but the battle was as lively as could be asked for. Houck had to keep in close, it was his only safety, for Williams certainly knows how to flay a man from long distance. Houck boxed with a splintered thumb, but this is nothing unusual for a man so husky that he could keep on going with three ribs cracked. The decision should go to Williams.[23]

Official records list the fight as both a draw and a newspaper-decision win for Leo.

Three days later, Leo fought Al McCoy, a former middleweight champion, in a six-rounder on March 31 at Frank Erne's Gymnasium in Lancaster. McCoy had lost the middleweight title on November 14, 1917, when Mike O'Dowd kayoed him in six rounds at the Clermont Avenue Ring in Brooklyn. As expected, Leo's fans were excited to finally see these two superlative fighters meet in the squared circle.

Yet, something was amiss. Newspaper advertisements for the upcoming super-bout were scanty. In addition, the outcome of the fight as reported by the *Evening Public Ledger* was reduced to a stingy two-sentence description. "In the wind-up at the Erne Club last night Leo Houck, of this city, gave Al McCoy a severe lacing. In the final round Houck knocked the Brooklynite through the ropes out of ring."[24]

Several days later, Al McCoy's manager, L.P. Flynn, publicly exposed Leo's bout as a set-up with a total ringer and bum who was *not* Al McCoy, the former middleweight champion. In a letter to the *Harrisburg Telegraph*, Flynn asserted that promoter Frank Erne had hoodwinked the public with his chicanery by billing Leo's opponent as Al McCoy. Flynn demanded justice against Erne, the small-town "backyard promoter," and called for police surveillance over boxing in all backwoods towns like Lancaster that, according to Flynn, routinely swindle the public and defame reputable fighters like Al McCoy.[25]

Naturally, Erne did what any promoter does once the jig is up. He went into damage control and immediately responded to the newspapers by slightly bending the truth. One fact regarding Erne's shenanigans was accurate. He had written to Flynn and inquired about obtaining an agreement for Al McCoy to fight Leo. However, the price for McCoy's services was too high and completely nonnegotiable. Suddenly, Erne found himself on the spot and backed into a corner. There is no evidence to support the existence of any prefight publicity for the Houck-McCoy contest, but most likely, there was some local buzz. Erne needed to deliver an opponent and miraculously obtained the services of Al Thiel, a journeyman middleweight boxer from Brooklyn, who billed himself as the "New Al McCoy." He fit the frame-up perfectly, had almost the same name, and immediately agreed to sign for the fight.

Erne remained defiant throughout the "switcheroo scandal" and took exception to being called an underhanded "bootblack" by Flynn. Erne had even tricked himself into believing that he actually had signed the "Real Al McCoy." He backpedaled with an anxious plea delivered to the *Harrisburg Telegraph*. Erne's statements to the newspaper are both funny and entertaining, especially when he describes his role in the predicament as that of a victim persecuted for no good reason.

> I was so badly fooled when the Al McCoy who appeared here last Monday night was not the original Al McCoy, but it was several hours before the fight when I discovered the mistake, and then it was too late for a public announcement.
>
> The entire affair is unfortunate. The fight was as good as though Houck had boxed the original. The fans who saw it will bear me out in this statement. Letters, such as Flynn's from out-of-town managers who persistently try to drain every cent they can from the small town club, and then kick them when their back is turned have long been a source of contention, not only with me but with every other Lancaster fight promoter, whether they are in or out of the business now. I know the fans will give me a square deal.[26]

Official records list Al McCoy, Al Theil, and the "New Al McCoy" as Leo's opponents. Leo was awarded the newspaper decision win over all three.

After three months of difficult bouts, Leo needed an easy opponent. Duke Kelly, Leo's manager, answered and delivered Joe Allison, aka Kid Henry, a light heavyweight from Philadelphia. Leo fought Allison in an eight-rounder on April 4 at Penns Grove A.C. in New Jersey. Allison had an odd boxing record. He had fought over a period of twelve years, accumulating a total of but thirteen fights and four wins. In addition, he had completely missed the years 1916 and 1917.[27] Allison's involvement in boxing appeared to be more of a hobby than a serious professional career. By all accounts, Allison was exactly what Leo needed as a tune-up in preparation for his final rematch with Harry Greb twenty-one days later.

The next day, Lancaster fans were astonished as they read the *Evening News* coverage about how Allison got the early drop on an unguarded Leo Houck. "Joe Allison, of Wilmington, sprang a surprise here tonight by decisively defeating Leo Houck, of Lancaster, in every one of the eight rounds at the Penns Grove A.C. weekly show. Allison scored a clean knockdown in the first round, Houck taking the count of four."[28] All official records list the fight as a newspaper-decision loss for Leo.

After a twenty-one-day layoff, Leo fought future middleweight champion Harry Greb on April 25 in a ten-rounder at Carney Auditorium in Erie, Pennsylvania. The match was their third and final contest. Greb's hometown newspaper, the *Pittsburgh Daily Post*, bragged about their homeboy by stating, "Houck, while he is still good enough to whip some middleweights, is little more than a set-up for Greb, who has beaten him easily several times."[29] Certainly, there was some truth to the newspaper's judgment about Leo. The phenomenal climb of Greb's career and his youthfulness did indeed contrast noticeably with the downward trajectory of Leo's career. Greb had started his professional career during 1913 and ever since had rapidly ascended the middleweight ranks by defeating all comers who dared to cross the ropes. On the other hand, Leo had started his professional career during 1902 and by 1913 had established himself as a premier middleweight boxer and number-one ranked contender. After the final match with Greb in Erie, until the end of his career several years later, Leo had only a few more opportunities to battle a current middleweight or light heavyweight champion for his title.

The *Philadelphia Inquirer* reported that the house was packed but added little detail to the thirty-minute fracas.

> The Pittsburgher forced the fighting in every round and carried the fight to his opponent at all times. He danced rings around Houck, who was on the defensive from the start.
>
> Only in two frames, the fifth and the seventh, did Houck show any aggressiveness; in these rounds he landed some heavy body blows at close range.[30]

During the fifth round, Referee Stephens cautioned both men to fight and claimed that Greb held his punches.[31] The Houck-Greb boxing trilogy that started on January 14, 1919, ended as another win by Greb.

Three days later, on April 28, Leo fought light heavyweight Larry Williams in a six-rounder at Frank Erne's Gymnasium in Lancaster. The bout was their third and final contest. The fight had absolutely no consequence in moving the needle either way regarding Leo's ranking. In fact, the rest of the season promised more of the same type of opponents for Leo—a revolving succession of third-tier fighters whom he would clobber. In any event, Leo deserved some easy opponents, some easy money, and a long layoff to ponder his future as a prizefighter. Official records awarded Leo a newspaper-decision win over Williams and also called the fight a draw.[32]

The next four months were pure Nirvana for Leo. By May 17, he had signed up to play baseball with the Eighth Ward Club in Lancaster. Opening day was on a Sunday, and Ollie Ruoff, the manager of the Eighth Ward Club, promised to pry the lid off the Carsonia Park diamond in Reading during their first game against the Kaufmann Professionals.[33]

Leo completely surprised the public four months later, during August, with a terse public announcement that he was retiring from boxing. The *Evening News* reported that promoter Herman Taylor tried to make arrangements for Leo to box Clay Turner at the Atlantic City Sporting Club and stated, "Leo sent word back that he was through with the boxing game forever."³⁴ The newspaper story contained no speculation as to why Leo suddenly decided to hang up his gloves. The fact that Leo had decided to remain mum on the subject hardly came as a surprise. Throughout his career, public comments from Leo to the press were sparse, and when he did comment, his statements typically described what he intended to do to an opponent, especially if an opponent had pulled some shenanigans or fouled him during a prior bout.

Almost one month later, Leo changed his mind about retiring and visited Atlantic City on September 12 to fight Wild Bert Kenny in an eight-rounder. Kenny, a light heavyweight from Prince Edward Island, Canada, was having a miserable season during 1919, fighting nine times and winning only once.³⁵ Leo had previously defeated Kenny in 1915. Kenny was a "gamer" but totally outclassed by Leo.

The *Pittsburgh Daily Post* reported that Leo won the fight going away, stating, "Houck had the entire eight rounds. Kenny hung in a clinch to avert the K.O. In this session Houck sent over a number of telling blows with his dangerous left."³⁶ All official records have listed the contest as a newspaper-decision win for Leo.

Twenty-five days later, on October 6, the newly established National Sporting Club conducted its first boxing show of the season at Frank Erne's Gymnasium. Leo fought six rounds against KO George Samson in the wind-up. Samson, a light heavyweight journeyman boxer from Philadelphia, fought and lost to Leo a total of six times during 1919 and 1920.³⁷

The *Pittsburgh Post-Gazette* reported that KO Samson made a great showing but lacked Leo's aggressiveness. Leo's hard-hitting style earned him another easy win on points.³⁸ One day before Thanksgiving, Leo fought Samson in a rematch at Frank Erne's Gymnasium. Samson was wobbly during the fifth round but he held on to finish the contest.³⁹ Leo was awarded another easy newspaper-decision win.

During the next eighteen days, while Leo was on layoff, he accepted a position as the first boxing coach for the Franklin and Marshall Academy boxing team.⁴⁰ The *Harrisburg Telegraph* reported, "This is the first time in the history of local sports that attention has been given to the ring game. A schedule of the schools on the football roster is being adopted and the local boxers will form a team to box at home and away."⁴¹ Twenty-two years later, Leo's son, Edward, attended Franklin and Marshall Academy during 1941 prior to his entry into the United States Army, where he served as a combat infantryman in the European Theater during World War II.

On December 12, eight days after accepting the coaching position at Franklin and Marshal Academy, Leo fought Harry Applegate, a neophyte middleweight from Philadelphia, at the York A.C. boxing show. Leo kayoed Applegate during the second round, ending his professional boxing career within less than a six-minute time frame. Applegate never fought in another professional bout.⁴²

Leo's last fight of the season, three days later on December 15, was an exciting six-round wind-up at Frank Erne's Gymnasium. Wild Bert Kenny was on a continuous losing streak that started on August 28, 1919. Most of the fans who attended the contest believed that Wild Bert was "all in" and had already figured that the fight would be easy for Leo. The fans received their Christmas bonuses early, witnessing an unexpected and stunning slam-fest in which both Leo and Wild Bert took turns knocking each other down during the second round. Leo recovered, regained the lead, and ultimately reined in the newspaper-decision win.⁴³

In retrospect, the most outstanding and noteworthy events of Leo's 1919 boxing season were his three fights with Harry Greb, the up-and-coming middleweight champion. Unfortunately, Leo had injured his left thumb during his first fight of the season on January 14 against Greb. The injury had continued to plague Leo during his rematch with Greb on March 6. A completely healthy Leo Houck might have been able to gain a win or draw with Greb. However, Greb was so thoroughly dominant in the middleweight ranks at this point in his career that the odds against Leo winning were probably six to one.

In addition, a win over Mike Gibbons by Leo during 1919 could have partially erased the sting of his three losses to Greb. Once again, Leo's injured thumb had persisted in bothering him and had ruined any chance against the fleet-footed Gibbons. The best Leo could muster was "survival by clinch."

From May until the end of August, Leo had concentrated on playing baseball. Today, Leo's sons, Edward and Joseph Hauck, both believe that their father's lengthy layoffs playing other sports during any boxing season hindered his career and revealed a lack of follow-through by his managers to keep Leo singularly committed to boxing.[44] On the other hand, Leo might have simply fired any manager who tried to persuade him to give up baseball, football, or basketball during any boxing season.

Age and lack of ring speed were not the problem for Leo during most of 1919. The injured thumb had plagued Leo constantly and forced him to change his style of fighting, which resulted in lackluster fights and a lot of hissing and booing from the fans. He had a legitimate right to beef about the injury, but never did so publicly.

Overall, the 1919 season was a success in spite of the injured left thumb. Leo ended the season with eleven wins, two draws, and five losses.

11

Grandpa Draws with Tunney, 1920

During the first week in January, Leo played basketball at the St. Joseph's Hall in Lancaster, against Locust Gap. The *Mount Carmel Item*, like many local and regional newspapers, typically advertised Leo's appearance in any game by including the wording, "With Leo Houck," in order to maximize ticket sales.[1]

Three days after the basketball game, on January 10, Leo fought KO Samson in a six-rounder at the National A.C. in Philadelphia. The contest kicked off the beginning of the season for both fighters. Leo, now into his eighteenth year of professional boxing, continued to demand about $500 for a six- round bout.[2] The semifinal match was their third meeting and resulted in a newspaper-decision win for Leo.

Leo's next fight on January 21, against Eddie Revoire at the Olympia A.C. in Philadelphia was another tune-up bout prior to Leo's upcoming rematch with Roddy MacDonald. The Revoire-Houck fight, their third and last meeting, resulted in another newspaper-decision win for Leo.[3]

On February 3, Leo fought Roddy MacDonald in a fifteen-round contest at the Armouries in Halifax, Nova Scotia. Leo had experienced several bizarre circumstances in the ring during his career, including Harry Mansfield's "Werewolf of London" imitation in 1911, the "Fiasco in Frisco" against Billy Murray in 1914, and the "Al McCoy Switcheroo Bout" in 1919. The Houck-MacDonald fight added yet another new and stupefying situation to the jumble.

> There is a reason why the referee's decision was against Leo Houck, last Tuesday night, after a fifteen round bout with Roddie MacDonald, at Halifax, N.S. Houck only arrived home yesterday afternoon after being storm-bound for eleven hours between Boston and New York. When interviewed this morning concerning the fight, Houck said, "It was one of the easiest fights of my career and any sober referee would have given me the decision. A man by the name of Leithan, was the third man in the ring. He was visibly under the influence of liquor and was not capable of rendering a decision on anything. His verdict was not pleasing to the fans and caused a near riot. It was far from pleasing to me, because it knocked me out of $150.00 extra."[4]

After the MacDonald contest, Leo took an extended layoff before his next match on March 11 against KO Samson at the Germantown A.C. in Philadelphia. Duke Kelly, Leo's manager, had padded his schedule up until the end of May with journeymen boxers and "ham and eggers" like Samson. The match with Samson, their fourth, was another easy win for Leo.

After the fight with Samson, the *Reading Times* took a good-natured jab at Leo with a byline, "Houck, a Grandpa, Comes Back." The newspaper described the thirty-two-year-old boxer as an "old man" but also called him "The Pride of Lancaster" and reported that "Grandpa Houck" had recently made a good showing by slamming and easily out-pointing KO Samson.[5]

Five days after the Samson-Houck match, Leo fought Johnny Howard in an eight-rounder at Schutzen Park in Bayonne, New Jersey. Howard was a very good middleweight who had scored a no-decision win on May 2, 1919, over light heavyweight champion Battling Levinsky. Almost four years had elapsed since Leo first fought and defeated Howard at the Lancaster A.C. Howard had four years to prepare a defense against Leo's trademark punch, a steady left-hand jab, but was unable to avoid being hit. The capacity crowd witnessed a close fight, but Leo prevailed and received the newspaper-decision win.

On May 10, at the conclusion of another extended layoff, Leo fought Rudy Martinez, a middleweight maiden, in a six-rounder at Frank Erne's Gymnasium in Lancaster. The match was a terrible pairing and a perplexing starting point for Rudy's first professional bout. In fact, placing Rudy, a greenhorn boxer, into the ring with a seasoned professional like Leo was reckless. The *Reading Times* had jokingly called Leo a "Grandpa," but he was far from it. Leo was clearly in the twilight of his career but had never been knocked out, was superbly conditioned, and at this point, was twenty to thirty pounds heavier than his opponent. The fight lasted five and a half rounds with Rudy covering up throughout. During the sixth round, Leo put the youngster to sleep.[6]

Five days after the bout with Rudy Martinez, Leo fought KO Samson in a six-rounder in Columbia, Pennsylvania. The fight was so unspectacular that the local and regional newspapers published only the outcome—another newspaper-decision win for Leo.

On May 19, four days after the Samson bout, Leo and Anna's fourth child, Leo E., was born. Two more children later joined their growing family after Leo's professional boxing career had ended. They were Thomas W. on March 19, 1926, and Joseph M. on September 6, 1934.

On the last day of May, Leo fought K.O. Sullivan, of Shenandoah, Pennsylvania, in a ten-rounder at Railway Park in Pottsville. The bout was close, with Leo excelling at infighting while Sullivan dominated with long-range punches. Leo was awarded a newspaper-decision win.[7] After the Sullivan bout, Leo took another extended layoff of five months.

Leo returned to the ring on October 22 when he fought Frankie Farron from Yakima, Washington, in a six-round tune-up bout in Lancaster. Farron's first professional bout, a loss, occurred in Yakima on January 16, 1920. He then traveled all the way across the United States for his second bout, against Leo on October 22 in Lancaster.[8] Farron lost to Leo and quit the boxing game.

The very next day, Leo fought Fay Keiser in a ten-rounder at the Roller Rink in Cumberland, Maryland. The fight with Keiser, directly on the heels of the Farron contest, was the first time in Leo's career that he fought back-to-back bouts without even a day's rest. Leo had defeated Keiser during their first meeting in 1916. Fighting a boxer like Keiser without any downtime, and on the road, was risky. Keiser was an underrated and remarkably tough boxer who could easily be described as a top-ranked middleweight contender. He had wins over Buck Crouse and Herman Miller, and two wins over Harry

Greb.[9] Official records list three different outcomes for the Houck-Kaiser fight: a draw, a win for Leo, and a loss for Leo.

On November 12, Leo substituted for Jeff Smith of Bayonne, New Jersey, in a ten-rounder at the Sportsman Club in Camden. Smith had become ill before his scheduled bout against KO Sullivan from Shenandoah. KO Sullivan had been knocked out by Gene Tunney on April 5, 1920, and had remained idle afterwards for a period of almost seven months. The timing of Leo's fight with Sullivan was perfect. Leo needed the tune-up bout with Sullivan in order to prepare for an upcoming contest on November 25 with former Marine Gene Tunney, the American Expeditionary Forces light heavyweight champion from 1918 to 1919.

The *Pittsburgh Post-Gazette* reported that Leo knocked Sullivan down in the third and fourth rounds. During the tenth round Leo attempted to belt out Sullivan, but was unable to do so.[10] Official records list the outcome of the bout as both a win and a loss for Leo.

On November 13, one day before Leo's thirty-second birthday, Wilber Hemphill, Leo's close friend, asked his boss, Willis Shenk, the manager of Bogar Sporting Goods Store, for a day off to hunt rabbits. Shenk obliged, and off Wilber went to the countryside surrounding Terre Hill, and returned later that evening with his limit of rabbits. Suddenly, he wondered what to do with all of the cottontails. Wilber remembered that his pugilist buddy, Leo, had a birthday the next day and decided to reduce the abundance of game by giving him a birthday supper. Anna Hauck, Leo's wife, agreed to both prepare the rabbits with all of the trimmings at her home, and invite the guests. After the repast, the visitors commenced to singing and dancing. "Speed" Brinkman, Lancaster's leading vocalist, gave a delightful impersonation of George M. Cohan, to the accompaniment of Roy Kreider on the piano. Even Leo made a brief speech.[11]

Four days later, the *Evening News* published a report that Leo had been offered a match with the French boxer Georges Carpentier.[12] On October 12, 1920, Carpentier had made a mess out of Battling Levinsky, the light heavyweight champion, when he knocked him out during the fourth round in Jersey City. The *Courier* also validated the offer from Carpentier's camp and added some specifics regarding a proposed agreement. The newspaper reported, "Agents for Carpentier have had a hard time to get anyone from the other side to meet the French champion and Houck was offered the job because he was a good clever fighter and hard hitter, likely to give the Frenchman a stiff argument."[13] Leo was far from being washed-up in the fight game. The offer once again validated Leo's status as a legitimate light heavyweight contender, and earned him some newfound recognition as one of the most durable boxers in the pugilistic world. The proposed bout between Carpentier and Leo was to be held in Paris. Regrettably, the bout never materialized. More than likely, Leo nixed the offer because of his aversion to lengthy overseas journeys.

On Thanksgiving Day, Leo fought Gene Tunney in a six-round contest at the Olympia A.C. in Philadelphia. Tunney, "The Fighting Marine," had eleven fights and eleven victories under his belt in 1920, prior to his contest with Leo. During the next six years, Tunney's boxing prowess dazzled the fistic world and, in due course, positioned him auspiciously in 1926 as the heir presumptive to the heavyweight crown then owned by Jack Dempsey.

Tunney entered the ring at 175 pounds and Leo at 173 pounds.[14] A local newspaper reported the fight and titled the article "Houck-Tunney Battle Good Draw."

Tunny [sic throughout] in the early rounds used a long fight to good effect and startled the immense crowd by fancy footwork. Houck seemed at sea when Tunny was jabbing and dancing away and Leo looked like a badly beaten dancer. In the closing rounds, however, Houck's body blows began to tell upon Tunny who lost most of his speed and outward direction of his jab. With the jab out of his opponent Leo began to get in close without being stung and a right hand body wallop had Tunny weary at the finish.

Houck swung many a wicked right hand blows to the body in eight rounds. Tunny was badly marked about the stomach and chest when the bout ended.[15]

The *Wilkes-Barre Record* also reported the Houck-Tunney bout as a draw.[16] Official boxing records all awarded the win to Tunney.

Tunney had reinjured his right hand during a prior bout on October 25 against Paul Samson-Koerner. Despite the injury, he kept his commitments for two successive fights against Leo. Jack Cavanaugh, Tunney's biographer, asserted that Tunney fought Leo exclusively left-handed on November 25 and clearly out-pointed him.[17] Cavanaugh's statement that Tunney dominated the contest as a one-handed boxer contrasts with the *Wilkes-Barre Record*'s report that the fight was a hard-fought draw.

Four days later, Leo substituted for Frank Maguire in a six-rounder in Williamsport, Pennsylvania. Maguire was too ill to fight his opponent, Leo Leonard, a middleweight from Edwardsville, Pennsylvania. Leonard agreed to fight Houck, who weighed in at 181 pounds. Over 1,600 fans in attendance were rewarded with a great battle. The *Wilkes-Barre Record* reported, "Leonard fought the young giant for six rounds and put up an A-1 battle without losing a thing. The fans were strong for the Edwardsville boy, who weighed in at 156 pounds."[18] Official records list the fight as both a draw and a win for Leo.

Several days after the bout with Leonard, Leo traveled to Jersey City and completed training for his last bout of the season, a ten-round rematch against Gene Tunney on December 7 at the 4th Armory Regiment in Jersey City. The Lancaster gamblers were reported to have been backing Leo very liberally to "stay the limit" against Tunney.[19] Frank Bagley, Tunney's manager, told the press that his boxer's injured right hand had healed well enough to continue fighting and that he had already made arrangements for Tunney to fight again six days after the bout with Leo, against Boston heavyweight Dan O'Dowd at the Flower A.C. in Rochester, New York.[20]

The *Evening World* described the Tunney-Houck semifinal bout and reported that Tunney entered the ring at 175 pounds and Leo at 180.

The first four rounds were tame, Houck continually backing away until Harry Ertle, the referee, cautioned him to show more pep. After that he did but Tunney's superior height and reach made him hard to get at.

Tunney broke his left hand during the fourth round. Houck took a nine count in the seventh round from a right swing that landed high. He recovered in game fashion and gave James a fine "shiner" in the eighth. In the tenth Tunney mauled his man around the ring but Houck covered his jaw and stayed though badly punished.[21]

The *New-York Tribune* stated, "Neither man made any effort to mix until the sixth round, when the referee threatened to throw the pair out of the ring unless they got busy, whereupon Tunney opened up with a bevy of jabs and uppercuts which gave him the decision."[22]

The *Evening News* also reported that Tunney had broken his left thumb during the bout.[23] Tunney's broken thumb early on during the bout, as reported by both the *Evening News* and the *Evening World*, might have been the reason for the tentative nature of the fight during the opening six rounds. Moreover, the prior report by Tunney's manager Frank Bagley that his fighter's right hand was healed might have been an overstatement. Tunney not only broke his left thumb during the fight, but may have also been bothered by a right hand that was still fractured, or at least very sore. After the second fight with Leo, Tunney had a lengthy layoff of almost seven months, confirming the seriousness of the damage to both hands and the necessity for a lengthy period of rehabilitation.

Boxing fans remember Tunney's second win over Leo, but have long since forgotten the tragic wind-up fight afterwards between Al Roberts, the "Staten Island Adonis," and Mickey Shannon, the "Idol of Newark." During the fifth round, Roberts sent Shannon down for the count of nine. In the next round, Roberts floored Shannon and his head thudded flatly onto the canvas. He was carried to his corner. Physicians summoned from the arena discovered that Shannon had suffered a fractured skull.[24] Shannon was transported to the hospital, never regained consciousness, and subsequently died from shock and internal hemorrhaging.[25] An investigation into the underlying cause of Shannon's death concluded that the padding installed underneath the canvas floor in the ring was severely deficient, comprising only two thin sheets of wrapping paper. The New Jersey Boxing Commission was at fault and was chastised publicly for not attending to details by inspecting and ensuring that adequate padding was installed underneath the canvas prior to the boxing show.[26]

Leo ended the 1920 boxing season on a sour note. The two losses to Tunney may have been a tipping point that signaled the end of his boxing career. The offer to fight Georges Carpentier earlier in the season was Leo's final opportunity to possibly win a light heavyweight championship, something he never accomplished over Battling Levinsky while he held the title. Carpentier had knocked out Levinsky during round four in Jersey City on October 12, 1920, and won the world light heavyweight championship. Leo had received his offer to fight Carpentier early in November 1920. The timing for a Houck-Carpentier match was fortuitous. Unfortunately, Leo declined the opportunity to fight Carpentier after he had won the world light heavyweight title. Instead, Leo resumed his regular routine by starting the next spring season playing basketball. Something else had also captured Leo's attention. Leo knew that Georges Carpentier was slated to fight heavyweight champion Jack Dempsey in July 1921. In an about-face, Leo completely abandoned his next boxing season and signed on as one of Dempsey's sparring partners at his Atlantic City training camp.

12

Leo and Jack Dempsey, 1921

From January through April, Leo decided to concentrate exclusively on playing basketball. He had signed on with two teams, the Lancaster Five and the Keenan Club Five.

Before the end of March an intriguing offer also surfaced for Leo. The *Evening News* reported, "It is announced from Lancaster that Leo Houck, the veteran middleweight of that city, has been engaged for Jack Dempsey's training camp to prepare for the Carpentier fight."[1]

Dempsey established his training camp early in May and lived in a two-story home near a former aerodrome in Atlantic City. A boxing ring and an outdoor arena with bleachers were constructed and completely fenced in.[2] Dempsey entertained the many reporters who showed up for a scoop before the official opening of training camp in the middle of May. During one lengthy interview and photo session, Dempsey plainly had had enough. He grabbed one reporter, playfully roughed him up, and teased him by saying, "You reporters have it too soft."[3] Dempsey needed to be occupied every waking moment and often read his fan mail, which ranged from folks wanting to borrow money for a business venture to a woman who said she wanted to "bet the farm" on him while forewarning him that she was not a good loser.[4]

The first contingent of sparring partners was due to arrive in training camp before the end of May. Dempsey had told Jack Veiock, the sports editor for the International News Service (I.N.S.), "I want strong, aggressive fellows who will tear into me in earnest. I believe Houck and Miller will be valuable sparring partners. There will be others too."[5]

Leo arrived at Dempsey's training camp on May 16. Some of the other pugilists expected were Henry Miller, Martin Bourke, Jimmy Darcey, Jeff Clark, Martin Cross, Chuck Wiggins, and Eddie Chara. More would arrive and depart in a carefully planned rotation.[6] Even wrestler Bull Montana participated in the training. After a session of sparring with the boxers, Montana and Dempsey would push and shove each other around the ring to strengthen the muscles used while clinching with an opponent.[7]

Former heavyweight champion James J. Corbett submitted an article written for the I.N.S. titled "Leo Houck and Other Sparring Partners Are Happy When Bell Sounds." He described Leo's first day in the ring with Dempsey.[8]

> First, Dempsey sparred with Jack Renault, a heavyweight from Canada. At the end of the third round Dempsey decked Renault with a well placed blow to the head. Leo was next in the rotation and kept Dempsey busy. Corbett gave Leo points for taking the blows but noted that he was lucky the champ had on the big gloves. After Leo escaped unscathed, Alex Trambitas, a welterweight from the West

coast, was next. He had witnessed the first two sessions with Renault and Leo and quickly decided to pull on the headgear. Trambitas never saw it coming. Dempsey brought up one of his knees in the third round and caught Trambitas squarely under the chin, which lifted him up, sent him through the ropes, and spilled him right onto his head outside the ring.[9]

Several days later, Dempsey sparred three rounds each with Clifford, Leo, Renault, and Trambitas. The first session ended prematurely for Clifford when he was laid out by Dempsey with a short right to the chin during the first round. Afterwards, Dempsey said, "I don't like to do it, but I have to."[10] Renault managed to stay in the ring throughout his session, but Leo got it much worse during his turn. This time around, Leo put on the headgear. During the first round Leo caught a solid straight left in the face and was flattened right onto his back. By the end of the second round, Leo returned to his corner bleeding from both the mouth and nose. Leo limped through the third round and managed to stay on his feet. Dempsey went a bit easier on Trambitas but never let up on him. One feature remained constant throughout every session. Dempsey always put on a glaring fighting face, no matter who sparred with him. However, after the sessions were over, Dempsey grinned and showed his lighter side.[11]

The ground rules for Dempsey's sparring sessions were plain. He explained his strategy to the *Pittsburgh Post-Gazette* after the May 19 sparring session.

> I'm afraid I roughed the boys up today. I don't like to do it but it is the only way I can gradually work myself to a real fighting edge. I cannot fight in public before the bout with Carpentier, so I've got to fight here. Every man Kearns hires comes here with that understanding. He tells them what to expect and we will pay them for it. None of them will work with me for more than 10 days. I expect to have a new batch every week.[12]

The next day, Dempsey worked only one round each with Clifford, Renault, and Leo. Clifford, who was almost knocked out the day before, decided to protect himself by wearing headgear, which provided a modicum of security. Still, Dempsey threw a left hook that landed over Clifford's right eye and within several minutes it completely swelled shut. Dempsey "had to do it," just like he told the newspapers the day before. Both Leo and Renault cruised through their turns in the ring and finished unscathed.

There was a reason for the one-round sessions with Dempsey. The next day four bouts, all eight-round contests, were held in the open-air arena at Dempsey's camp. Two of the boxers who appeared in the boxing show were Leo and Alex Trambitas. The one-round session with Dempsey the day before had sharpened them and kept both fresh for their bouts. Leo fought Dan O'Dowd, a heavyweight from Boston, in the wind-up. According to the *Pittsburgh Post-Gazette*, Leo disappointed the fans by persistent holding. O'Dowd landed some painful body shots but also failed to deliver a good performance.[13] Official records list the fight as a newspaper-decision loss for Leo.

Dempsey resumed training after a day off, and for the first time allowed the public to watch him, after paying the admission price of 50 cents. After almost being knocked out twice, Jack Clifford had enough and left training camp. Leo was also mysteriously unavailable. Larry Williams had recently joined the training camp and was scheduled to spar with Dempsey, but never appeared. Babe Herman, a featherweight from Sacramento, and Alex Trambitas were both present and sparred with Dempsey. Herman and Trambitas were dwarfed by Dempsey, who outweighed them by seventy and ninety pounds, respectively.[14] Both men demonstrated their speed in the ring and were difficult for Dempsey to hit. Trambitas had steadily become a favorite for Dempsey. He liked the way Trambitas boxed and how he never seemed to back down. However, Dempsey was all business in the ring. After a while, he would show Trambitas who was the boss and knock him around the ring like a house cat batting its toy about the living room floor.

On that same day, Dempsey's opponent, Georges Carpentier, officially opened his training camp in Atlantic City. His training schedule was quite different from Dempsey's and consisted of one day of work followed by a day of rest, leading up to their July 2 bout.[15]

A newsmonger from the New York press had fabricated a story about Leo and attempted to label him as "missing in action" or deserting training camp after his absence of two or three days. The reporter's story even managed to upset Dempsey, who was afraid that Leo might not return. The camp already had an insufficient number of sparring partners.[16] Dempsey huddled with his manager, Jack Kearns, over the dwindling number of sparring partners. They both decided to up the pay, since the word was out that Dempsey would not hesitate to knock out any welterweight or heavyweight who was unable to get out of his way during any training session.[17]

Leo did return home to Lancaster for several days. However, he did not abandon his responsibilities as Dempsey's sparring partner. Leo told the press, "I have been boxing for almost twenty years and have never been knocked off my feet and have never been rendered dizzy. Now that I am about to retire I can't see why I should permit Dempsey to knock me woozy. It isn't that Dempsey really hurt me while boxing with him but, oh, what a headache the next morning."[18]

On May 27, both Leo and Jack Renault returned to training camp. Each sparred with Dempsey two rounds. The *Wilkes-Barre Record* stated, "Dempsey worked best with Houck, and he was on the receiving end of whatever hard punching the champion did during that afternoon."[19] Afterwards, Dempsey and Bull Montana, the wrestler, entertained the crowds with an impromptu wrestling match. Dempsey grabbed Montana by the ears, rushed him to the ropes, and bounced his head off of the right ring post. Montana hollered in pain and refused to continue. He yelled out to the crowd that Dempsey was too rough.[20] Dempsey's training camp provided action-packed boxing, moments of hilarity, and occasional celebrity visits to a public audience, who could not get enough of the entire spectacle.

The next day, Renault and Dempsey collided heads in a corner during their fourth round of sparring. The fast-paced action resulted in an open cut over Dempsey's left eye. The cut reopened an old wound, first inflicted during a sparring session with middleweight Robert Buckley, aka Jamaica Kid, while Dempsey had been preparing for his July 4, 1919, bout against heavyweight champion Jess Willard.[21] Most boxers would have quit sparring for the day after suffering a cut above the eye. Instead, Dempsey continued to box and sparred two rounds with Leo.[22]

The next day, Dempsey sparred two rounds each with Williams, Leo, and a newcomer to camp, middleweight Patsy Cline, aka the Harlem Phantom or "Irish Patsy." All Dempsey's sparring partners wore headgear. Williams brawled with Dempsey and gave him the best workout, but ultimately paid for it after he crossed Dempsey on the chin early during the second round. Dempsey then hooked furiously into Williams's midsection and bounced him around the ring with a succession of alternating rights and lefts to his head. By the end of the second round, Williams was drooping and almost out. During the next sparring session, Dempsey slowed the pace with Leo and in general took it easy on him in comparison to Williams.

Irish Patsy received his formal introduction and trial by fire against Dempsey. Patsy entered the ring and immediately put Dempsey to work by fast-stepping around the ring. Dempsey soon caught up with Patsy and flattened him with a right-hand blow during the first round. During the second round, Dempsey almost knocked Patsy out of the ring.[23] Without a doubt, Patsy earned his lumps and deserved the kudos for surviving his employer's initial onslaught.

A large crowd gathered for the next training session on May 30, the largest since camp had started two weeks previously. Over 1,500 spectators packed the open-air arena. Early that morning, Dempsey completed six miles of roadwork accompanied by his three dogs.

The inclement weather and cold breezes off the ocean that day failed to prevent several hundred devoted female admirers of Dempsey from attending the sparring sessions. One noticeable trend had recently emerged during the training camp: more and more ladies were attending the public sparring sessions. Dempsey had noticed the attention from the fairer sex and soon altered his appearance by stepping into the ring clean-shaven and wearing colorful full-length tights.[24]

Once again, Larry Williams, the 180-pound heavyweight, was almost knocked out by Dempsey during their two-round scuffle. He pressured and roughed-up Williams by pushing him around the ring. After the shoving contest, Dempsey delivered a series of wicked body blows accompanied by several shots to Williams's head. The second round ended badly as Dempsey reopened a previous cut over Williams's right eye with the last punch of the session. The *Altoona Tribune* reported, "Williams is proving to be the best sparring partner for the champion as he fights back all the time."[25]

After Williams, Renault and Leo had their turns in the ring with Dempsey. The *Altoona Tribune* reported that Dempsey was unable to do much with either of them because they retreated and generally covered up. Dempsey jolted Renault hard on the chin twice and delivered a severe left hook to the body during their session. Leo typically anchored the daily sparring sessions with Dempsey and was sent down on his haunches early in the first round after Dempsey sledge-hammered him with a straight left.[26] By the second round, Leo had recovered completely and gave the champion some fast-paced action.[27]

Dempsey began a four-day rest period after the day's workout. During the interim, Jack Kearns, Dempsey's manager, traveled to New York to find fresh sparring partners who would remain in training camp until the day of the fight with Carpentier. Promoter Tex Rickard met and consulted with Jack Kearns while he was in New York, in order to iron out the final details for the championship bout.[28]

Six days later Dempsey sparred with Martin Burke, Jack Renault, and Larry Williams. Renault never made it past the first round. Dempsey pummeled him severely and knocked him out with a series of short jabs to the stomach and ribs, followed up by crushing punches to the jaw. Burke received his fair share of blows from Dempsey during their two-round session. Williams sparred with Dempsey last and reopened the cut over his eye with a head butt during their second round of sparring. The cut that was healing favorably was now enlarged and deeper, and required one stitch to close it properly. Unfortunately, Dempsey, for the time being, was now forced to confine his training to roadwork, rope skipping, and other forms of exercise.[29]

The unanticipated halt to Dempsey's sparring sessions meant that Leo was out of work. He drew his pay and left on the train for his home in Lancaster. Prior to his departure, Leo told the press that he was satisfied with his performance and the amount of punishment he endured from the champion.[30]

By late June, the cut over Dempsey's left eye had healed completely. He had continued to train intensively while the cut healed, but wore headgear for every sparring session thereafter. Dempsey had sparred with a total of ten different boxers during the training camp: Jack Renault, Larry Williams, Eddie O'Hara, Joe Benjamin, Irish Patsy Cline, Alex Trambitas, Battling Ghee, Babe Herman, Jack Clifford, and Leo Houck, along with Bull Montana, who grappled with Dempsey after the daily sparring sessions.

In a "Special to the *New York Times*," a reporter claimed that Alex Trambitas, Battling Ghee, Jack Clifford, and Leo Houck were unable to stand the "gaff" while sparring with Dempsey.[31] The statement and the reporter had little credibility. Clifford took his licks and left camp after almost being knocked out twice. Trambitas may have been the gutsiest boxer of all. His seventy-pound weight difference clearly put him at a disadvantage when sparring with Dempsey. Battling Ghee had joined training camp later and was personally selected by Jack Kearns to provide both speed and rugged competition for the champion. Leo, the first boxer to arrive at training camp, also took his lumps and never complained, though Dempsey floored him several times. After 190 professional bouts, spanning some twenty years, Leo had been knocked down only a total of three times.

Seven days before the championship fight, Dempsey started to taper off his rigorous schedule of training. He continued to demonstrate some light boxing for the public, and usually completed his workouts with moderate gymnasium exercises. The entire training camp lasted approximately two months.

Several days before the championship fight, Dempsey relocated to a private residence in Jersey City, in order to have quiet and seclusion. All the members of his training camp were sworn to secrecy not to reveal the home's location.[32]

On July 2, both Dempsey and Carpentier stepped into the ring at Boyle's Thirty Acres in Jersey City, before one hundred thousand spectators. Dempsey weighed in at 190 pounds, a fifteen-pound advantage over Carpentier at 175.

In his book, *Ten-and Out!* Alexander Johnson meticulously detailed the action-packed four-round championship bout and described Dempsey beforehand as a "ferocious tramp" about to assault a "Greek God," Carpentier.[33]

> From the first gong Dempsey forced the fighting, but Carpentier boxed beautifully and suddenly landed the first blow of the fight, a snappy left to the jaw. The blow plainly enraged Dempsey, who followed his familiar tactics, boring in savagely and finally sinking a left to Carpentier's body. Right here the Frenchman made a mistake. Instead of backing away and making a long range fight of it, he elected to stand and exchange punches with the heavier champion. Dempsey was slashing in blows now, right and left, right and left. They came so fast that they gave Carpentier no time to get set. But finally he slipped between the whirling fists and drove in a right uppercut that staggered Dempsey. For an instant his knees sagged, but then he was up again and pouring in a destructive stream of rapid-fire smashes. As the round ended one of Dempsey's lefts flattened the Frenchman's nose and all but flattened him.
>
> In the second Dempsey came out of his corner with one of his most berserk rushes. He drove into Carpentier with a veritable tattoo of blows. The Frenchman, boxing well, kept the champion off with his left and about the middle of the round drove in a terrific right, which caught Dempsey on the side of the cheek just a couple inches above the vulnerable spot. Even so, Dempsey staggered, his knees sagged, and he gave every indication of trouble. But almost before the spectators could realize that the powerful champion had been really hurt by his antagonist, he was fighting back and quickly fell into a clinch. Before the round was over he knocked Carpentier through the ropes.
>
> When the third round opened Dempsey was himself again. He charged with his accustomed fury, raining blows on body and face. Carpentier had always claimed that he broke the thumb of his right hand in the blow that staggered Dempsey in the second round. He may have, but certainly hit

Dempsey with a right in that third round and even drove him up against the ropes for a moment. However, Dempsey's blows were four to one for the Frenchman, and they carried such a sting that Carpentier was tottering as the round ended. Dempsey made a quick finish of it in the fourth. In the first charge he knocked Carpentier down for a count of nine. As he rose the champion charged in, brushed aside the Frenchman's guard, and ended the fight with a crushing right to the jaw. He was out for five minutes after Dempsey carried him to his corner.[34]

The knockout victory by Dempsey transmitted a resounding and direct message to the pugilistic world. He had plainly demonstrated in four rounds that he deserved the title of World Heavyweight Champion. So much so, that afterwards he simply dismissed or ignored any other pretenders to the throne, and did not fight again that year or during 1922, but did return to the ring on July 4, 1923, when he successfully defended his heavyweight title against Tommy Gibbons.

Of course, Dempsey's win was also a triumph for Leo and the other boxers who had sparred and trained with the champion during the 1921 training camp.

Dempsey's training camp had reinforced one incontestable and personal truth about Leo—that he could still absorb the unmerciful punches and forceful rushes of a heavyweight champion determined to knock him out. All of the excitement created during the training camp had fully compensated Leo for the void he had created for himself during 1921, when he temporarily suspended his own boxing career. Dempsey, Bull Montana, and the nine other sparring partners of the historic training camp provided an important diversion for Leo, and more importantly served as a rejuvenating catalyst for his return to boxing the following year, his last as a prizefighter.

13

"Triunfo en Cuba," 1922

During the first week of January, Leo, the team captain for the Keenan A.C. basketball team, helped hand the Lebanon Independents their first defeat of the season.[1] Leo continued playing basketball until March 13, when he fought his first opponent of the season, Sergeant Ray Smith, a heavyweight from Camden, in an eight-rounder in Lancaster. Smith had lost his last five matches leading up to this contest and had recently been knocked out on January 6, 1922, by Jack Renault, one of Dempsey's sparring partners during his 1921 training camp.[2] Smith was eight inches taller but failed to exploit his height advantage over Leo during their contest. Leo won easily and received the newspaper- decision win.

Thirty-five days later, Leo fought Lewis Schupp, aka the New Holland Ploughboy from New Holland, Pennsylvania, in an eight-rounder in Lancaster. The contest was an awful mismatch. Schupp, a mediocre regional boxer, practiced some slugging early on during the fight, but eventually Leo tied the poor fellow up, hooked sharply to his opponent's body, and then straightened him up with hard left-hand punches. Schupp was in way over his head and missed every attempt he made at trying to lead.[3] The newspaper-decision win belonged to Leo.

Young Herman Miller fought Leo for the fourth and last time on May 1 in an eight-round match at the Orpheum Theater in York. Miller was on the skids and had been losing consistently since September 6, 1920. The fight ended as win on points for Leo.

The type of fighters Leo fought from March to May provided little competition for him, but paid well and extended his boxing career. The first three fights of the season received almost no attention in the local press, and it appeared that Leo's final season would conclude with more of the same type of contests. The press was unaware that Leo's abysmal tune-up bouts had served as an important component of a larger and somewhat stealthy plan. Duke Kelly and Leo had been tight-lipped with the press during this time frame and managed to pull a fast one on the public.

During the second week in May, both Leo and his sparring partner, Jule Ritchie, a middleweight boxer from Lancaster, surprised local and regional boxing fans who read about and saw the photographs of both boxers arriving in Havana, Cuba, on board the steamship *Cuba*. Leo announced that they would both participate in a series of fights on the tropical isle. The trip, which normally would have produced a lot of publicity beforehand, received little or no attention from the local newspapers in Lancaster or Harrisburg.

Mike Castro, Cuba's flyweight champion and host to Leo and Jule while in Cuba, along with several hundred fans, boxing promoters, and local pugilists, met them when they arrived at the dock. Havana's leading paper, *La Nacion*, published over seven columns in the newspaper about the boxers, each with an explanatory streamer above the articles. A sports editor from the *Lancaster Intelligencer* received a communication from Leo soon after their arrival, but details concerning the scheduled bouts had yet to be decided.[4]

Within days after their arrival in Cuba, Leo was scheduled to fight heavyweight "Kid Cardenas" on May 1. Cardenas's second professional fight on January 16, 1921, had produced a knockout win over Louis Smith, the Cuban heavyweight champion. Five months later, Smith knocked out Cardenas in a rematch and reclaimed the Cuban light heavyweight championship.[5]

Jule Ritchie had been scheduled to fight against "Panama" Joe Gans and later Nero Chink. The advertisement about Richie's bouts was purely hype. His sole role while in Cuba was to train and spar with Leo in preparation for his upcoming fights.

Joseph Hauck, Leo's son, recollected his father's story that the battle with Cardenas had to be close because a lopsided fight or knockout could possibly result in the cancellation of Leo's next bout with Santiago Esparraguera.[6] Leo's strategy against Cardenas may have been intuitive, motivated by advice from his sparring partner Jule, or influenced by some inside information that he had gleaned from his host Mike Castro. The fight lasted the entire ten rounds and Leo was awarded the win on points.

Only two days before his bout with Leo, light heavyweight Santiago Esparraguera, aka El Cabo (The Corporal), fought and knocked out Kid Cardenas. Joseph, Leo's son, recollected that his father always referred to Esparraguera as "Asparagus."[7] The daring of "Asparagus" in accepting a fight two days before his bout with Leo revealed an obvious lack of worry or concern about Leo's record and abilities. As far as Leo was concerned, his strategy leading up to the fight with "Asparagus" was well conceived. Leo's calculated fight plan against Cardenas was about to pay another dividend against "Asparagus," a fighter completely unaware that he was about to enter a trap.

Two days later, on June 17, Leo fought Esparraguera, the Cuban light heavyweight champion, at Nuevo Fronton in Havana. The event ended abruptly during the fourth round when Leo served the crowd a wilted stalk of "Asparagus" by way of a knockout.

Leo deserved a star turn for his masterful plan and performance against two of Cuba's premier boxers. Local and regional newspaper coverage of Leo and Ritchie's return to Lancaster two weeks later was nonexistent. Moreover, Kid Cardenas and Santiago Esparraguera have never been identified as opponents who belong to the grouping of champions and future champions that Leo had defeated during his career.

Thirty-seven days after the fight with Santiago Esparraguera, Leo returned to the ring on July 24 in Lancaster, and fought Frankie Britton, a middleweight from Philadelphia. The fight was an eight-rounder and received no attention from the local newspapers. Leo was awarded the newspaper-decision win.

Leo's next bout, on August 28, was another eight-rounder in Lancaster against Jim Holland, a heavyweight from Baltimore. Once again, the newspaper coverage was negligible. The catchy headlines and descriptive stories about Leo's boxing matches during the height of his career were now reduced to a meager sentence or two. The outcome of the contest was another newspaper-decision win for Leo.

On October 2, Leo fought Jackie Clark, a middleweight from Allentown, Pennsylvania. The eight-round wind-up bout managed to garner some attention from the *Pittsburgh Post-Gazette*. "Leo Houck of Lancaster shaded Jackie Clark of Allentown, former A.E.F. middleweight champion, in a sensational and rough eight round windup here tonight. Clark had the better of the milling at long range but Houck excelled in close fighting."[8]

On October 23, Leo fought another eight-rounder against Lew Schupp in Lancaster. The *Pittsburgh Post-Gazette* reported that Leo won easily and administered a terrific beating to his opponent by effectively delivering left jabs throughout the bout.[9] The *Reading Times* claimed that Schupp out-fought Leo and gave him the battle of his life during all eight rounds.[10] Official records list the fight as a newspaper-decision win for Leo.

After the fight with Schupp, Leo looked forward to ending the year by playing in a proposed semiprofessional basketball cage circuit league that would include teams from Harrisburg, Lebanon, York, Steelton, and Lancaster.[11]

During November, Leo started to consider his future outside the ring. By all accounts, Leo never mentioned the possibility of retiring at the end of the 1922 season, at least not to the newspapers. However, Leo had heard about a possible job opening at Penn State College and decided to investigate.

Years later, Leo described in his own words his career-changing meeting with Hugo Bezdek after the football game between Penn State and the University of Pennsylvania.

> "Someone," he used to remark, "told me that Penn State was interested in boxing and needed a coach, so on the day their football team came to Philadelphia to play Penn I went down. I don't remember the score anymore, but I knew State got licked. Still, I decided to see about this job so I went up to Hugo Bezdek's room right after the game. Bez was coaching the football team, so, frankly, I didn't expect much of a reception at this time.
>
> "But, I knocked on the door and Bez invited me in. I told him what I had come down for and without even saying a word to me, he called to a guy who had the room next door.
>
> "'Neil,' he said, 'I want you to meet Penn State's new boxing coach.'
>
> "Later, I learned that the gentleman was Neil Fleming, then athletic director at State, and that's how I was hired as boxing coach up there."[12]

Before the end of the year, Leo received and turned down another job offer to assume the duties of head instructor in a boxing school located in Halifax, Nova Scotia. A prominent businessman affiliated with the school wanted Leo to train Edward Healy, a talented lightweight, and point him toward a challenge with Benny Leonard, aka the Ghetto Wizard and lightweight champion from 1917 until 1925.[13]

The 1922 boxing season ended as a great success for Leo. He had won all nine of his contests. Local newspaper sources at home had circulated rubbish about Leo being "all in" for several consecutive years before his action-packed trip to Cuba. His arrival and presence in Cuba had created a virtual stir in their boxing community. Leo humbly accepted the Cubans' enthusiastic attention and celebrity treatment. For whatever reasons, Leo's two victories in Cuba during his last year of professional boxing have, for the most part, been overlooked or forgotten.

Leo's professional boxing career started in 1902 when he was fourteen years old. He earned one silver dollar and a new pair of boxing gloves for his first fight. Over the next twenty years and two hundred fights, he established himself as one of the premier middleweights in the nation. His ability to continue fighting successfully in all weight classes without ever being knocked out is no minor footnote in boxing history, but rather an enduring individual pugilistic masterpiece.[14]

Legends and legendary sports figures like Leo emerge only from time to time. Their actions and accomplishments etch indelible collective memories into the American experience. Leo was prepared to embark on a new journey—coaching at Penn State—and had no way of knowing that some legends can, indeed, be born twice.

Part III

The Penn State Years

14

Penn State's First Legendary Coach

When Leo arrived at State College in 1922, official boxing guidelines already in practice at the collegiate level provided him with a solid framework of rules and regulations on which to base his program. More specifically, in 1921 Joseph E. Raycroft, Princeton professor and the War Department's chief administrator for Army training camp activities during World War I, had developed and promulgated essential guidelines that pertained to the fundamental boxing skills, physical training, and rules for Army boxing. Later, he suggested that they could also be adapted to the collegiate boxing environment. The next year, R. Tait McKenzie, who was a physical educator from the University of Pennsylvania, Lieutenant Commander William A. Richardson of the United States Military Academy, and Allan Winter Rowe from the Massachusetts Institute of Technology, modified Raycroft's original precepts and established a concrete set of rules to govern intercollegiate boxing. These rules were subsequently approved by the National Collegiate Athletic Association (NCAA) and later sanctioned by the Intercollegiate Boxing Association (IBA).[1]

Another event which occurred that same year involved William A. Rocap, sports editor for the *Public Ledger*, who was also a boxing referee, and the writer who had covered Leo's triumph over Harry Lewis in France in 1911. Acting in his post as the current chairman of the Pennsylvania State Boxing Commission, Rocap gathered a contingent of like-minded boxing officials and shared his ideals with them about "the spirit and principals at the heart of college boxing."[2] Together they formed an association, which was subsequently approved by the IBA. In order to solidify the arrangement, all association members agreed to receive their direction solely from Francis C. Grant, the secretary of the IBA. He would approve all official assignments of referees and judges from the association, prior to any collegiate match.[3]

Hugo Bezdek, the Penn State Athletic Director, embraced the subsequent implementation of standardized practices for collegiate boxing and the adherence to officially sanctioned guidelines. He also possessed the "gut instincts" and common sense to hire Leo F. Houck to lead the way as their new boxing coach. Penn State class yearbooks and archival athletic photographs reveal that in addition to coaching boxing, Leo also performed the collateral duties of an athletic trainer and coach for the baseball team.[4]

Penn State's first boxing match occurred on May 9, 1919, at the University of Pennsylvania in Philadelphia. The contest was believed to be the nation's first dual meet.[5] From 1920 through 1930, Penn State boxing surpassed football as the most popular winter sport.[6] In addition, "Penn State, as a pacesetter in the field, served as host to the first Eastern IBA tournament in 1924 and the first National Collegiate tournament in 1932."[7]

Penn State's collegiate boxing rivals included the University of Pennsylvania, Virginia Military Institute, Navy, Army, Catholic University, Notre Dame, Temple, Michigan Institute of Technology, Western Maryland, Georgetown, the University of West Virginia and Syracuse.

Penn State Boxing History describes the rivalry between Penn State and Annapolis as one of the most prominent and hard-fought collegiate rivalries within the IBA. Coach Hamilton Murrel Webb, aka Spike Webb, who commanded the midshipmen from Annapolis, was described as the "Boxing Boss," while Leo was referred to as "King Man." Often, only one point separated the teams' scores at the conclusion of an event. One constant practice became commonplace whenever both teams met. Formal attire or tuxedos were worn by the coaches and boxing officials. Recreation Hall (Rec Hall) was always jammed to the rafters for dual meets and tournaments held at Penn State. The facts regarding the intensity of the rivalry are staggering. "In the first eight years of the Eastern IBA tournament, each team emerged the winner four times. Navy's individual champions from 1924 through 1931 numbered 10. Penn State's added up to 18. It was that close all the way."[8] After the 1931 IBA tournament, Annapolis formally ended their participation in intercollegiate boxing.

Several of Leo's most notable boxing students experienced the heights of fame, success, and bitter defeat. Julius Epstein, an IBA bantamweight champion at Penn State in 1929, and his identical twin brother, Phillip, who also boxed for Leo and became an intramural boxing champion, both graduated and headed for the glamour and glitz of Hollywood. They wrote plays and screenplays, and pitched their work unrelentingly to any movie studio executive who would give them the time of day. They both hit pay dirt, along with co-writer Howard Koch, by writing the script for the Academy Award–winning movie *Casablanca*, starring Humphrey Bogart and Ingrid Bergman. The movie earned the Epstein brothers an Academy Award for the Best Adapted Screenplay.[9]

Another standout student of Leo's was heavyweight Steve Hamas from Passaic, New Jersey. Leo had approached Hamas, the only Penn State athlete to earn five letters in one year, and on the spot recruited him for the boxing team.[10] Hamas's first boxing match occurred on the same day Leo recruited him.[11] Hamas was a powerhouse in the ring and earned the IBA heavyweight collegiate championship title in 1929. After college, Hamas turned professional. One of his most notable fights was a win against former heavyweight champion Max Schmeling on February 2, 1934, at Convention Hall in Philadelphia.[12] The rematch with Schmeling on March 10, 1935, was a devastating calamity. Hamas was injured while training for the rematch and was pressed into the contest by his manager before having had an opportunity to heal sufficiently. Schmeling beat Hamas terribly and sent him to the hospital for a total of ten days. Hamas retired from boxing afterwards and went on to lead a quiet life as a salesman.[13]

Leo never intended to use the Penn State boxing team as a nursery in order to develop amateur boxers into professional fighters. Quite the opposite, Leo believed wholeheartedly that boxing, as a collegiate sport, was the perfect setting to develop the science of boxing in its purest form. Leo's philosophy was simple. He believed that any of his students who entered the ring was a winner and had in essence proven his manhood. More importantly, each developed his own character significantly by understanding that pugilism was first and foremost based on an understanding of the fistic art of "give and take."[14]

William "Billy" Soose, from Farrell, Pennsylvania, was another superstar protégé of Leo's and an IBA middleweight collegiate champion in 1937. Before Soose attended Penn State, he had already become a three-time Golden Gloves champion. During his sophomore year at Penn State, Soose was credited with winning all seventeen of his bouts by knockouts.[15] His accomplishments were so overpowering that they immediately caught the attention of IBA officials. The IBA immediately focused on the likelihood of other seasoned amateurs like Soose, who wanted to continue their boxing careers at the collegiate level. In a short period of time, the IBA leveled the playing field by passing a rule that prohibited any amateur boxer who formerly competed in Golden Gloves competitions from competing at the collegiate level.[16] Soose turned professional in 1941 and amassed an amazing record of thirty-four wins, six losses, and one draw.[17]

Another one of Leo's outstanding boxers, Gil Filegar, deserves a special mention. He was a two-time IBA collegiate champion from Penn State, first in 1926 as a lightweight, and then in 1928 when he competed as a featherweight. Other Penn State boxers also achieved dual and triple IBA championships. However, none of the other champions had composed and dedicated a poem to their beloved coach.

Leo Houck

Leo Houck was a fighter
So illustrious was his name
Within this year it was chosen
For the boxing Hall of Fame.
He had the art of perfection
Of courage and boxing skill
He was known the world over
This youngster from Cabbage Hill.

Many the champions challenged
Many who met defeat
They could not cope with the matter
With those flying fists and feet.
His fans were cheering loudly
When the Kid went for the kill
They could hear the smack of leather
Way back on Cabbage Hill.

But he was quiet and humble,
With never a want to boast.
Over two-hundred times he battled
As he traveled from coast to coast.
Seldom was he a loser
And the crowds received a thrill
As they watched in fascination
The master from Cabbage Hill.

Oh, Leo Houck was a fighter
A fighter of world renown.
A middleweight unbeaten
But he never could wear the crown.
With the title bouts denied him,
He stayed in the game until
The time that he must retire
And return to Cabbage Hill.

> So great was his love of boxing
> That he taught the things that he knew
> To the Nittany Lion ring men
> And they were champions too.
> Not because they were winners
> But because they had the will
> He was known as the "old professor"
> Who now lived on "College Hill"
>
> But the final round had ended
> And the uncrowned champ is gone
> The lessons of life he taught us
> And his memory linger on.
> Yes, Leo Houck left us
> And the mighty heart is still
> May he wear the crown of an angel
> As he travels on Glory Hill.
>
> Gil Filegar[18]

Early in January 1945, Leo was granted an indefinite leave of absence from Penn State. The *Stars and Stripes* newspaper reported that Leo Houck, along with Harry J. Rockefeller, Athletic Director of Rutgers University, New Brunswick, New Jersey; Robert "Red" Rolfe, basketball and baseball coach at Yale University, New Haven, Connecticut; Charles Berry, American League baseball umpire from Easton, Pennsylvania; and Ed Zanfrieni, Athletic Director at Dartmouth University, Hanover, New Hampshire, were selected to join the United States Army Special Services Unit and travel to Iceland to conduct Army coaching clinics and promote morale.[19] "While his duties in the new assignment were not specifically outlined, Houck said he expected to concentrate on boxing instructions at the clinics, which will be attended by athletic officers of the area."[20] Before arriving in Greenland, which was the first port of call, the party visited wounded servicemen from the European theater in an Army hospital at Presque Isle, Maine.[21] An earlier newspaper story, "Leo Houck Selected for U.S. Army Special Service Unit," mentioned that Leo would serve as a civilian consultant. The civilian service status was incorrect. A photograph of Leo while in Greenland shows him in an Army uniform and identifies him as Major Leo Florian Houck. He is pictured with three Penn State graduates who are also in uniform, Lt. Clarence Smith, 1945 (Army); Lt. Anthony Rubino, 1938 (Navy); and Lt. Wayne Vonarx, 1938 (Navy).[22]

During World War II, three of Leo's sons served bravely in the military. Leo E., a glider pilot in the United States Army Air Corps, landed American paratroopers behind enemy lines in Holland and France. Edward, a combat infantryman, served in Western Europe. Thomas, who immediately enlisted in the Navy on his eighteenth birthday, served on board a ship in the Pacific Theater.[23] Leo's youngest son, Joseph, was only eleven years old in 1945, but later went on to serve his nation in the United States Marine Corps.

After Leo returned home from the Special Services tour, which also included visits to Army hospitals, he was moved to comment publicly about one outstanding problem that needed an immediate remedy. He recommended that additional resources be directed toward the treatment and recovery of the sick and wounded servicemen in all Army hospitals.[24]

Leo returned to Penn State several months later after his obligation to the United States Army ended. Participation in Penn State's boxing program remained vigorous and constant throughout Leo's entire tenure at the helm. Collegiate boxing, for the most part, had delineated an era of rugged rough-and-tumble American individualism and its competitive application to one's own pursuit of success in the world. Many World War I soldiers who learned how to box while in the military enrolled in college after returning home from the war. Those same veterans greatly influenced and perpetuated the growing interest and participation in collegiate boxing after 1919.

In his book, *The Six-Minute Fraternity*, E.C. Wallenfeldt clearly echoed a similar theme and believed that individual initiative, power, and domination were the underpinnings and sought-after values that contributed toward the robustness of a capitalistic society during the first years of the United States' existence.[25] However, he goes on to identify the contrasting behaviors and values of compassion, charity, and respect for human dignity in one's life, and states that they are equally important in order to become a successful human. Wallenfeldt's observations, ranging from the display of aggression in the ring to compassionate behaviors practiced outside of the ring, yielded his conclusion that collegiate boxing was overall a clear indicator of oppositional and differing values.[26] His observations were perceptive, and over time that clash of values became apparent when the enthusiasm for and participation in boxing at the collegiate level dropped significantly, and forced many colleges to eliminate their boxing programs. Penn State was among this number.

In a little over a generation, interest in boxing at Penn State started to falter and finally succumbed completely in 1954, when boxing officially ended. The appetite for boxing at Penn State had diminished most significantly between 1949 and 1954. On May 30, 1954, Penn State University's Public Information Department released their reasons for eliminating Penn State's intercollegiate boxing program.

> State College, Pa. May 29 — Public apathy and scheduling difficulties, combined with continued non-acceptance of the sport as an educational activity, today prompted Penn State to drop boxing from its intercollegiate program, effective immediately.
>
> Athletic Director E.B. McCoy, who announced the decision, said the university's 13 member Athletic Advisory Board had unanimously recommended the action after a year-long study indicated there no longer was any great enthusiasm for the sport among students, faculty, and alumni. Penn State fielded teams for 36 straight years.
>
> McCoy explained that scheduling difficulties had been accentuated in late years by a steady drop in the number of institutions participating in the sport. He pointed out that it was now necessary to go far afield for competition since only four Eastern schools of comparable size and tradition still field teams.
>
> "No institution ever takes a step like this without considerable forethought," the Penn State Athletic Director observed. "This would be particularly true of this University because of our long and distinguished record as a supporter of intercollegiate boxing.
>
> "There's no question, however, that there has been a change of heart in recent years and our people now look upon boxing as a sport of questionable value, and one which it has become increasingly difficult to defend because of its continued non-acceptance by the vast majority of our educational institutions."[27]

From 1922 to 1949, Leo Houck had established, built, nurtured, and maintained one of the most highly regarded and competitive intercollegiate boxing programs in the United States. His numerous accomplishments are indisputable and clearly annotated for posterity. Leo may have agreed that the Penn State boxing record stands on its own as a collective achievement; but he might also have suggested that his real accomplishments did not reside in the win-loss column, but in the development of youthful sluggers

Leo F. Houck (right) playing handball with fellow Penn State coaches during August 1949. Others, left to right: Bob Higgins, Joe Bedenk and John Lawther. After Leo's boxing career had ended, he continued to sustain a high level of physical conditioning by playing handball. He firmly believed that all athletes needed to maintain their fitness throughout the year by participating regularly in some type of sporting activity (courtesy Michael Hauck, Leo F. Houck's grandson).

into young men of worth and responsibility. Leo had a very simple and matter-of-fact philosophy about collegiate boxing and the boys who elected to participate. His pugilistic charges at Penn State devotedly followed his straightforward advice in the ring, by practicing and applying an uncomplicated formula that was sometimes described as an oversimplification: "Keep your left working in his face and hit him with your right when you get a chance."

> He never said one critical thing about a member of his own team. Everybody did well according to Leo, only he didn't put it exactly that way. Boxing, he'd point out, is a difficult science. Boys shouldn't expect it to be learned in college. It was an achievement, he'd honestly inform you, just to get in the ring. Now and then, Leo would express a great liking for an opponent, the member of another college team. We'd know his opinion of the young man was extremely high if he'd say, "Well, he's a pretty good boy."[28]

This is an overview of Leo Houck's coaching achievements at Penn State from 1922 to 1949:

Team Championships:
NCAA—1932
IBA (Eastern)—1924, 1927, 1929, 1930, 1935, 1936, 1940

Individual Coaching Record:
Dual Meets—Won 88, Lost 71, Tied 17
Team Titles—IBA 7, NCAA 1
Champions—IBA 48, NCAA 5

Dual Meet Record:
Won 101, Lost 97, Tied 23[29]

Founded:
The Eastern Intercollegiate Boxing Association—1923[30]

Anecdotal stories about Leo's tenure at Penn State abound. Many of his friends, students, boxing opponents, and rival coaches have been interviewed throughout the years. Their stories about Leo have been recorded and published in numerous newspaper articles and feature stories about his life. The greatest example is a compilation of reminiscences about Leo found in L. Shaw's feature article titled "Leo Florian Houck: Fred's Mentor."[31] The stories are often humorous, lighthearted, and touching tributes that recognize and highlight Leo's unwavering commitment to his family, faith, morals, genuine interest in his friends and students, and his consummate professionalism. These characteristics earned him a resounding and unsurpassed status of respect and popularity on campus, from both the academic and student population.

15

Leo and the Pennsylvania State Athletic Commission

Late in November 1949, Leo addressed an audience from the Second Guessers Club at the Stock Yards Hotel in Lancaster. In addition to providing a brief overview of his professional boxing and coaching career, he also mentioned that his dedication to boxing, commitment to honesty in the sport, overall philosophy about professional boxing, and reputation as a coach at Penn State fulfilled all the qualifications required for a recently vacated position on the Pennsylvania State Athletic Commission.[1] Leo had decided to leap headfirst into Pennsylvania politics by seeking Mr. Leo Raines's recently vacated position on the State Athletic Commission. He was denied the position. Leo's guest appearance at the Second Guessers Club allowed him to address the issues involved in cleaning up the current and objectionable state of boxing in Pennsylvania.

The audience was captivated by Leo's dissertation on what exactly was wrong with boxing in 1949.

> Boxing is a great sport, but today it lacks teachers and real leaders. Frankly, I'm disappointed with amateur boxing, for in some of the matches that I have seen in Golden Gloves competitions, which is supposed to be the peak of amateurs, I have seen teen boys who do not know how to stand or how to hold their balance. To me boxing is like a trade that requires about four years of apprenticeship. You've got to work hard to learn the art.
>
> As for our professional boxing today, it is controlled by the politicians and the gamblers. Why couldn't I get a job as a commissioner here in Pennsylvania? I have devoted all my life to boxing and yet today there is no room for me as a Commissioner.[2]

The audience might have been aware that Leo had recently undergone major surgery at St. Joseph's hospital in Lancaster. He had experienced severe abdominal pains while at Penn State, collapsed, and had to return home immediately for treatment. Leo was still convalescing but did intend a return to Penn State and coaching. However, his overall condition was serious and threatened to jeopardize his future plans and well-being.

The next day after Leo's appearance at the Second Guessers Club, the *Evening News* published an interview with Leo in which he answered questions about his previous bid for a political appointment with the State Athletic Commission. He followed up by shedding some light on his current bid for an appointment to the Commission.

> Regarding Leo's first bid for an appointment to the Commission he said, "I couldn't get an appointment as a boxing commissioner in this state because of politics.... I sought an appointment as a member of the boxing commission. That was when Governor [Gifford] Pinchot was Governor. The Governor called me to an interview at his home in Milford. Everything seemed set. Somehow the

appointment was blocked and the only reason being named was that Pinchot's party was the Republicans (and sometimes the Bull Moose Party) while mine was the Democratic Party."

During his second and current bid for an appointment Al Clark from the *Evening News* asked Leo if he actually was a candidate for the vacancy. Houck responded, "You want a 'yes' or 'no' answer to that one, so I'll say that I wouldn't turn down the post if it was offered to me."

Leo responded to his earlier public statements that boxing was controlled by gamblers and politicians. Hock said, "Boxing today in forty-seven states is controlled by one powerful group—the New York Group."

Finally, Leo touched on an issue of major importance, that of ring safety and officiating. He said, "I have made a study of ring injuries and what causes ring fatalities. I find in most cases several injuries and deaths could have been halted by an official with common sense and the courage to stop the bout when the ring men were knocked helpless by an opponent."[3]

Leo's assertion about the "New York Group" and their stranglehold over boxing was no casual generalization. The New York City–based International Boxing Club (IBC) controlled all boxing promotions. James Norris, who owned the primary interest in the IBC, and mobster Frankie Carbo, who controlled both the Boxing Managers Guild of New York and the International Boxing Managers Guild, combined forces to create a devious union that arranged staged matches and controlled all the fighters. The upshot of their lengthy and unseemly partnership produced thrown fights, cheating on purses, and decisions about who got title shots. "Monkey business" in the fight game under the reign of these principals remained absolute until 1959, when the Justice Department prosecuted Norris and Arthur M. Wirtz, the owners of the IBC, and nailed them both on antitrust violations. They were ordered to sell their mutual interests in the IBC in New York and Illinois, liquidate their holdings in Madison Square Garden, and reduce the number of championship bouts that were advertised as IBC venues. As for Carbo, he was initially sentenced to two years in prison for underhanded matchmaking and managing, but improved on that deal soon afterwards by earning twenty-five more years in jail for extortion.[4]

Early in December, the *Lancaster Intelligencer* urged Governor James H. Duff to appoint Leo to the State Athletic Commission. The newspaper endorsed Leo one hundred percent by recognizing that he was wholly committed and qualified to eliminate the festering grip of gambling and underhanded political machinations that were ruining professional boxing. The newspaper also suggested that a statewide drive of circulating petitions, signed by the residents of Pennsylvania on Leo's behalf, may help him cinch the vacancy on the State Athletic Commission.[5]

Unfortunately, Leo never received an appointment to the Pennsylvania State Athletic Commission. At this point, his condition after the surgery had worsened and he was soon confined to his home. Returning to Penn State in the fall of 1949 was now out of the question. However, Leo was still alert, mobile, and able to receive visitors at home. The somber news about Leo soon reached his multitude of friends and colleagues at Penn State, so they decided to write him a cheerful get-well letter. George Graham, his longtime friend and owner of Graham's Store, authored the letter. Signing stations were available at Graham's, the Cathaum Theater, the Student Union at Old Main, and the Corner Room. Over 10,000 signatures were expected.[6] In five brief paragraphs the letter conveys a heartfelt message throughout to their friend and beloved coach.

November 1949
Leo Houck
Lancaster and State College

Dear Leo:

Greetings from your army of Penn State College friends who love and admire you very much! Salutations from all the boys who come into Graham's each day and who miss seeing you on the bench or in front of the candy counter or on the chair in front of the radio or maybe back of the register with your hand in the barrel.

Felicitations from all the Freds you greeted every day; from all the people you knew and many, many more who knew you as Leo or Lem or Professor or Doctor—terms of friendliness and affection.

Best wishes from our communities' leading citizens and the College's highest officials to the smallest urchin whose illegal entrance to Recreation Hall you aided and abetted.

Hurry back, Leo, State College hasn't been the same this fall; Penn State just can't get along without you.

Sincerely,[7]

Twenty-eight days after the letter-writing campaign at Penn State, Leo passed away on January 21, 1950, in his sleep at 2:30 p.m. The cause of death was a carcinoma of the large bowel. He was sixty-one years old.

Funeral services were held on January 25 at the Sullivan Funeral Home in Lancaster. In an excerpt from a collection of stories titled "Anecdotes About Leo Houck Stir Lively Memories of His 27 Years at Penn State," Ed Malmed, a 1933 alumnus of Penn State who attended Leo's viewing, stated that he believed Leo would have liked the simplicity of the arrangements and described them as "nothing fancy." While Malmed and some other mourners talked, Anna Hauck joined them. She said, "He was such a good man, always—and he never had anything—anything. He was always so poor. What did people see in him? It's so nice they're here tonight. We thank you so much. We can't talk. Nothing comes out."[8]

On the same day at 10:30 a.m., over five hundred friends and relatives attended the Requiem High Mass at the St. Joseph's Catholic Church in Lancaster. Monsignor Schweich, who conducted the Mass, was assisted by Father Owen Gallager, Catholic Chaplain of Pennsylvania State College, and Major Charles L. Diamond, Chaplain at the New Cumberland Army Depot. The Reverend Richard Mitchell of Baltimore, a former parishioner at St. Joseph's Catholic Church, served as the master of ceremonies. Father Gallager conducted the graveside service at St. Joseph's Cemetery. Monsignor Schweich told the mourners that Leo's qualities of honesty and fairness in athletic contests extended equally into his everyday life.

> There is a striking parallel in the training of boxers or for that matter, of any athlete, in order to be successful and respected, and in that of a Christian making life a training ground for the eternal victory—the Kingdom of Heaven.
>
> Our departed friend, Leo Houck, Monsignor Schweich said, "was a successful athlete in several sports because he trained carefully and kept all the rules; so too he lived his life in regards to his religious duties to God and his fellow man."[9]

Leo's pallbearers were boxers from the current Penn State boxing team and included Charles Drazanovich, captain of the boxing team, John Bolger, Bob Keller, Paul Smith, Frank Cross, Curtis Crooks, Paul Heims, and Charles Wilson. Former Penn State boxing standouts, Steve Hamas and Billy Soose, who later achieved fame as professional fighters were also in attendance.

The list of local honorary pallbearers included Professor Charles W. Mayser, Ally Albright, E.T. Hager, Ed Stumpf, Harry Goodhart, Richard C. Danz, George W. Kirchner, George Crudden, Jr., Harold J. Eager, John Sullivan, Harry J. Marshall, Harry R. Haldy, and William Hemphill. A large contingent of honorary pallbearers from Penn State were: William W. Shade, boxing manager and representative of the student body, Randall Graham, representing the people of State College, H.R. Gilbert, graduate manager of athletics, Ridge Riley, executive secretary of the Alumni Association,

Eddie Sukowski, acting coach of Penn State's boxing team, Chuck Werner, head track coach, and George T. Smith, representing the church and community. The U.S. Naval Academy also sent two representatives, Lt. Commander Tony Robins and Lt. Jr. Grade Hillis Hume. Charles Havens, of the University of Western Maryland, and president of the Eastern Intercollegiate Boxing Association and J. DaGrosse, newly appointed head of the Pennsylvania Athletic Association also attended.[10]

A list of other notable individuals in attendance included these:

Nate Cartmel, of Forest Hills, N.Y., ex–Penn State track coach; Joe Miller, of New York City, former Penn State athletic great; Joe McGuigan, of Philadelphia, a well known referee and son of the man who at one time served as Houck's manager; and Charles Berry, American League baseball umpire; Joe Bedenk, head football coach at Penn State who acted as official representative of the college; his two assistants, Al Michaels and James O'Hara; Charles Speidel, wrestling coach; James Coogan, sports public relations official of the college; Samuel Donato, one of Leo's 145-pound champions; James Gilligan, member of the college athletic board; H.R. Gilbert, graduate manager of athletics; Rudolph Valentino, a native of Lancaster who is a member of Penn State's swimming and wrestling teams; Hinkey Hayes, former Penn State football great; Dr. A.H. Griess, team physician of the college; Brian Hayes, old-time referee from Philadelphia; Charles Ettinger, Allentown fight promoter; Bill Jeffreys, Penn State soccer coach, Nick Thiel, lacrosse coach; and Ray Conger, campus recreation director.[11]

On Sunday, December 3, Anna Hauck gathered with friends and relatives at Stumpf Athletic Field in Lancaster for the dedication and unveiling of the Leo F. Hauck Memorial. The ceremony took place during halftime at the Lancaster Presidents football game. After the invocation by the Reverend Philip A. Liebich, St. Joseph's Catholic Church, and opening remarks by Charles Ettinger, an Allentown boxing promoter and lifelong friend of Leo's, Anna Hauck unveiled the memorial. Harry Goodhart, the chairman of the memorial committee, read a passage from a letter written by former heavyweight champion Gene Tunney to Dr. Herbert Beck, the primary force guiding the memorial committee. "I do hope you have a proper ceremony and that the person you select to do the unveiling will be worthy of the man who bore the name Leo Hauck."[12]

After the unveiling of the memorial, which was placed at the entrance to Stumpf Field, the Lancaster Presidents football team presented Anna Hauck with a floral wreath. Dr. Herbert Beck wrote the inscription for Leo's memorial.

> In an era of top middleweight and lightweight boxers, 1905–1920, Leo Hauck rose through them all to become "uncrowned middleweight champion of the world." Always a clean sportsman and a gentleman. He was a credit to the world of boxing and to his native town, Lancaster; he was an ideal pattern for the youth of America.
> Erected by his many friends of the world of sports.
> 1950

The memorial was eventually moved to James Buchanan Park at nearby Franklin and Marshall College and close to the North Museum at the corner of Race and Buchanan Avenues in Lancaster.[13] Leo's memorial now resides in close proximity to the statue of James Buchanan, America's fifteenth president.

Sixty-five years after Leo's death, Edward Hauck, Leo's son, offered his own thoughts about his father.

> Where Leo departs abruptly from most of the herd is his innate humility. From the perspective of a son: Leo never exhibited evidence in word or deed of wanting more material embellishments, grasping for wealth or scheming for another buck. While he attended to bodily cleanliness (shaving, showering, et al.) his dress was acceptable drab. I recall one or two suits, tweedy and gray, set off with white shirt and tie. About the house he was usually attired in an old pair of pants, which my mother

threatened to dispatch with the trash; worn shoes to match and topped off by a well-worn sweatshirt from Penn State gear.

Leo in my memory never wore a piece of jewelry (only women wore wedding rings) although he did possess a Hamilton pocket watch. Trousers in those days included a waist pocket. In the early forties at a dinner ceremony in his honor by the Lancaster County Penn State Alumni, Leo was presented with a Hamilton watch with an appropriate inscription. Leo was appreciative, obviously, but never wore that watch or any wristwatch. He presented it to me when I returned home after my discharge from the World War II Army infantry. I have since passed it on to our youngest son and namesake.

Leo's religious faith and beliefs never wavered. He attended Sunday Mass without fail; and I'm sure from time to time during the week. Leo always found positives when discussing opponents. I assume that is why they always greeted Leo with a handshake and smile when they were in contact after their contests.

Leo's Lancaster friends when he was a young man were his friends when they were older. I've mentioned many times the experience that my older brother, Leo, and I recalled when we trailed after him on a walk to downtown Lancaster. He frequently bumped into old athletes he competed with (baseball, basketball); local politicians, sports writers, etc., all worthy of a chat. Of course, my brother and I were in turns fascinated or bored; but nonetheless, we remembered these walks.

Memorial to Leo F. Hauck in Buchanan Park, close to Franklin & Marshall College, Lancaster, Pennsylvania (courtesy LancasterHistory.org, Lancaster, Pennsylvania, John Hauck Collection, MG-63, JH-04-06-43).

Leo made many friends among fellow coaches at Penn State and with members of the faculty, all attesting to Leo's ability as a teacher, more impressive, since his formal education was deficient: but he could be described as an autodidact.

Leo's life was determined, unknowingly, by his innate humility. I don't believe any person who knew Leo as a personal friend or casual acquaintance thought of him other than as a genuine "good guy."[14]

On June 10, 2012, sixty-two years after Leo's death, he was honored and memorialized by the International Boxing Hall of Fame (IBHOF). Leo was considered an "Eligible Old-Timer" for the honor as early as 1964.[15] The induction ceremony was held in Canastota, New York, where the IBHOF is located. Edward and Joseph, Leo's sons, attended the event and accepted the honor on their father's behalf. Edward also addressed the audience for a two-minute period. On this day, Thomas "Hitman" Hearnes, a former middleweight champion; Freddie Roach, trainer of champion Manny Pacquiao; ring announcer Michael Buffer; and broadcaster Al Bernstein were also inducted.

The *Intelligencer Journal* neatly summed up Leo's boxing career in an article titled "Houck Headed to Hall of Fame."

> No other fighter who ever came out of this city, and few who ever fought anywhere, mastered the art of self-defense so thoroughly.
>
> He was the master of the jab, the feint, the uppercut and all other fine points of the game. His was a skill that brought the unbegrudged compliment from Johnny Wilson, a former middleweight champ of that era, that Leo was the greatest fighter he had ever met.[16]

In addition to the IBHOF, Leo was also inducted into the Pennsylvania Sports Hall of Fame by the Central Chapter in 1972, and the Ring Magazine Hall of Fame in 1969.

Leo's wife, Anna, passed away nineteen years after her husband, at age seventy-nine, on April 6, 1969. They are survived by their sons, Edward Hauck and Joseph Hauck, who both currently reside in Lancaster, Pennsylvania.

Appendix: Leo F. Houck's Professional Fight Record

Archival newspaper reports have been used as the primary source for verifying all of Leo F. Houck's fights and their outcomes. Other official published fight records have been reviewed, but are used only as comparative guidelines. Differences do exist between some of the fight outcomes when official fight records are compared to the newspaper reports. However, the total number of variations is minimal. In some cases, newspaper accounts have yielded one, two, or three different outcomes for one particular fight. All newspaper-decision outcomes discovered for those fights are listed on Leo F. Houck's fight record in the Appendix. This record in no way represents an attempt by the author to alter or challenge existing fight records or to find fault with the hard work and dedication of other individuals who have meticulously reconstructed the numerous fight records of the early 1900s boxers.

Key: **NDW** Newspaper-Decision Win; **NDL** Newspaper-Decision Loss; **NDD** Newspaper-Decision Draw; **KO** Knockout; **TKO** Technical Knockout; **DQ** Disqualification; **PTS** Points; **W** Win

Year/Date	Opponent	City/State	Outcome	Rounds
1902				
October 1	Carl Kreckel	Lancaster, PA	NDD	4
1903				
December 10	Leo (Baldy) Fritsch	Prince Street Hall Lancaster, PA	NDW	4
1904				
October 20	Herb Eshelman "Young Warren"	Mannerchor Hall Lancaster, PA	NDL	4
1905				
February 17	Walter "Shorty" Groff	Lancaster A.C. Lancaster, PA	NDW	6
April 17	Pinky Evans	Lancaster A.C. Lancaster, PA	NDD	6

Appendix

Year/Date	Opponent	City/State	Outcome	Rounds
1906				
January 24	Young Jack Hanlon	Lancaster A.C. Lancaster, PA	NDW	6
February 21	Tommy Dugan	Lancaster A.C. Lancaster, PA	W-KO	2
March 7	Sam Parks	Lancaster A.C. Lancaster, PA	NDW	6
April 18	Sam Parks	Lancaster A.C. Lancaster, PA	NDD	6
May 17	Jimmy Livingston	Lancaster A.C. Lancaster, PA	W-KO	4
June 6	Hugh McCann	Lancaster A.C. Lancaster, PA	W-KO	5
October 18	Jack Britton	Lancaster A.C. Lancaster, PA	NDW	6
1907				
January 24	Young Marshall	Lancaster A.C. Lancaster, PA	W-KO	2
February 21	Young Kid Broad	Lancaster A.C. Lancaster, PA	W-TKO	2
April 4	Young Kid Broad	Lancaster A.C. Lancaster, PA	NDW	6
April 25	Buck Eagan	Lancaster A.C. Lancaster, PA	NDW	6
June 12	Reddy Moore	Lancaster A.C. Lancaster, PA	NDD	6
October 17	Frankie Moore	Lancaster A.C. Lancaster, PA	NDD	6
November 14	Kid Beebe	Lancaster A.C. Lancaster, PA	NDW	6
December 12	Kid Beebe	Lancaster A.C. Lancaster, PA	NDW	6
1908				
January 16	Kid Daly	Lancaster A.C. Lancaster, PA	NDW	6
February 20	Tommy O'Keefe	Lancaster A.C. Lancaster, PA	NDL	6
March 19	Percy Cove	Lancaster A.C. Lancaster, PA	NDL	6
April 16	Willie Lucas	Lancaster A.C. Lancaster, PA	NDD	6
April 25	Phil Griffin	Philadelphia A.C. Philadelphia, PA	NDL	6
October 15	Harry Kegel	Lancaster A.C. Lancaster, PA	W-TKO	2
November 19	George Decker	Lancaster A.C. Lancaster, PA	NDD	6

Year/Date	Opponent	City/State	Outcome	Rounds
December 17	Phil Griffin	Lancaster A.C. Lancaster, PA	NDW	6
1909				
January 14	Eddie McAvoy	Lancaster A.C. Lancaster, PA	NDL	6
February 4	Jack Britton	Lancaster A.C. Lancaster, PA	NDW	6
February 18	Kid Locke	Lancaster A.C. Lancaster, PA	NDD	6
February 23	Grover Hayes	Chestnut Street Auditorium Harrisburg, PA	NDW	6
March 4	Young Kid Broad	Lancaster A.C. Lancaster, PA	NDW	6
March 18	Jack Britton	Lancaster A.C. Lancaster, PA	NDD	6
March 27	Grover Hayes	National A.C. Philadelphia, PA	NDD	6
May 14	Tommy O'Keefe	Lancaster A.C. Lancaster, PA	NDW	6
October 14	Mike Fleming	Lancaster A.C. Lancaster, PA	NDW	6
November 11	Joe Sieger	Lancaster A.C. Lancaster, PA	NDD	6
November 25	Joe Hirst	National A.C. Philadelphia, PA	NDL NDD	6
December 2	Young Kid Broad	Lancaster A.C. Lancaster, PA	NDW	6
December 16	Kid Locke	Lancaster A.C. Lancaster, PA	NDW	6
December 20	Young Nitchie	Academy Hall Reading, PA	NDW	10
1910				
January 20	Joe Hirst	Lancaster A.C. Lancaster, PA	NDL	6
January 29	Mickey Gannon	National A.C. Philadelphia, PA	NDW	6
February 10	Tommy O'Keefe	Lancaster A.C. Lancaster, PA	NDW	6
February 12	Young Erne	National A.C. Philadelphia, PA	NDD NDL	6
February 16	Paddy Lavin	Academy Hall Reading, PA	NDD NDL	10
March 3	Young Nitchie	Lancaster A.C. Lancaster, PA	NDW	6
March 9	Jack Cardiff	Academy Hall Reading, PA	NDW	10

Year/Date	Opponent	City/State	Outcome	Rounds
March 15	Young Loughery	Douglas A.C. Philadelphia, PA	NDW	6
March 17	Joe Hirst	Lancaster A.C. Lancaster, PA	NDW	6
March 31	Young Erne	Lancaster A.C. Lancaster, PA	NDW	6
April 7	Young Loughrey	Academy Hall Reading, PA	NDD	10
April 15	Young Erne	Douglas A.C. Philadelphia, PA	NDW	6
April 21	Dick Nelson	New Haven, CT	DRAW	12
April 26	Frank Perron	Armory, Boston, MA	LOSS–DQ	2
April 30	Johnny Willetts	National A.C. Philadelphia, PA	NDW	6
May 4	Young Loughrey	Wilmington, DE	NDL	15
June 16	Joe Hirst	Lancaster A.C. Lancaster, PA	NDW	6
June 23	Young Loughrey	Lancaster A.C. Lancaster, PA	NDW	6
August 23	Harry Lewis	Armory Boston, MA	NDW	12
September 17	Harry Lewis	National A.C. Philadelphia, PA	NDW	6
September 28	Jimmy Dolan	Lancaster A.C. Lancaster, PA	W-TKO	4
October 1	Young Otto	National A.C. Philadelphia, PA	NDW	6
October 7	Young Loughrey	Nonpareil A.C. Philadelphia, PA	NDW	6
October 11	Tommy Quill	Armory A.A. Boston, MA.	W-KO	8
October 17	Jimmy Gardner	National A.C. Philadelphia, PA	NDW	6
October 27	Fred Corbett	Lancaster A.C. Lancaster, PA	W-TKO	3
October 29	Frank Klaus	National A.C. Philadelphia, PA	NDW	6
November 11	Frank Mantell	Rhode Island A.C. Thorton, RI	NDW	15

1911

Year/Date	Opponent	City/State	Outcome	Rounds
February 2	Battling Levinsky	Lancaster A.C. Lancaster, PA	NDW	6
February 4	Tom McMahon	National A.C. Philadelphia, PA	NDW	6
February 14	Frank Klaus	Armory A.A. Boston, MA	NDL	12

Leo F. Houck's Professional Fight Record

Year/Date	Opponent	City/State	Outcome	Rounds
February 23	Harry Mansfield	Lancaster A.C. Lancaster, PA	NDW	6
March 13	Harry Ramsey	American A.C. Philadelphia, PA	NDW	6
March 16	Battling Levinsky	Lancaster A.C. Lancaster, PA	NDW	6
May 3	Harry Lewis	Hippodrome Paris, France	W-PTS	20
June 16	Joe Thomas	Lancaster A.C. Lancaster, PA	NDW	6
September 16	George Chip	National A.C. Philadelphia, PA	NDW NDL	6
September 21	Frank Mantell	National S.C. NYC, NY	NDW	10
September 28	Harry Ramsey	Lancaster A.C. Lancaster, PA	NDW	6
October 18	Frank Klaus	American A.C. Philadelphia, PA	NDW NDL NDD	6
October 24	Battling Levinsky	Armory A.A. Boston, MA	NDW	12
November 3	Harry Ramsey	Nonpareil A.C. Philadelphia, PA	NDD	6
November 15	Buck Crouse	Duquesne Gardens Pittsburgh, PA	NDL	6
December 9	Buck Crouse	National A.C. Philadelphia, PA	NDW NDD	6

1912

Year/Date	Opponent	City/State	Outcome	Rounds
January 1	Jack Dillon	Auditorium Indianapolis, IN	L-TKO	6
April 20	Bob Moha	National A.C. Philadelphia, PA	NDW	6
April 23	Peck Miller	Lancaster A.C.	NDW	6
May 7	Buck Crouse	Pilgrim A.A. Boston, MA	NDL	12
May 23	Jack Fitzgerald	Lancaster A.C. Lancaster, PA	NDW	6
June 13	George Chip	Rossmere Park Lancaster, PA	NDW	6
September 19	Peck Miller	Lancaster A.C. Lancaster, PA	NDW	6
September 27	Billy Papke	Olympia A.C. Philadelphia, PA	NDW	6
October 9	Eddie McGoorty	National A.C. Philadelphia, PA	NDW	6
October 28	Jack Fitzgerald	Scranton, PA	NDW	6
November 8	Dave Smith	Olympia A.C. Philadelphia, PA	NDW NDD	6

Appendix

Year/Date	Opponent	City/State	Outcome	Rounds
November 15	Larry Williams	Lancaster A.C. Lancaster, PA	W-KO	4
November 25	Emmett "Kid" Wagner	Town Hall Scranton, PA	NDW NDD	6
1913				
January 15	Freddie Hicks	Lancaster A.C. Lancaster, PA	NDW	6
January 22	Jack Dillon	Olympia A.C. Philadelphia, PA	NDL NDD	6
February 10	Al Rogers	Lincoln A.C. Altoona, PA	NDW NDD	6
March 27	Dick Gilbert	Lancaster A.C. Lancaster, PA	NDW	6
May 7	George "KO" Brown	St. Nicholas Arena NYC, NY	NDW	10
May 29	Buck Crouse	Lancaster A.C. Lancaster, PA	NDW NDL	6
September 6	Tommy Bergin	National A.C. Philadelphia, PA	NDW	6
October 9	Jack Dillon	Rocky Springs Park Lancaster, PA	NDW NDD	6
November 15	George Chip	National A.C. Philadelphia, PA	NDW	6
December 20	Joe Borrell	National A.C. Philadelphia, PA	NDW	6
1914				
January 17	Joe Borrell	National A.C. Philadelphia, PA	NDL	6
February 23	Billy Murray	Coffroths Arena Daly City, CA	L-TKO	14
April 21	George Chip	Grand Opera House Youngstown, OH	NDW NDD NDL	12
September 7	Tommy Gavigan	Wright Field Youngstown, OH	W-TKO	11
November 14	Young Ahearn	National A.C. Philadelphia, PA	NDL	6
November 16	Emmett "Kid" Wagner	Lancaster A.C. Lancaster, PA	NDW NDL NDD	6
1915				
March 22	Jack Toland	Lancaster A.C. Lancaster, PA	W-KO	3
March 27	George Ashe	Irving A.C. Brooklyn, NY	NDW	10
March 30	Al Grayber	Fairmont A.C. Philadelphia, PA	NDW	6
April 8	George "KO" Brown	Bijou Theater Atlanta, GA	NDW	10

Year/Date	Opponent	City/State	Outcome	Rounds
April 22	Young Ahearn	Irving A.C. Brooklyn, NY	NDL	10
May 19	Frank Mantell	Rhode Island A.C. Providence, RI	NDW	12
May 26	Mike Gibbons	St. Nicholas Arena New York, NY	NDL	10
June 7	Young Ahearn	Capitol District Albany, NY	NDL NDW	10
July 26	Sailor Grande	Lancaster A.C. Lancaster, PA	NDD	6
September 10	Bert Kenny	New Polo A.C. New York, NY	NDW NDL	10
September 14	Young Herman Miller	Lancaster A.C. Lancaster, PA	W-KO	6
September 30	Johnny Howard	Lancaster A.C. Lancaster, PA	NDW	6
November 11	Bill Fleming	Meriden, CT	Never Occurred	—
November 15	Al Rogers	Frohsinn Hall Altoona, PA	NDW	6
November 16	Sailor Grande	Douglas A.C. Philadelphia, PA	NDL	6
November 22	Willie Baker	Olympia A.C. Philadelphia, PA	NDW	6
1916				
February 14	Billy Berger	Lancaster A.C. Lancaster, PA	NDW	6
February 29	Battling Brandt	York, PA	NDW	6
March 7	Eddie Revoire	Auditorium York, PA	NDL	6
March 13	K.O. Sullivan	Lancaster A.C. Lancaster, PA	NDW	6
March 29	Jack Reck	Orpheum Theater Harrisburg, PA	NDW	6
April 7	Young Herman Miller	Coliseum Hall York, PA	NDW	6
April 25	Ralph Erne	Coliseum Hall York, PA	NDW	6
May 15	Jack Reck	Lancaster, PA	NDW	6
December 9	Al Grayber	Power Auditorium Pittsburgh, PA	NDD	6
December 27	Fay Keiser	Cumberland, MD	NDW	10
1917				
January 21	Eddie Revoire	Lancaster A.C. Lancaster, PA	NDW	6
March 30	Dummy Ketchell	Lancaster A.C. Lancaster, PA	NDW	6
April 6	Tommy Burke	Lancaster, A.C. Lancaster, PA	NDW	6

Year/Date	Opponent	City/State	Outcome	Rounds
May 7	Jackie Clark	Lancaster, A.C. Lancaster, PA	NDW	6
May 16	Battling Levinsky	York, PA	NDL	6
May 22	See Saw Kelly	Lancaster A.C. Lancaster, PA	W-KO	3
September 18	Young Herman Miller	York, PA	NDW NDD	6
October 22	Jack McCarron	Lancaster A.C. Lancaster, PA	NDW	6
October 26	Willie Meehan	Philadelphia, PA	NDW	6
November 19	Buck Crouse	Lancaster A.C. Lancaster, PA	NDW	6
December 10	KO Willie Loughlin	Lancaster A.C. Lancaster, PA	NDW	6
December 25	George Ashe	Lancaster A.C Lancaster, PA	NDW	6

1918

Year/Date	Opponent	City/State	Outcome	Rounds
January 1	Chuck Wiggins	National A.C. Philadelphia, PA	NDW	6
February 22	Jack McCarron	Cambria A.C. Philadelphia, PA	NDW NDL NDD	6
March 4	Chuck Wiggins	Frank Erne's Gymnasium Lancaster, PA	NDW	6
March 11	Johnny Wilson	Douglas A.C. Chelsea, MA	NDW	12
April 15	Johnny Wilson	Douglas A.C. Chelsea, MA	NDL	12
April 23	Clay Turner	Frank Erne's Gymnasium Lancaster, PA	NDW	6
May 27	Gunboat Smith	Frank Erne's Gymnasium Lancaster, PA	NDW NDD	6
July 4	Jeff Smith	Frank Erne's Gymnasium Lancaster, PA	NDW	6
July 30	Pete Malone	Chester Armory Chester, PA	NDW	12
December 25	Battling Levinsky	Frank Erne's Gymnasium Lancaster, PA	NDL	6

1919

Year/Date	Opponent	City/State	Outcome	Rounds
January 14	Harry Greb	Arena Armory A.A. Boston, MA	NDL	12
January 20	Battling Kopin	Frank Erne's Gymnasium Lancaster, PA	W-KO	3

Year/Date	Opponent	City/State	Outcome	Rounds
February 2	Bob Grant	Frank Erne's Gymnasium Lancaster, PA	W-KO	1
February 20	Roddy MacDonald	Halifax, N.S. Canada	NDW NDD	15
February 24	Zulu Kid	Frank Erne's Gymnasium Lancaster, PA	NDW	6
March 6	Harry Greb	Fulton Opera House Lancaster, PA	NDL	6
March 14	Jack Clifford	Cambria A.C. Philadelphia, PA	NDW	6
March 25	Mike Gibbons	Coliseum Saint Louis, MO	NDL	6
March 28	Larry Williams	Orpheum Theater Harrisburg, PA	NDW	6
March 31	Al Theil	Frank Erne's Gymnasium Lancaster, PA	NDW	6
April 4	Joe Allison	Penns Grove A.C. Penns Grove, NJ	NDL	8
April 25	Harry Greb	Carney Auditorium Erie, PA	NDL	10
April 28	Larry Williams	Frank Erne's Gymnasium Lancaster, PA	NDW NDD	6
September 11	Bert Kenny	Atlantic City, NJ	NDW	8
October 6	KO Samson	Frank Erne's Gymnasium Lancaster, PA	NDW	6
November 24	KO Samson	Frank Erne's Gymnasium Lancaster, PA	NDW	6
December 12	Harry Applegate	York A.C. York, PA	W-KO	2
December 15	Bert Kenny	Frank Erne's Gymnasium Lancaster, PA	NDW	6
1920				
January 10	KO Samson	National A.C. Philadelphia, PA	NDW	6
January 21	Eddie Revoire	Olympia A.C. Philadelphia, PA	NDW	6
February 3	Roddy MacDonald	Armouries Halifax, N.S., Canada	NDL	15
March 11	KO Samson	Germantown A.C. Philadelphia, PA	NDW	6
March 16	Johnny Howard	Schutzen Park Bayonne, NJ	NDW	8

Year/Date	Opponent	City/State	Outcome	Rounds
May 10	Rudy Martinez	Frank Erne's Gymnasium Lancaster, PA	W-KO	6
May 15	KO Samson	Columbia Lancaster, PA	NDW	6
May 31	KO Sullivan	Railway Park Pottsville, PA	NDW	10
October 22	Frankie Farron	Frank Erne's Gymnasium Lancaster, PA	NDW	6
October 23	Fay Keiser	Roller Rink Cumberland, MD	NDD	10
November 12	KO Sullivan	Sportsman Club Camden, NJ	NDW	10
November 25	Gene Tunney	Olympia A.C. Philadelphia, PA	NDD NDL	6
November 29	Leo Leonard	Williamsport, PA	NDD	10
December 7	Gene Tunney	4th Armory Regiment Jersey City, NJ	NDL	10
1921				
May 21	Dan O'Dowd	Atlantic City, NJ	NDL	8
1922				
March 13	Sgt. Ray Smith	Frank Erne's Gymnasium Lancaster, PA	NDW	8
April 17	Lew Schupp	Frank Erne's Gymnasium Lancaster, PA	NDW	8
May 1	Young Herman Miller	Orpheum Theater York, PA	NDW	8
May 20	Kid Cardenas	Havana, Cuba	W-PTS	10
June 17	Santiago Esparraguera	Nuevo Fronton Havana, Cuba	W-KO	4
August 28	Jim Holland	Frank Erne's Gymnasium Lancaster, PA	NDW	8
October 2	Jackie Clark	Frank Erne's Gymnasium Lancaster, PA	NDW	8
October 23	Lew Schupp	Frank Erne's Gymnasium Lancaster, PA	NDW NDL	8
1923				
May 7	Buck Ashton	Frank Erne's Gymnasium Lancaster, PA	NDW	8
1926				
August 9	Sailor Jack Grady	Rossmere Park Lancaster, PA	W-TKO	3

Chapter Notes

Chapter 1

1. On May 6, 1886, the Ancient and Noble Order of the Knights of St. John was established in the United States by a special act of legislature. The Order of the Knights of St. John was introduced into the Gold Coast, now Ghana, in 1933. Meanwhile, in July 1992, the name was changed to the Knights of St. John International to reflect its global status. Running concurrently with the Knights and Ladies is the Cadets and Junior Auxiliaries. These are the nursery stages of the Order in which young boys and girls, as future leaders, are groomed to take over from the older Knights and Ladies. www.johncadet.freeservers.com.

2. Leo Houck's recollections and stories about his boxing career were chronicled and written by him for the *Lancaster Daily Intelligencer*, Lancaster, Pennsylvania. The newspaper column appeared periodically and was titled "My Twenty Years of Boxing." John Hauck Collection, MG-63, LancasterHistory.org.

3. The official date for Leo Houck's first professional fight with Carl Kreckel was October 1, 1902, and was validated by Leo's brother John Hauck during the 10th Annual Dinner of the Veterans Boxers Association. Harry Pegg, "Leo Houck," *The Veteran Boxer* (Summer 1945): pg. 2.

4. *Lancaster New Era*, Lancaster, Pennsylvania, July 17, 1926. Leo Houck joined the *Lancaster New Era* staff in 1926. He wrote a series of stories about his fights, which included personal views and previously unknown facts.

5. *Daily Intelligencer Journal*, Lancaster, Pennsylvania, January 23, 1950.

6. Interview with Joseph Hauck conducted by Randy L. Swope, 2015. This quote refers to Leo's devotion to assisting his mother after she was widowed.

7. *The Veteran Boxer*, "Leo Houck," by Harry Pegg, Summer Issue, 1945.

8. *Lancaster New Era*, July 17, 1926, Story written by Leo Houck.

9. Joseph and Edward Hauck recollected that Bob Fitzsimmons was Edward Hauck's favorite boxer during an interview conducted by Randy L. Swope, 2015.

10. Frank (Frankie) Hauck suffered with polio while he was a youngster. His mother constantly massaged his stricken legs, which prevented him from losing his ability to walk. Frank had a permanent limp after his recuperation from polio, but learned how to box and accrued a record of approximately fifteen bouts. Later, Frank entered the military and served during World War I. Interview with Edward and Joseph Hauck conducted by Randy L. Swope, 2015.

11. *Daily Intelligence Journal*, January 30, 1950.

12. *Lancaster New Era*, December 12, 1950. The story was written by Johnny Hauck, Leo's youngest brother.

13. Interview with Edward and Joseph Hauck conducted by Randy L. Swope, 2015.

14. The Lancaster Red Roses were part of the Tri-State League from 1905 to 1912, and again in 1914. Leo played for the Red Roses, Class-Level B, in 1911 at age twenty-two. Leo's statistics for 1911 included 10 games played, 32 at bats, 4 hits, and a cumulative batting average of .125. Home games were played at Stumpf Field in Lancaster, Pennsylvania. https://www.baseball-reference.com/minors/team.cgi?id=98c4b495.

15. German Immigration to the U.S. in the 1800s, State Historical Society of Wisconsin, Madison, 1977.

16. Marc Oliff, "Cabbage-Hill Against the World: Profile of a Neighborhood," *Journal of the Lancaster County Historical Society* 86, No. 4 (1982): pg. 122.

17. John Davies, "Memories of 'The Hill,'" *Journal of the Lancaster County Historical Society* 101, No. 4 (2000): pg. 172.

18. Joseph Hauck explained that the neighborhood offered everything needed for daily living, thereby eliminating any unnecessary trips into downtown Lancaster. Interview with Joseph Hauck, conducted by Randy L. Swope, 2015. See also the *Journal of the Lancaster County Historical Society* 101, No. 4 (2000).

19. Interview with Joseph and Edward Hauck conducted by Randy L. Swope, 2015.

20. Oliff, "Cabbage-Hill Against the World," pg. 125.

21. St. Mary's Catholic Church was located at the corner of Prince and Vine Streets. The new church, St. Joseph's Catholic Church, was located nearby on St. Joseph's and West Strawberry Street.

22. *A History of Saint Joseph's Roman Catholic Church, Lancaster, Pennsylvania, 1849–1999*, Lancaster Historical Society, Lancaster, Pennsylvania.
23. Interview with Joseph Hauck conducted by Randy L. Swope, 2015.
24. *A History of Saint Joseph's Roman Catholic Church*.
25. Andrew O'Toole, *Sweet William: The Life of Billy Conn* (Bloomington: University of Illinois Press, 2008), pg. 130.
26. Ernest R. May and the editors of *Life*, *The Progressive Era*, vol. 9 (New York: Time Inc., 1964), pg. 18.
27. Jodelle L. Bryant, "From Vaudeville to the Silver Screen: Popular Entertainment in Lancaster, 1900–1930," *Journal of the Lancaster County Historical Society* 95, No. 4 (1993): pg. 110.
28. Ibid.
29. Hamilton Watch Company program titled "A Tribute to an Illustrious Hamiltonian, Leo Hauck," John Hauck Collection, MG-63, LancasterHistory.org.
30. Joe Hauck verified his (Edward's) grandfather's work schedule by accident when recycling some leather-bound timekeeping record books from the Hamilton Watch Company. Edward Hauck's timekeeping record showed a seven-day work week consisting of twelve-hour daily shifts. His payment for a week's work amounted to $9.45. Interview with Joseph Hauck conducted by Randy L. Swope, 2015.
31. Davies, "Memories of 'The Hill,'" a recollection from Mrs. Clara Schwartz, a resident of Cabbage-Hill, pg. 172.

Chapter 2

1. *Lancaster New Era*, July 17, 1926. Story written by Leo Houck.
2. "My Twenty Years of Boxing," by Leo Houck, John Hauck Collection, MG-63, LancasterHistory.org.
3. Tom O'Hara compiled a record of 22 bouts: Won (11), Lost (9), Draw (1), www.boxrec.com.
4. Article from "Hauck's Corner," titled "The Grim Reaper Strikes," by Johnny Hauck. John Hauck Collection, MG-63, LancasterHistory.org.
5. Ibid.
6. *Daily Intelligencer Journal*, January 23, 1950.
7. John Hauck worked at the Armstrong Cork Factory in Lancaster. As a youngster he boxed a total of 10 fights, all six-rounders. At 15 years old he managed a young boxer named Young Metz. Later as an adult John coached the St. Joseph's Church boxing teams. John Hauck wrote and reported on boxing for the local Lancaster newspapers and chronicled Leo's boxing career, as well as his coaching career at Penn State. John corresponded with professional boxers throughout the world and was active in many veteran boxing organizations. These accomplishments earned him the distinction of being recognized as an authority on the subject of boxing, and international recognition as a boxing historian. *Lancaster Intelligencer Journal*, January 7, 1970.
8. *Daily Intelligencer Journal*, John Hauck Collection, MG-63, LancasterHistory.org.
9. *The Veteran Boxer*, "Leo Houck," by Harry Pegg, Summer Issue, 1945, pg. 2.
10. James B. Roberts and Alexander G. Skutt, *The Boxing Register* (Ithaca, NY: McBooks Press, 2006), pg. 152.
11. Johnny Hauck, "The Grim Reaper Strikes."
12. *Daily Intelligencer Journal*, John Hauck Collection, MG-63, LancasterHistory.org.
13. Harry H. Hensel was a boxing promoter and sportswriter/editor for the *Lancaster Daily Intelligencer*. H. Walter Schlichter was a boxing promoter, referee, and sports editor for the *Philadelphia Item*, Philadelphia, Pennsylvania. Both men promoted fights for the Lancaster A.C. boxing shows. The Lancaster A.C. fights were held at the Maennerchor Hall in Lancaster on Prince Street.
14. "My Twenty Years of Boxing," *Lancaster Daily Intelligencer*, John Hauck Collection, MG-63, LancasterHistory.org.
15. *Lancaster New Era*, July 17, 1926. Story written by Leo Houck.
16. "My Twenty Years of Boxing," *Lancaster Daily Intelligencer*, Lancaster, Pennsylvania, John Hauck Collection, MG-63, LancasterHistory.org.
17. Interview with Joseph and Edward Hauck, conducted by Randy L. Swope, 2015.
18. Johnny Hauck, "The Grim Reaper Strikes," John Hauck Collection, MG-63, LancasterHistory.org.
19. Bill Paxton, *The Fearless Harry Greb* (Jefferson, NC: McFarland, 2009), pg. 11.
20. Ibid.
21. Roberts and Skutt, *The Boxing Register*, pgs. 54–55.
22. Charles A. Lindbergh, *The Spirit of St. Louis* (New York: Charles Scribner's Sons, 1953), Preface.
23. Pennsylvania Department of State, State Athletic Commission, www.dos.pa.gov.

Chapter 3

1. Jersey Jones, "Leo the Lion," *The Ring* (April 1950): pg. 26.
2. Arthur "Bugs," "The Champ of Chumps, *Everlast Boxing Record 1924* (New York; Everlast Sport Publishing), pg. 21.
3. *Harrisburg Telegraph*, Harrisburg, Pennsylvania, May 18, 1906.
4. *Harrisburg Telegraph*, May 29, 1906. Gilmore Day was named after Patrick S. Gilmore, "Father of the American Band" (December 1829–September 1892). www.ouririshheritage.org
5. Roberts and Skutt, *The Boxing Register*, pgs. 74–75.
6. "Leo Houck Tells of First Kayo Thrill," *Lancaster New Era*, May 15, 1926.
7. Sportswriters reported that Leo occasionally took it easy on an opponent when ahead on points. Leo did let up on some opponents when he realized that he had enough points to win or knew the decision would favor him. Discussions with Leo's sons, Edward and Joseph, corroborated what the sportswriters suspected. Their father admitted at home that it was not necessary to punish the less skilled oppo-

nent when leading overwhelmingly on points and there was no threat of being knocked out. In addition, Leo recognized that most fighters had families to feed, so he saw no point in injuring an opponent who may have to fight again the same week. Interview with Edward and Joseph Hauck, conducted by Randy L. Swope, 2015.

8. A technical knockout or TKO differs from a true knockout; it usually occurs when a boxer is deemed unfit to continue and the referee ends the bout. This may be to protect a boxer who is being unduly punished by his opponent, or as a result of an injury such as a bad cut, broken nose, or broken jaw. Sometimes the boxer's second, trainer or manager may ask the referee to stop it, or throw in the towel; or the boxer himself may retire on his own volition. www.boxrec.com.

9. *Harrisburg Telegraph*, March 25, 1907.

10. *Harrisburg Daily Independent*, April 5, 1907. To "shade" is to have the better of the boxing opponent: www.boxrec.com.

11. *Harrisburg Telegraph*, April 26, 1907.

12. A boxer earns points, from officials, generally ringside judges, during a bout through punches to an opponent's head and body, knockdowns, defense, and the like. A boxer can also lose on points. A boxer who accumulates more points at the bout's conclusion wins the decision or a win on points—unless the bout ends by knockout, technical knockout, or no contest. www.boxrec.com.

13. *Courier*, Harrisburg, Pennsylvania, June 11, 1907.

14. *Harrisburg Telegraph*, June 8, 1907.

15. *Courier*, November 10, 1907.

16. The wind-up is the final boxing match of a boxing show, which occurs after the conclusion of all the preliminary bouts during the same show. The wind-up is sometimes called the "main event."

17. *Harrisburg Telegraph*, November 15, 1907.

18. *Harrisburg Daily Independent*, November 15, 1907. Leo was awarded the win on points.

19. *Harrisburg Daily Independent*, November 16, 1907.

20. *Courier*, November 24, 1907.

21. *Courier*, December 1, 1907.

22. *Courier*, November 24, 1907.

23. *Courier*, December 1, 1907.

24. Newspaper sportswriters of the early 1900s often described the Philadelphia boxers as "Quaker City Lads" or "Quaker City Boys" because Pennsylvania was settled in the 17th century by Quakers, led by William Penn.

Chapter 4

1. *Harrisburg Telegraph*, January 17, 1908.
2. *Courier*, February 9, 1908.
3. "Kid Beebe," www.boxrec.com.
4. *Harrisburg Daily Independent*, February 21, 1908.
5. *Courier*, March 15, 1908.
6. *Lancaster New Era*, 1926.
7. *Harrisburg Telegraph*, March 20, 1908.
8. Willie "Kid Lucas," Lightweight, Record: 58-20-22, with 11 KO: www.phillyboxinghistory.com.
9. *Harrisburg Telegraph*, April 17, 1908.
10. *Courier*, October 18, 1908.
11. *Courier*, November 15, 1908.
12. *Harrisburg Telegraph*, November 20, 1908.
13. *Harrisburg Telegraph*, December 18, 1908.
14. *Harrisburg Telegraph*, January 15, 1909.
15. *Ibid.*
16. Leo Houck's Ring Record, BoxRec, www.boxrec.com; IBRO, www.ibroresearch.com.
17. *Boston Daily Globe*, Boston, Massachusetts, February 5, 1909.
18. The *Boston Daily Globe* and the *Harrisburg Telegraph* both reported the fight as a win for Leo Houck.
19. *Harrisburg Daily Independent*, February 19, 1909.
20. *Harrisburg Telegraph*, February 19 1909.
21. *Lancaster New Era*, May 22, 1926.
22. Jim Driscoll, a champion featherweight from Cardiff, Wales (1880–1924), amassed a ring record of 53 wins, 4 losses, and 6 draws during his career. Roberts and Skutt, *The Boxing Register*, pgs. 112–113.
23. *Harrisburg Telegraph*, February 23, 1909.
24. *Harrisburg Daily Independent*, February 24, 1909.
25. *Lancaster New Era*, May 15, 1926.
26. Jack Britton, BoxRec, www.boxrec.com.
27. Semi-wind-up is the fight prior to the wind-up or main event.
28. *Pittsburgh Daily Post*, Pittsburgh, Pennsylvania, March 29, 1909.
29. Tommy O'Keefe (Thomas Crilly), Philadelphia, Pennsylvania, lightweight, active from 1905 to 1916. Ring Record, 78-35-24, with 8 KO. www.phillyboxinghistory.com.
30. *Harrisburg Telegraph*, May 15, 1909.
31. Roberts and Skutt, *The Boxing Register*, pgs. 55–255. References the total bout schedules for the "Old Timers." There are numerous examples of boxers who fit the criteria of fighting once a week for any given year.
32. *Courier*, November 7, 1909.
33. *Courier*, November 21, 1909.
34. A journeyman is a boxer who has little or no expectations of winning his fights, thus he is said to be "along for the journey." They are generally competent boxers who possess solid boxing skills and/or the ability to absorb punishment. Often they are aspiring novices or even prospects, but are found to have limitations that relegate them to the role of journeyman.
35. *Harrisburg Daily Independent*, November 12, 1909.
36. *Courier*, November 28, 1909.
37. *Harrisburg Telegraph*, December 7, 1909.
38. Leo Houck Ring Record, www.boxrec.com.
39. *Courier*, December 26, 1909. The *Philadelphia Item* referenced, Leo Houck, www.boxrec.com.
40. "Young Kid Broad," or William Broad, from Philadelphia, had a lengthy boxing career extending from 1905 to 1921. www.boxrec.com.

41. *Harrisburg Telegraph*, December 17, 1909.
42. *Reading Times,* Reading, Pennsylvania, December 18, 1909.
43. The *Reading Times*, Reading, Pennsylvania, December 21, 1909.
44. *Ibid.*
45. *Lancaster New Era,* May 22, 1926.
46. *Harrisburg Telegraph,* January 6, 1910. Quinsy is an inflammation of the tonsils, accompanied by the formation of pus. *Webster's Dictionary, Unabridged*, 2nd ed. (World Publishing, 1957), pg. 1481.

Chapter 5

1. Allen Bordner, "Boxing: A Jewish Sport," December 16, 2007. www.myjewishlearning.com.
2. *Harrisburg Telegraph,* January 21, 1910.
3. *Ibid.*
4. Roberts and Skutt, *The Boxing Register,* pgs. 198–199.
5. John Hauck Collection, MG-63, LancasterHistory.org.
6. Leo Houck, "My Twenty Years of Boxing," *Lancaster Daily Intelligencer,* April 5, 1921.
7. *Harrisburg Telegraph,* February 4, 1910.
8. "Houck Tells of Three Bouts with 'Yi Yi' Erne," *Lancaster New Era,* July 3, 1926.
9. *Ibid.*
10. *Reading Times,* February 11, 1910.
11. *Courier,* February 13, 1910.
12. "Houck Tells of Three Bouts with 'Yi Yi' Erne," *Lancaster New Era,* July 3, 1926.
13. *Pittsburgh Daily Post,* February 14, 1910.
14. *Reading Times,* February 14, 1910.
15. Leo Houck, "My Twenty Years of Boxing," *Lancaster Daily Intelligencer,* April 5, 1921.
16. *Daily Intelligence Journal,* January 23, 1950. A second is a person other than a coach who stands in a boxer's corner during a bout and gives him advice and assistance between rounds. A team of seconds is also called the boxer's corner. www.boxrec.com.
17. *Reading Times,* February 17, 1910.
18. *Harrisburg Telegraph,* February 17, 1910.
19. Leo Houck, "My Twenty Years of Boxing," *Lancaster Daily Intelligencer,* April 5, 1921.
20. *Reading Times,* March 10, 1910.
21. James J. Jefferies, heavyweight champion from 1899 to 1905. Jefferies was considered one of the greatest heavyweights in boxing history. Roberts and Skutt, *The Boxing Register,* pgs. 144–145.
22. Leo Houck, "My Twenty Years of Boxing," *Lancaster Daily Intelligencer,* April 8, 1921.
23. *Lancaster New Era,* December 18, 1926.
24. *Harrisburg Telegraph,* March 16, 1910.
25. The report by the *Public Ledger* was undated and appeared as an excerpt in Leo's column "My Twenty Years of Boxing," *Lancaster Daily Intelligencer,* April 8, 1921.
26. *Harrisburg Telegraph,* March 17, 1910.
27. Leo Houck, "My Twenty Years of Boxing," *Lancaster Daily Intelligencer,* April 8, 1921.
28. *Harrisburg Telegraph,* March 29, 1910. The Jefferies-Johnson fight on July 4, 1910, was a heavyweight world championship fight held in Reno, Nevada. The current champion, James Jefferies, was defeated and knocked out in the fifteenth round. Leo Houck did not fight in any of the preliminary bouts for the Jefferies-Johnson bout. Roberts and Skutt, pgs. 144–145.
29. *Harrisburg Telegraph,* April 1, 1910.
30. *Lancaster New Era,* July 3, 1926.
31. Leo Houck. "My Twenty Years of Boxing," *Lancaster New Era,* July 3, 1926.
32. Leo Houck. "My Twenty Years of Boxing," *Lancaster New Era,* April 15, 1921.
33. *Lancaster New Era,* July 3, 1910.
34. *Lancaster Daily Intelligencer,* April 15, 1921.
35. Young Erne, BoxRec, www.boxrec.com.
36. Dick Nelson, BoxRec, www.boxrec.com.
37. *Lancaster New Era,* September 4, 1926.
38. Frank Perron, BoxRec, www.boxrec.com
39. Leo Houck was never fond of extended stays away from his family during his boxing career. He admitted it made him homesick. Interview with Edward and Joseph Hauck conducted by Randy L. Swope during 2015.
40. *Harrisburg Daily Independent,* April 27, 1910.
41. Frank Perron, BoxRec, www.boxrec.com.
42. *Harrisburg Daily Independent,* April 30, 1910.
43. *Lancaster New Era,* October 23, 1926.
44. William Mellody, BoxRec, www.boxrec.com.
45. *Harrisburg Telegraph,* May 5, 1910.
46. *Harrisburg Telegraph,* May 9.1910.
47. *Harrisburg Telegraph,* May 19, 1910.
48. "Houck's Death Is Blow to Lancaster. He Was One of Boxing's Greatest," by George Kirchner, John Hauck Collection, MG-63, LancasterHistory.org.
49. *Harrisburg Telegraph,* June 17, 1910.
50. Leo Houck, "My Twenty Years of Boxing," *Lancaster Daily Intelligencer,* April 19, 1921.
51. *Lancaster New Era,* September 11, 1926.
52. *Harrisburg Telegraph,* June 22, 1910.
53. *Lancaster Daily Intelligencer,* April 19, 1921.
54. Leo Houck, "My Twenty Years of Boxing," *Lancaster Daily Intelligencer,* April 19, 1921.
55. *Ibid.*
56. *Harrisburg Telegraph,* August 22, 1910.
57. Harry Lewis, BoxRec, www.boxrec.com.
58. *Harrisburg Telegraph,* August 22, 1910.
59. The John Hauck Collection, MG-63, LancasterHistory.org.
60. *Harrisburg Telegraph,* August 24, 1910.
61. Leo Houck, "My Twenty Years of Boxing," *Lancaster Daily Intelligencer,* April 19, 1921.
62. *Harrisburg Telegraph,* August 24, 1910.
63. *Lancaster Daily Intelligencer,* April 22, 1910.
64. *Harrisburg Telegraph,* September 16, 1910.
65. Leo Houck, "My Twenty Years of Boxing," *Lancaster Daily Intelligencer,* April 22, 1921.
66. Joe Sieger, BoxRec, www.boxrec.com.
67. *Harrisburg Telegraph,* September 29, 1910.
68. *Ibid.*
69. Arthur Susskind, BoxRec, www.boxrec.com.
70. Leo Houck, "My Twenty Years of Boxing," *Lancaster Daily Intelligencer,* April 22, 1921.
71. A Sunday punch is a slang term for a boxer's

best calculated or usually effective punch. BoxRec, www.boxrec.com.

72. From the movie *Cool Hand Luke* (1967) starring Paul Newman and George Kennedy, directed by Stuart Rosenberg and produced by Gordon Carrol for Warner Bros.–Seven Arts Studio. Turner Classic Movies, www.tcm.com.

73. *Lancaster Daily Intelligencer*, April 22, 1921.

74. *Lancaster New Era*, December 18, 1926.

75. *Harrisburg Telegraph*, October 12, 1910.

76. W.C. Heinz and Nathan Ward, *The Book of Boxing* (New York: Bishop Books, 1992), pg. 62. Paraphrased from Dempsey-Carpentier, by Irvin S. Cobb, "He makes a xylophone of the challenger's short ribs."

77. *Harrisburg Telegraph*, October 12, 1910.

78. Roberts and Skutt, pg. 153.

79. Nat Fleisher, *50 Years at Ringside* (New York: Fleet, 1958), pg. 281.

80. *Scranton Truth*, Scranton, Pennsylvania, October 18, 1910.

81. *Washington Post*, Washington, D.C., November 27, 1910.

82. *Delaware County Times*, Chester, Pennsylvania, October 19, 1910; *Harrisburg Telegraph*, Harrisburg, Pennsylvania, October 18, 1910.

83. A tune-up is a relatively insignificant bout that a boxer engages in to try out his reflexes and skills, usually in preparation for a forthcoming bout of greater importance. www.boxrec.com.

84. Fleisher, *50 Years at Ringside*, pg. 260.

85. *Boston Daily Globe*, October 28, 1910.

86. Fleisher, pg. 260. Sports epithet coined by Tad McGeehan, which referred to all boxers in general.

87. *Lancaster Sunday News*, November 27, 1960.

88. *Ibid.*

89. *Lancaster New Era*, November 13, 1926.

90. *Boston Daily Globe*, November 12, 1910.

91. *Harrisburg Telegraph*, December 5, 1910.

92. *Pittsburgh Daily Post*, January 4, 1911.

Chapter 6

1. *New York Times*, December 25, 1910.

2. *Washington Post*, January 15, 1911.

3. Roberts and Skutt, *The Boxing Register*, pg. 160.

4. *Harrisburg Telegraph*, December 12, 1910.

5. *York Daily*, York, Pennsylvania, January 14, 1911.

6. Jack Cavanaugh, *Tunney* (New York: Random House, 2006), pgs. 93, 119.

7. *Harrisburg Telegraph*, February 3, 1911.

8. *New Castle Era*, February 6, 1911.

9. *Ibid.*

10. *Ibid.*

11. *Ibid.*

12. *New Castle News*, March 21, 1911.

13. Thomas McMahon, BoxRec, www.boxrec.com.

14. Nat Fleisher, *The Ring Record Book and Boxing Encyclopedia* (New York: The Ring Bookshop, 1955), pg. 96.

15. *Boston Globe*, February 15, 1911.

16. Fleisher, *Ring Record Book*, pg. 96.

17. *Harrisburg Telegraph*, February 15, 1911.

18. *Harrisburg Telegraph*, February 22, 1911.

19. Leonard Maltin, Spencer Green, and Rob Edelman, eds., *Leonard Maltin's Classic Movie Guide* (New York: Plume, 2010), pg. 736.

20. *Lancaster New Era*, August 28, 1926.

21. Leo's younger brother Frankie appeared on the undercard for the same boxing show and lost to Tatters Lyle of Columbia.

22. *Harrisburg Telegraph*, February 18, 1911.

23. *Washington Post*, February 19, 1911.

24. *Wilkes-Barre Record*, March 2, 1911.

25. Harry Ramsey fought and lost to middleweight notables Joe Thomas, Jack Fitzgerald, Tommy Sullivan, Eddie McGoorty, Bob Moha, and Jack Dillon. BoxRec, www.boxrec.com.

26. *Harrisburg Telegraph*, March 14, 1911.

27. *Harrisburg Telegraph*, March 10, 1911.

28. Hugo Kelly, BoxRec, www.boxrec.com.

29. *Harrisburg Telegraph*, March 17, 1911.

30. The RMS *Lusitania* was torpedoed and sunk by a German U-Boat on May 15, 1915, during World War I. www.history.com.

31. *Harrisburg Telegraph*, May 3, 1911.

32. *Ibid.*

33. "Leo Houck Is Now World's Champion," *Philadelphia Public Ledger*, MG-63, John Hauck Collection, LancasterHistory.org.

34. *Parisian News & Notes*, Paris, France, May 13, 1911. John Hauck Collection, MG-63, LancasterHistory.org.

35. *Ibid.*, John Hauck Collection, MG-63.

36. *Lancaster New Era*, May 3, 1957.

37. The round-by-round description was excerpted from two sources: *Parisian News & Notes*, by special correspondent F.H. Lucas, May 13, 1911, and the *Lancaster New Era*, in an article that recounted the entire fight as reported by *The Mirror of Life*, London, England, May 3, 1957.

38. *Lancaster New Era*, May 3, 1911.

39. The American press never endorsed Leo as the new middleweight champion of the world after his victory over Lewis. In fact, Lewis fought primarily as a welterweight but did defeat some middleweight opponents while in Europe and France. The Lewis-Houck fight was a middleweight bout and both fighters weighed in at 158 pounds. However, the match was not a middleweight championship bout. The referee announced Leo as the new world's' middleweight champion after the fight, but American sportswriters knew that Leo needed to defeat Billy Papke in order to claim the middleweight title.

40. William H. Rocap, "Leo Houck Is Now World's Champion," *Public Ledger*, John Hauck Collection, MG-63, LancasterHistory.org.

41. Interview with Edward Hauck and Joseph Hauck conducted by Randy L. Swope during 2015.

42. *Parisian News & Notes*, May 13, 1911.

43. *Williamsport Sun-Gazette*, Williamsport, Pennsylvania, May 9, 1911.

44. *Ibid.*

45. *Harrisburg Telegraph*, May 19, 1911.
46. Joe Thomas was identified incorrectly by the *Harrisburg Telegraph* as a former middleweight champion. He may have been a welterweight champion and had achieved significant victories in 1906 over Honey Melody and Harry Lewis. BoxRec, www.boxrec.com.
47. *Harrisburg Telegraph*, June 16, 1911.
48. *Harrisburg Telegraph*, June 20, 1911.
49. *Lebanon Courier and Semi-Weekly Report*, Lebanon, Pennsylvania, June 6, 1911.
50. *Harrisburg Telegraph*, June 10, 1911.
51. *Ibid*.
52. *Harrisburg Telegraph*, July 25, 1911.
53. *Harrisburg Telegraph*, September 13, 1911.
54. *Harrisburg Telegraph*, September 18, 1911.
55. *Pittsburgh Post-Gazette*, September 17, 1911.
56. *New York Times*, September 21, 1911.
57. *Harrisburg Telegraph*, September 22, 1911.
58. *Ibid*.
59. *Harrisburg Telegraph*, September 26, 1911.
60. Fleisher, *50 Years at Ringside*, pg. 260. The humorous sports epithet "Cauliflower Industry" was coined by Bill McGeehan, sports editor for the *New York Herald Tribune*.
61. *Harrisburg Telegraph*, September 29, 1911.
62. Frank Klaus, BoxRec,www.boxrec.com.
63. *Harrisburg Daily Independent*, October 19, 1911; *Harrisburg Telegraph*, Harrisburg, Pennsylvania, October 19, 1911.
64. *Pittsburgh Daily Post*, October 19, 1911; *Pittsburgh Post-Gazette*, Pittsburgh, Pennsylvania, October 19, 1911.
65. *Harrisburg Daily Independent*, October 19, 1911.
66. *Ibid*.
67. Fleisher, *50 Years at Ringside*, pg. 260.
68. *Boston Globe*, October 25, 1911.
69. *Harrisburg Daily Independent*, October, 30, 1911.
70. *York Daily*, November 4, 1911.
71. Billie Papke, BoxRec,www.boxrec.com.
72. Buck Crouse, BoxRec, www.boxrec.com.
73. *Harrisburg Telegraph*, November 8, 1911.
74. *Altoona Tribune*, Altoona, Pennsylvania, November 9, 1911.
75. *New Castle News*, November 16, 1911.
76. *Boston Daily Globe*, November 16, 1911.
77. *Harrisburg Telegraph*, December 11, 1911.
78. *Boston Daily Globe*, December 10, 1911.
79. Roberts and Skutt, *The Boxing Register*, pgs. 84–85.
80. *Harrisburg Telegraph*, December 20, 1911.

Chapter 7

1. *Pittsburgh Daily Post*, December 31, 1911.
2. *Harrisburg Telegraph*, January 12, 1912.
3. *Allentown Democrat*, Allentown, Pennsylvania, January 25, 1912.
4. Interview with Edward Hauck and Joseph Hauck conducted by Randy L. Swope during 2015.
5. Georges Carpentier became the European middleweight champion on February 29, 1912, with a win over Jim Sullivan. BoxRec, www.boxrec.com.
6. The *Delaware Daily Times,* Chester, Pennsylvania, February 24, 1912.
7. In retrospect, Leo's indecisiveness about a return trip to France during 1912 made little sense. A fight with Georges Carpentier would have produced a capacity crowd at the Hippodrome in Paris and earned Leo the largest purse of his career thus far.
8. *Evening Report*, Lebanon, Pennsylvania, March 1, 1912.
9. Interview with Edward Hauck and Joseph Hauck conducted by Randy L. Swope, 2015.
10. *Lancaster New Era*, June 19, 1926.
11. Some boxing registers list the April 12 bout scheduled with Peck Miller as a newspaper-decision win for Leo while other sources do not list the fight. The newspaper archives do not report a cancellation for the April 12 fight. Conversely, there is no newspaper report that describes or provides an outcome for an April 12 contest.
12. *Pittsburgh Post-Gazette*, April 22, 1912.
13. *Lancaster New Era*, October 16, 1926.
14. *Harrisburg Telegraph*, April 16, 1912.
15. Buck Crouse, BoxRec, www.boxrec.com.
16. *Altoona Tribune*, May 10, 1912.
17. *Pittsburgh Daily Post*, May 8, 1912.
18. *Pittsburgh Post-Gazette*, May 10, 1912
19. *Altoona Tribune*, May 10, 1912.
20. *Pittsburgh Daily Post*, May 12, 1912.
21. *Altoona Tribune*, May 10, 1912.
22. *Pittsburgh Post-Gazette*, May 10, 1912.
23. *Harrisburg Telegraph*, May 15, 1912.
24. *Harrisburg Telegraph*, May 17, 1912.
25. Jack Fitzgerald, BoxRec, www.boxrec.com.
26. *Lebanon Daily News*, May 24, 1912.
27. *Lebanon Daily News*, May 31, 1912.
28. *Harrisburg Telegraph*, June 14, 1912.
29. Interview with Joseph Hauck conducted by Randy L. Swope, 2015.
30. Peck Miller, BoxRec,www.boxrec.com.
31. *Harrisburg Daily Independent*, September 20, 1912.
32. Fleisher, *Ring Record Book*, pg. 96.
33. *Delaware County Daily Times*, September 24, 1912.
34. *Lebanon Daily News*, September 17, 1912.
35. *Lancaster Sunday News*, September 23, 1962.
36. *Ibid*.
37. *Ibid*.
38. *Washington Post*, September 28, 1912.
39. Eddie McGoorty, BoxRec,www.boxrec.com.
40. *Lancaster New Era*, November 6, 1926.
41. "Mike Gibbon may be carrying the coveted prize around in his physique hidden in his shift form and protected by two automatic-like hands." *Allentown Democrat*, October 19, 1912.
42. *Scranton Truth*, October 29, 1912.
43. Dave Smith, BoxRec, www.boxrec.com.
44. *Scranton Truth*, November 9, 1912.
45. Herbert G. Goldman, *Boxing: A Worldwide Record of Bouts and Boxers* (Jefferson, NC: McFar-

land, 2012), pg. 575, lists the Dave Smith–Leo Houck bout as a draw.
46. *Harrisburg Telegraph*, November 13, 912.
47. *Wilkes-Barre Record*, November 16, 1912.
48. *Wilkes-Barre Record*, November 28, 1912.
49. Goldman, *Boxing: A Worldwide Record of Bouts and Boxers*, p. 576, lists the fight as a win for Leo Houck.
50. *Wilkes-Barre Record*, November, 22, 1912.
51. *Allentown Democrat*, December 6, 1912.
52. *Scranton Republican*, December 12, 1912.
53. *Harrisburg Telegraph*, January 16, 1913.
54. *Ibid.*
55. *Reading Times*, January 16, 1913.
56. *York Daily Record*, January 16, 1913.
57. Jack Dillon, BoxRec, www.boxrec.com.
58. *Harrisburg Telegraph*, January 20, 1913.
59. *Allentown Leader*, January 23, 1913.
60. *Harrisburg Telegraph*, January 23, 1913.
61. *Harrisburg Daily Independent*, January 23, 1913.
62. A "Great White Hope" was an up-and-coming white boxer, whom white people hoped would reclaim the heavyweight title from a black champion. www.oxforddictionaries.com.
63. Johnny Hauck, "In This Corner," *Lancaster Independent*, February 8, 1938.
64. *Ibid.* The Philly sportswriter mentioned in the article was not identified.
65. *Evening Report*, February 8, 1913.
66. Al Rogers, BoxRec,www.boxrec.com.
67. *Reading Times*, February 12, 1913.
68. *Scranton Truth*, March 4, 1913.
69. *Courier*, March 2, 1913.
70. *Evening Report*, March 21, 1913.
71. Dick Gilbert, BoxRec, www.boxrec.com.
72. *Harrisburg Telegraph*, March 24, 1913.
73. *Harrisburg Telegraph*, March 28, 1913.
74. *New Castle News*, April 28, 1913.
75. *Pittsburgh Post-Gazette*, April 15, 1913.
76. *Harrisburg Telegraph*, April 1, 1913.
77. *Allentown Democrat*, May 8, 1913.
78. *Harrisburg Daily Independent*, May 27, 1913.
79. *Harrisburg Daily Independent*, May 21, 1913.
80. Buck Crouse, BoxRec, www.boxrec.com.
81. *Pittsburgh Press*, May 23, 1913.
82. *Harrisburg Telegraph*, May 30, 1913.
83. *Pittsburgh Daily Post*, May 31, 1913.
84. *Reading Times*, June 26, 1913.
85. *Altoona Tribune*, September, 6, 1913.
86. Tommy Bergin, BoxRec,www.boxrec.com.
87. *Allentown Leader*, September 3, 1913.
88. *Harrisburg Telegraph*, September 8, 1913.
89. *Reading Times*, October 2, 1913.
90. *Harrisburg Telegraph*, September 30, 1913.
91. *Harrisburg Telegraph*, October 10, 1913.
92. Alexander Johnson, *Ten and Out* (New York: Ives Washburn, 1927), pg. 292. The second Chip-Klaus fight occurred on December 23, 1913.
93. *Wilkes-Barre Record*, November 17, 1913.
94. *Scranton Republican*, November 17, 1913.
95. *Scranton Truth*, November 17, 1913.
96. *Allentown Leader*, January 3, 1914.
97. *Allentown Democrat*, November 18, 1913.
98. *Pittsburgh Post-Gazette*, December 29, 1913.
99. Joe Borrell, BoxRec, www.boxrec.com.
100. *Allentown Democrat*, December 23, 1913.
101. *Wilkes-Barre Record*, December 23, 1913.
102. *Scranton Republican*, December 23, 1913.

Chapter 8

1. *Harrisburg Telegraph*, January 19, 1914.
2. *New Castle Herald*, January 26, 1914.
3. *New Castle Herald*, January 20, 1914.
4. *Reading Times*, January 30, 1914.
5. Billy Murray, BoxRec,www.boxrec.com.
6. *Pittsburgh Daily Post*, February 25, 1914.
7. Jack Kearns was an American boxing manager who was most famous for managing Jack Dempsey, World Heavyweight Champion, from 1919 to 1926. International Boxing Hall of Fame, www.ibhof.com.
8. *Pittsburgh Daily Post*, April 3, 1914.
9. *Courier*, February 22, 1914.
10. *Reading Times*, March 6, 1914.
11. *Harrisburg Telegraph*, February 24, 1914.
12. *Scranton Republican*, March 7, 1914.
13. Kearns's plan for Murray had limited success. After the fight with Leo Houck he fought Jimmy Clabby as planned and had a draw. However, by the time Murray fought George Chip he had already lost the middleweight title to Al McCoy on April 7, 1914. Kearns then brought Murray East, and believed that he would be in demand as a contender and make a lot of money. There was little interest from the reigning middleweights in the East who ignored Murray. Al McCoy fought and won over Murray twice in New York. After that, Murray returned to California.
14. *Scranton Republican*, February 23, 1914.
15. *Scranton Republican*, April 8, 1914.
16. Fleisher, *Fifty Years at Ringside*, pg. 260. "Cauliflower Industry" referred to the damaged ears of boxers, which looked like cauliflowers.
17. *New Castle Herald*, April 20, 1914.
18. *New Castle News*, April 21, 1914.
19. A match between Leo and McCoy occurred during 1919, two years after he lost the middleweight title on November 14, 1919. However, the match was a sham: Leo's opponent was Al Thiel, who billed himself as the "New" Al McCoy. BoxRec, www.boxrec.com.
20. Interview with Edward Hauck conducted in 2016 by Randy L. Swope.
21. *Pittston Gazette*, May 2, 1914.
22. *Delaware County Daily Times*, August 15, 1914.
23. Tommy Gavigan, BoxRec, www.boxrec.com.
24. *New Castle Herald*, August 12, 1914.
25. *Allentown Leader*, September 8, 1914.
26. *Pittsburgh Daily Post*, September 8, 1914.
27. Young Ahearn, BoxRec, www.boxrec.com.
28. *Pittsburgh Daily Post*, November 15, 1914.
29. *York Daily*, November 16, 1914.
30. *Scranton Republican*, November 16, 1914.
31. *Scranton Republican*, October 26, 1914.

32. "Kid Wagner," BoxRec,www.boxrec.com.
33. *Scranton Republican*, November 19, 1914.
34. *Wilkes-Barre Record*, November 17, 1914.
35. *Pittsburgh Post-Gazette*, November 17, 1914.
36. Dropsy, in pathology, is an abnormal infiltration of the tissues with a watery fluid or the collection of such fluid in any body cavity. *Webster's New Twentieth Century Dictionary*, 2nd ed. (World Publishing, 1957), pg. 559.
37. Jack Toland, BoxRec, www.boxrec.com.
38. *Harrisburg Telegraph*, March 23, 1915.
39. George Ashe, BoxRec,www.boxrec.com.
40. *Scranton Republican*, March 29, 1915.
41. *Evening Public Ledger*, March 31, 1915.
42. *Pittsburgh Daily Post*, March 31, 1915.
43. *Lebanon Daily News*, March 31, 1915.
44. *Atlanta Constitution*, April 1, 1915.
45. George "KO" Brown, BoxRec, www.boxrec.com.
46. *Atlanta Constitution*, April 9, 1915.
47. *New Castle Herald*, April 22, 1915.
48. *Evening News*, Wilkes-Barre, Pennsylvania, April 23, 1915.
49. *Scranton Republican*, April 26, 1915.
50. *Scranton Republican*, May 1, 1915.
51. *Scranton Republican*, April 24, 1915.
52. Frank Mantell, BoxRec, www.boxrec.com.
53. *Scranton Republican*, May 22, 1915.
54. *New Castle Herald*, May 25, 1915.
55. Johnson, *Ten and Out*, pg. 292.
56. *Wilkes-Barre Record*, May 27, 1915.
57. *Harrisburg Daily Independent*, May 27, 1915.
58. *Harrisburg Telegraph*, May 27, 1915.
59. *Allentown Democrat*, May 27, 1915. Damon Runyon (1884–1946) was an American journalist and short story writer, best known for his book *Guys and Dolls*, written in the regional slang that became his trademark. He covered the New York baseball clubs as well as various other sports topics, and developed his style of focusing on human interest rather than strictly reporting the facts. At the peak of his popularity he was one of the most productive and highly paid writers in New York. www.britannica.com/biography/Damon-Runyon.
60. "Young Ahearn" did fight Mike Gibbons on January 18, 1916, and lost by a knockout. Gibbons knocked out Ahearn the first time on June 13, 1913. BoxRec, www.boxrec.com.
61. *Allentown Democrat*, June 8, 1915.
62. *Reading Times*, July 28, 1915.
63. *Scranton Republican*, July 28, 1915.
64. *Courier-News*, Bridgewater, New Jersey, September 11, 1915.
65. *York Daily*, September 4, 1915.
66. Herman Miller, BoxRec, www.boxrec.com.
67. *York Daily*, September 15, 1915.
68. *Harrisburg Telegraph*, September 23, 1915.
69. *Wilkes-Barre Times Leader*, October 1, 1915.
70. *Harrisburg Telegraph*, October 1, 1915.
71. *York Daily*, October 16, 1915.
72. *Meriden Daily Journal*, Meriden, Connecticut, November 11, 1915.
73. Tommie Houck, BoxRec, www.boxrec.com.
74. Al Mason, BoxRec, www.boxrec.com.
75. *Altoona Tribune*, November 6, 1915.
76. *Altoona Tribune*, November 16, 1915.
77. *New Castle News*, November 16, 1915.
78. *New Castle Herald*, November 29, 1915.
79. *Allentown Leader*, November 23, 1915.
80. Willie Baker, BoxRec, www.boxrec.com.
81. *York Daily*, November 22, 1915.
82. *Pittsburgh Daily Post*, November 23, 1915.
83. *Allentown Leader*, November 23, 1915.
84. Billy Berger, BoxRec, www.boxrec.com.
85. *Harrisburg Telegraph*, February 15, 1915.
86. *Altoona Tribune*, February 24, 1916.
87. *York Daily*, March 1, 1916.
88. *Ibid.*
89. *Reading Times*, March 7, 1916.
90. *Reading Times*, March, 8, 1916.
91. *Ibid.*
92. *Harrisburg Telegraph*, March 14, 1916.
93. "K.O." Sullivan, BoxRec, www.boxrec.com.
94. *Harrisburg Telegraph*, March 14, 1916.
95. League Island in Philadelphia was accepted by the U.S. Navy in 1868 as the new site for the Navy shipyard, which later became known as the Philadelphia Ship Yard. By the year 2000 the shipyard closed and the land was once again owned by the city of Philadelphia. Historical Society of Pennsylvania, www.hsp.org.
96. Jack Reck, BoxRec,www.boxrec.com.
97. *Harrisburg Telegraph*, March 30, 1916.
98. *York Daily*, April 25, 1916.
99. Ralph Erne, BoxRec, www.boxrec.com.
100. *York Daily*, April 26, 1916.
101. Henry H. Hensel retired shortly before his death. In addition to managing the Lancaster A.C., he was a reporter for forty-nine years, 39 which were spent as a reporter for the *Intelligencer Journal* in Lancaster, Pennsylvania. Charles A. Rieker was a prominent Lancaster businessman and executive manager of the Rieker Star Brewer. He opened a gym at the brewery where many of the local fighters trained. Jack Milley also owned a gym and trained fighters, and was, by far, the most influential person in Leo's life after his father's death. Milley trained Leo for approximately ten years and treated Leo like a son. "Oldtime Boxers Pay Respect To Late Manager Charlie Rieker," article written by Johnny Hauck, John Hauck Collection, MG-63, LancasterHistory.org.
102. *Reading Times*, May 4, 1916.
103. *Reading Times*, May 6, 1916.
104. *Wilkes-Barre Times Leader*, May 15, 1916.
105. According to a *U.S. News and World Report* article comparing income in 1915 and 2015: during 1915 one was doing about average by making $678 a year, according to the Census Bureau of Labor Statistics, www.bls.com.
106. *Reading Times*, November 21, 1916.
107. *Harrisburg Telegraph*, December 21, 1916.
108. *Pittsburgh Daily Post*, October 3, 1916.
109. *Pittsburgh Daily Post*, December 8, 1916.
110. *Pittsburgh Press*, December 10, 1916.
111. *Harrisburg Telegraph*, December 21, 1916.

Chapter 9

1. *Harrisburg Telegraph*, January 23, 1917.
2. Dummy Ketchel, BoxRec, www.boxrec.com.
3. *Allentown Leader*, March 21, 1917.
4. Tommy Burke, BoxRec, www.boxrec.com.
5. *Harrisburg Telegraph*, April 17, 1917.
6. Jackie Clark, BoxRec, www.boxrec.com.
7. Harry Greb, BoxRec, www.boxrec.com.
8. *Allentown Leader*, May 8, 1917.
9. *Scranton Republican*, May 9, 1917.
10. *York Daily*, April 27, 1917.
11. Ibid.
12. *Harrisburg Telegraph*, May 2, 1917.
13. *Harrisburg Telegraph*, May 6, 1917.
14. *York Daily*, May 17, 1917.
15. See Saw Kelly, BoxRec, www.boxrec.com.
16. *Reading Times*, July 14, 1917.
17. *York Daily*, September 7, 1917.
18. *York Daily*, September 15, 1917.
19. *York Daily*, September 14, 1917.
20. *York Daily*, September 19, 1917.
21. Ibid.
22. *Harrisburg Telegraph*, October 2, 1917.
23. Jack McCarron, BoxRec, www.boxrec.com.
24. *Harrisburg Telegraph*, October 23, 1917.
25. *Allentown Democrat*, October 23, 1917.
26. "Fat Willie Meehan Beat Them All but Leo," *Lancaster Sunday News*, November 11, 1972.
27. Ibid.
28. *Pittsburgh Daily Post*, October 27, 1917.
29. "Fat Willie Meehan Beat Them All but Leo," *Lancaster Sunday News*, November 11, 1972.
30. *Harrisburg Telegraph*, November 14, 1917.
31. Buck Crouse, BoxRec, www.boxrec.com.
32. *Pittsburgh Post-Gazette*, November 20, 1917.
33. *Harrisburg Telegraph*, November 20, 1917.
34. *New Castle Herald*, November 20, 1917.
35. *Harrisburg Telegraph*, November 24, 1917.
36. "KO" Willie Loughlin, BoxRec, www.boxrec.com.
37. *Allentown Leader*, December 11, 1917.
38. Harry Greb, George Ashe, BoxRec, www.boxrec.com.
39. *Harrisburg Telegraph*, December 26, 1917.
40. *Evening News*, December 26, 1917.
41. Chuck Wiggins, BoxRec, www.box rec.com.
42. *Pittsburgh Post-Gazette*, January 2, 1918.
43. *Evening News*, January 26, 1918.
44. Jack McCarron, BoxRec, www.boxrec.com.
45. *Allentown Leader*, January 14, 1918.
46. *Pittsburgh Daily Post*, February 23, 1918.
47. *Allentown Leader*, February 23, 1918.
48. *Allentown Leader*, March 5, 1918.
49. *Harrisburg Telegraph*, March 9, 1918.
50. *Great Fighters and Boxers: Psychology of the Ring*, Book Three (New York: Marshall Stillman Association), John Hauck Collection, MG-63, LancasterHistory.org.
51. *Boston Post*, March 10, 1918.
52. *Pittsburgh Daily Post*, March 12, 1918.
53. *Sunday Lancaster Intelligencer Journal*, February 19, 2012.
54. *Scranton Republican*, April 6, 1918.
55. *Boston Post*, April 16, 1918.
56. *Reading Times*, April 16, 1918.
57. Clay Turner, BoxRec, www.boxrec.com.
58. Tommy Gibbons, BoxRec, www.boxrec.com.
59. *Evening News*, April 24, 1918.
60. *Wilkes-Barre Times Leader*, May 4, 1918.
61. Gunboat Smith, BoxRec, www.boxrec.com.
62. *Evening News*, May 28, 1918.
63. *Pittsburgh Daily Post*, May 28, 1918.
64. Interview with Edward Hauck and Joseph Hauck conducted by Randy L. Swope, 2015.
65. *Wilkes-Barre Times Leader*, July 29, 1918.
66. The Sun Shipbuilding Company was located in Chester, Pennsylvania. The company was established by the Pew family and developed by the Sun Oil Company. Sun Shipbuilding remained in operation from 1917 until 1989. The name of the company was changed later to the Sun Shipbuilding and Drydock Company. Ships were initially built to relieve shipping losses during World War I. The first ship, a 10,500-ton single-screw tanker was delivered to Sun Oil Company in December 1917. The shipyard was the largest in the world during World War II. www.sunship.org.
67. Riveting involves a four-person crew. The rivet heater uses a forge to treat the rivet to a glowing cherry-red color. With a set of tongs, the passer then takes the rivet and tosses it to the holder-on, also called the bucket upper, who catches the rivet in a can or bucket. The bucket upper then puts the hot rivet into matching holes between the two metal plates and holds the rounded head of the rivet in place with a riveting gun. The riveter is on the other side of the plate and drives the rivet into the hole, compressing it until it fits tightly and is finished off neatly to the edge of the plating. Caulkers follow the riveters, to seal the joints between the plating. Leo might have been a "holder-on" or possibly a "bucket-upper." The definite time frame for Leo's employment with the Sun Shipbuilding Company has not been validated but, most likely, lasted from June 1918 until the end of December 1918. www.sunship.org.
68. Jeff Smith, BoxRec, www.boxrec.com.
69. *Harrisburg Telegraph*, June 1, 1918.
70. *York Daily*, June 10, 1918.
71. *Delaware County Times*, July 15, 1918.
72. Robert Ripley, *Everlast Boxing Record 1924* (New York: Everlast, 1924), pg. 110.
73. *Delaware County Daily Times*, July 19, 1918.
74. Ibid.
75. Pete Malone, BoxRec, www.boxrec.com.
76. *Evening Public Ledger*, August 9, 1918.
77. "Battling Levinsky," BoxRec, www.boxrec.com.
78. *Harrisburg Telegraph*, December 26, 1918.
79. *Reading Times*, December 26, 1918.
80. *Harrisburg Telegraph*, December 26, 1918.

(Note 112 continued from previous chapter:)
112. Catchweight refers to boxers coming in at no specific weight requirement for their bout. Traditionally they would meet in the middle of their usual weight division. BoxRec, www.boxrec.com.

Chapter 10

1. Harry Greb, BoxRec, www.boxrec.com.
2. "Houck Loses the Verdict to Greb," John Hauck Collection, MG-63, LancasterHistory.org.
3. "Greb Gets Decision Over Houck at Boston," John Hauck Collection, MG-63, LancasterHistory.org.
4. "Battling Kopin," BoxRec, www.boxrec.com.
5. Glass jaw is a term describing a boxer's susceptibility to being knocked out or hurt by a punch to the head. www.boxrec.com.
6. *Harrisburg Telegraph*, January 24, 1919.
7. *Evening News*, February 17, 1919.
8. *Philadelphia Inquirer*, February 22, 1919.
9. See Appendix A.
10. "Zulu Kid," BoxRec, www.boxrec.com.
11. Harry Greb, BoxRec, www.boxrec.com.
12. "Outside the Ropes," John Hauck Collection, MG-63, LancasterHistory.org.
13. "Leo Houck Bested by Harry Greb's Fast Work," John Hauck Collection, MG-63, Lancasterhistory.org.
14. "Houck Beats Clifford," John Hauck Collection MG-63, LancasterHistory.org.
15. "Leo Houck Beats Clifford in 6-Round Cambria Bout," John Hauck Collection, MG-63, LancasterHistory.org.
16. *Scranton Republican*, March 17, 1919.
17. *Delaware County Daily Times*, April 1, 1919.
18. Paul H. Douglas, "Wages and Hours of Labor in 1919," *Journal of Political Economy* 29, No. 1 (1921): pgs. 78–80.
19. *Pittsburgh Daily Post*, March 26, 1919.
20. *Harrisburg Telegraph*, March 24, 1919.
21. Ibid.
22. Larry Williams, BoxRec, www.boxrec.com.
23. *Harrisburg Telegraph*, March 29, 1919.
24. *Evening Public Ledger*, Harrisburg, Pennsylvania, April 1919.
25. *Harrisburg Telegraph*, April 4, 1919.
26. *Harrisburg Telegraph*, April 7, 1919.
27. Joe Allison, BoxRec, www.boxrec.com.
28. *Evening News*, April 5, 1919.
29. *Pittsburgh Daily Post*, April 17, 1919.
30. *Philadelphia Inquirer*, April 27, 1919.
31. *Pittsburgh Post-Gazette*, April 26, 1919.
32. See Appendix A.
33. *Reading Times*, May 17, 1919.
34. *Evening News*, August 14, 1919.
35. Burt Kenny, BoxRec, www.boxrec.com.
36. *Pittsburgh Daily Post*, September 12, 1919.
37. "K.O." Samson, BoxRec, www.boxrec.com.
38. *Pittsburgh Post-Gazette*, October 7, 1919.
39. *Pittsburgh Daily Post*, November 25, 1919.
40. The Franklin and Marshall Academy was established in Lancaster, Pennsylvania. The academy was launched as a private preparatory school and wing of the Franklin College during 1787. Eventually, Marshall College, also in Lancaster, merged with Marshall College to form Franklin & Marshall College. The Franklin and Marshal Academy officially closed in 1943. During 1917 the Franklin and Marshall Academy was ranked as one of the top twelve private preparatory schools in the United States. Franklin & Marshall College, www.fandm.edu.
41. *Harrisburg Telegraph*, December 4, 1919.
42. *Pittsburgh Post-Gazette*, December 13, 1919.
43. *Pittsburgh Daily Post*, December 16, 1919.
44. Interview with Edward and Joseph Hauck conducted by Randy L. Swope, 2017.

Chapter 11

1. *Mount Carmel Item*, January 5, 1920.
2. *Reading Times*, January 28, 1920.
3. *Pittsburgh Daily Post*, January 22, 1920.
4. "Drunken Referee Gave Decision at Halifax," John Hauck Collection, MG-63, LancasterHistory.org.
5. *Reading Times*, March 12, 1920.
6. *Pittsburgh Daily Post*, May 11, 1920.
7. *Mount Carmel Item*, June 1, 1920.
8. Frankie Farron, BoxRec. www.boxrec.com.
9. BoxRec lists the second fight on May 31, 1915, as a win for Keiser. BoxRec, www.boxrec.com. Robert Ripley, ed., *The Everlast Boxing Record Book 1924*, lists the fight as a win for Keiser, pg. 100. Bill Paxton's biography, *The Fearless Harry Greb*, lists the fight as a win for Greb.
10. *Pittsburgh Post-Gazette*, November 13, 1920.
11. John Hauck Collection, MG-63, LancasterHistory.org.
12. *Evening News*, November 18, 1920.
13. *Courier*, November 21, 1920.
14. *New York Times*, November 26, 1920.
15. John Hauck Collection, MG-63, LancasterHistory.org.
16. *Wilkes-Barre Record*, November 30, 1920.
17. Jack Cavanaugh, *Tunney* (New York: Random House, 2006), pg. 68.
18. *Wilkes-Barre Record*, November 30, 1920.
19. *Evening News*, December 4, 1920.
20. *Evening World*, December 7, 1920.
21. *Evening World*, December 8, 1920.
22. *New-York Tribune*, December 10, 1920.
23. *Evening News*, December 10, 1920.
24. *New York Tribune*, December 9, 1920.
25. *New York Tribune*, December 10, 1920.
26. *Evening World*, December 9, 1920.

Chapter 12

1. *Evening News*, April 2, 1921.
2. *Evening Report*, May 12, 1921.
3. Ibid.
4. Ibid.
5. *New Castle News*, May 12, 1921.
6. *New York Times*, May 14, 1921.
7. *New York Times*, June 26, 1921.
8. *New Castle News*, May 18, 1921.
9. *Pittsburgh Post-Gazette*, May 20, 1921.
10. Ibid.
11. Ibid.
12. *Pittsburgh Post-Gazette*, May 21, 1921.
13. *Pittsburgh Post-Gazette*, May 22, 1921.
14. *Pittsburgh Post-Gazette*, May 24, 1921.
15. *Washington Post*, May 24, 1921.

16. *New Castle News*, May 25, 1921.
17. *New York Times*, May 26, 1921.
18. *Pittsburgh Post-Gazette*, May 29, 1921.
19. *Wilkes-Barre Record*, May 28, 1921.
20. *Ibid.*
21. *New York Times*, June 6, 1921.
22. *New York Times*, May 29, 1921.
23. *Pittsburgh Post-Gazette*, May 30, 1921.
24. *New York Times*, May 29, 1921.
25. *Altoona Tribune*, May 31, 1921.
26. *Ibid.*
27. *New York Times*, May 31, 1921.
28. *Ibid.*
29. *New York Times*, June 6, 1921.
30. *Ibid.*
31. *New York Times*, June 26, 1921.
32. *Ibid.*
33. Alexander Johnson, *Ten-and Out!* (Ives Washburn, 1927), pg. 213.
34. *Ibid.*, pg. 213–214.

Chapter 13

1. *Lebanon Daily News*, January 4, 1922.
2. Sgt. Ray Smith, BoxRec, www.boxrec.com.
3. *Philadelphia Inquirer*, April 18, 1922.
4. John Hauck Collection, MG-63, LancasterHistory.org.
5. Louis Smith, BoxRec, www.boxrec.com.
6. Interviews with Edward and Joseph Hauck conducted by Randy L. Swope during 2015 and 2016.
7. Interviews with Edward and Joseph Hauck conducted by Randy L. Swope during 2015 and 2016.
8. *Pittsburgh Post-Gazette*, October 3, 1922.
9. *Pittsburgh Post-Gazette*, October 24, 1922.
10. *Reading Times*, October 24, 1922.
11. *Harrisburg Telegraph*, November 14, 1922.
12. John Hauck Collection, MG-63, LancasterHistory.org.
13. *Courier*, January 7, 1923.
14. Leo fought in two more professional bouts. The fights were not intended as a comeback. Most likely, they were an opportunity for Leo to cash in on the generous purses the local "ham and eggers" had been earning. On May 7, 1923, Leo defeated Buck Ashton in Lancaster. Leo's last battle on August 9, 1926, earned him a TKO win over Sailor Jack Grady in Lancaster, Pennsylvania.

Chapter 14

1. E.C. Wallenfeldt, *The Six-Minute Fraternity* (Westport, CT: Praeger, 1994), pg. 2.
2. *Ibid.*, pg. 3.
3. *Ibid.*
4. L. Shaw, "Leo Florian Houck, Fred's Mentor," *Town and Gown Magazine*, 1985.
5. Penn State Boxing History, TN28445, Special Collections, Penn State University Libraries.
6. Lou Prato, *The Main Event*, February 14, 2014, www.bluewhiteonline.com.
7. Penn State Boxing History, TN28445, Special Collections, Penn State University Libraries.
8. *Ibid.*
9. *New York Times*, January 1, 2001.
10. The five letters included football, basketball, track, soccer, and lacrosse. New Jersey Boxing Hall of Fame, www.njboxinghof.org.
11. L. Shaw, "Leo Florian Houck: Fred's Mentor," *Town and Gown Magazine*, June 1985.
12. Steve Hamas, BoxRec, www.boxrec.com
13. Lou Prato, "The Main Event," February 14, 2014, www.bluewhiteonline.com.
14. Shaw, "Leo Florian Houck."
15. Prato, "The Main Event."
16. *Ibid.*
17. Billy Soose, BoxRec,www.boxrec.com.
18. Gil Fileger, "Leo Houck," John Hauck Collection, MG-63, LancasterHistory.org.
19. *The Stars and Stripes*, January 15, 1945
20. "Leo Houck Selected for U.S. Army Special Service Unit," John Hauck Collection, MG-63, LancasterHistory.org, Lancaster, Pennsylvania.
21. "Houck Makes Plea for Wounded Vets," John Hauck Collection, MG-63, LancasterHistory.org.
22. Major Houck, John Houck Collection, MG-63, LancasterHistory.org.
23. *Lancaster New Era*, 1944.
24. "Houck Makes Plea for Wounded Vets," John Houck Collection, MG-63 LancasterHistory.org.
25. Wallenfeldt, pg. 1.
26. *Ibid.*
27. Penn State Boxing History, TN28445, Special Collections, Penn State University Libraries.
28. "Friends of Leo Houck Hold Cracker Barrel Session," John Hauck Collection, MG-63, Lancaster History.org.
29. Penn State Boxing History, TN28445, Special Collections, Penn State University Libraries. Note: Additional information and statistics are available in TN28445 including individual NCAA and IBA champions up to and including, 1954.
30. "Letters to Leo," Town Topics, State College, Pennsylvania, November 17–23, 1949.
31. Shaw, "Leo Florian Houck."

Chapter 15

1. *Lancaster New Era*, November 29, 1949.
2. *Ibid.*
3. *Evening News*, November 30, 1949.
4. Roberts and Skutt, *The Boxing Register*.
5. "Leo Houck Should Be Named to State Athletic Commission," *Lancaster Intelligencer*, John Hauck Collection, MG-63, LancasterHistory.org.
6. "Letters to Leo," Town Topics, State College, Pennsylvania, November 17–23, 1949.
7. *Ibid.*
8. "Anecdotes About Leo Houck Stir Lively Memories of His 27 Years at Penn State," John Hauck Collection, MG-63, LancasterHistory.org.
9. "Monsignor Schweich Extols Virtues of Leo Houck as 500 Relatives, Friends Attend Last Rites for Famed Fighter," John Hauck Collection, MG-63, LancasterHistory.org.
10. *Ibid.*
11. *Ibid.*

12. *Daily Intelligencer Journal*, December 4, 1950.
13. The exact date for the movement of Leo's memorial to Buchanan Park is uncertain. However, the memorial was cited as residing in Buchanan Park on November 15, 1972, by the *Lancaster Intelligencer Journal*.
14. Edward Hauck's written profile about his father, Leo Houck, was written during 2015.
15. Eligible old-timer is a designation for boxers whose ring careers ended before 1929.
16. *Intelligencer Journal*, February 19, 2012.

Bibliography

Books

Bordner, Allen. *When Boxing Was a Jewish Sport*. Westport, CT: Praeger, 1998.
Cavanaugh, Jack. *Tunney*. New York: Random House, 2006.
Fleisher, Nat. *50 Years at Ringside*. New York: Fleet, 1958.
_____. *The Ring Record Book and Boxing Encyclopedia*. New York: The Ring Bookshop, 1955.
Goldman, Herbert G. *Boxing: A Worldwide Record of Bouts and Boxers*. Jefferson, NC: McFarland, 2012.
Heinz, W.C., and Nathan Ward. *The Book of Boxing*. Kingston, NY: Total Sports Illustrated Classics, 1999.
Johnson, Alexander. *Ten and Out*. New York: Ives Washburn, 1927.
Johnson, J.J., and D.S. Cogswell. *Uncrowned Champions*. San Francisco: Blurb, 2011.
Lindberg, Charles A. *The Spirit of St. Louis*. New York: Charles Scribner's Sons, 1953.
Little, Pat. *Penn State Then & Now*. Lemont, PA: Pat Little Photography, 1999.
May, Ernest R. *The Life History of the United States*, vol. 9: *The Progressive Era, 1901–1917*. New York: Time, 1964.
Paxton, Bill. *The Fearless Harry Greb*. Jefferson, NC: McFarland, 2009.
Ripley, Robert. *Everlast Boxing Record*. New York: Everlast Sport, 1924.
Roberts, James B., and Alexander Skutt G. *The Boxing Register: International Hall of Fame. Official Record Book*, 4th ed. Ithaca, NY: McBooks Press, 2006.
Wallenfeldt, E.C. *The Six-Minute Fraternity*. Westport, CT: Praeger, 1994.

Manuscript Collections

John Hauck Collection, MG-63, Lancaster Historical Society, Lancaster, Pennsylvania, LancasterHistory.org.

Special Collections and Archives

Boxing Photographic Files, TN28448, Penn State University Libraries, University Park, Pennsylvania.
Penn State Boxing History, TN28445, Penn State University Libraries, University Park, Pennsylvania.

Journals

Journal of the Lancaster County Historical Society 86, Number 4 (1982). Lancaster Historical Society, Lancaster, Pennsylvania, LancasterHistory.org.
Journal of the Lancaster County Historical Society 95, Number 4 (1993). Lancaster Pennsylvania, LancasterHistory.org.
Journal of the Lancaster County Historical Society 101, Number 4 (2000). Lancaster Historical Society, LancasterHistory.org.

Boxing Record Sources

BoxRec, www.boxrec.com.
International Boxing Research Organization, www.ibroresearch.com.

Author's Interviews

Edward B. Hauck, Leo Houck's son (interviews 2015, 2016, 2017).
Joseph M. Hauck, Leo Houck's son (interviews 2015, 2016, 2017).

Newspapers

Allentown Democrat
Allentown Leader
Altoona Tribune
Atlanta Constitution
Boston Daily Globe
Boston Post
Courier
Courier-News

Delaware County Daily Times
Evening News (Harrisburg)
Evening Public Ledger
Evening Report
Evening Report (Lebanon)
Evening World
Harrisburg Daily Independent
Harrisburg Telegraph
Intelligencer Journal (Daily)
Lancaster Independent
Lancaster Intelligencer
Lancaster Intelligencer Sunday Journal
Lancaster New Era
Lancaster Sunday Times
Lebanon Courier and Semi-Weekly
Lebanon Daily News
Meriden Daily Journal
Mirror of Life (London, England)
Mount Carmel Item
New Castle Herald
New Castle News
New York Herald Tribune
New York Times
New York Tribune
Parisian News & Notes (Paris, France)
Philadelphia Inquirer
Philadelphia Item
Philadelphia Public Ledger
Pittsburgh Daily Post
Pittsburgh Post-Gazette
Pittsburgh Press
Pittston Gazette
Reading Times
Scranton Republican
Scranton Truth
Stars and Stripes
Washington Post
Wilkes-Barre Record
Wilkes-Barre Times Leader-Evening News
Williamsport Sun-Gazette
York Daily
York Daily Record

Index of Persons

Ahearn, Young 95-6, 98-9, 100-1, 103, 170, 181, 182
Allison, Joe 129, 130, 173, 184
Applegate, Harry 131, 173
Ashe, George 97, 117-8, 121, 170, 172, 182-3
Ashton, Buck 174, 185

Baker, Willie 104, 106, 171, 182
Beebe, Kid 22-3, 37, 42, 166, 177
Berger, Willie 62, 65, 105, 171, 182
Bergin, Tommy 84, 170, 181
Borrell, Joe 74, 87-90 107, 121, 170, 181
Brandt, Battling 106, 171
Britton, Frankie 145
Britton, Jack 21, 25, 27, 35, 166-7, 177
Broad, Young Kid 21-2, 27-8, 39, 166-7, 177
Brown, George 47, 82, 98, 170, 182
Burke, Tommy 112-3, 171, 183

Cardenas, Kid 145, 174
Cardiff, Jack 33-4, 167
Chip, George 1, 11, 59, 60, 73, 78, 80, 86-9, 90-2, 94, 98-9, 101, 103, 105, 107, 116, 120, 128, 169, 170, 181
Clark, Jackie 113, 146, 172, 174, 183
Clifford, Jack 127, 139, 142, 173, 184
Corbett, Fred 45-6, 168
Cove, Percy 23, 166
Crouse, Buck 65-6, 68, 71-2, 76, 80, 82, 84, 88, 105, 107-8, 117, 134, 169, 170, 172, 180-1, 183

Daly, Kid 23, 166
Decker, George 24-5, 166

Dillon, Jack 11, 45, 50-1, 63, 68-9, 70, 72, 75-6, 78-9, 80-2, 84-5, 88, 96, 98, 102-5, 108, 113, 116, 118, 121, 169, 170, 179, 181
Dolan, Jimmy 43, 168
Duggan, Tommy 20, 166

Eagan, Buck 22, 166
Erne, Ralph 108, 171, 182
Erne, Young 35, 37, 167-8, 178
Eshelman, Herb 11, 13, 165
Esparraguera, Santiago 145, 174
Evans, Pinky 19, 165

Farron, Frankie 134, 174, 184
Fitzgerald, Jack 62, 72, 76, 169, 179, 180
Fleming, Bill 102, 171
Fleming, Mike 27, 126, 167
Fritsch, Leo 11, 165

Gannon, Mickey 30, 31, 35, 167
Gardner, Jimmy 45-6, 52, 168
Gavigan, Tommy 94-5, 170, 181
Gibbons, Mike 45, 75-6, 78, 81, 96, 98-9, 100, 102, 116, 120, 122, 127-8, 132, 171, 173, 182
Gilbert, Dick 81, 170, 181
Graber, Al 97, 110, 170, 171
Grady, Sailor Jack 174, 185
Grande, Sailor 101, 103-4, 171
Grant, Bob 126, 173
Greb, Harry 1, 110, 113, 117-9, 125-7, 129, 130, 132, 172-3, 176, 183-4, 187
Griffin, Phil 24-5, 166-7
Groff, Walter 13-4, 19, 165

Hanlon, Young Jack 20, 34, 166
Hayes, Grover 26-8, 167
Hicks, Freddie 78-9, 170

Hirst, Joe 28, 30, 32, 35, 39, 40, 167, 168
Holland, Jim 145, 174
Howard, Johnny 97, 102, 134, 171, 173

Kegel, Harry 24, 166
Keiser, Fay 110, 134, 171, 174, 184
Kelly, See Saw 114, 172, 183
Kenny, Bert 101, 131, 171, 173, 184
Ketchell, Dummy 112, 171, 182
Klaus, Frank 45-6, 48, 50-3, 59, 60, 62-5, 68, 73-6, 78-9, 81, 86, 105, 168-9, 180-1
Kopin, Battling 126, 172, 183
Kreckel, Carl 7-8, 165, 175

Lavin, Paddy 32-4, 167
Leonard, Leo 136, 174
Levinsky, Battling 11, 49, 52-3, 63-4, 66, 77-8, 81, 97, 112-4, 118, 123-4, 134-5, 137, 168-9, 172, 183
Lewis, Harry 1, 41-6, 48, 51-6, 59, 62, 70, 87, 121, 151, 168-9, 178-9, 180
Livingston, Jimmy 21, 166
Locke, Kid 25-6, 28, 33, 39, 124, 167
Loughlin, Willie 117, 121, 172, 183
Loughry, Young 36, 39, 40-1, 44, 168
Lucas, Willie 24, 166

MacDonald, Roddy 126, 133, 173
Malone, Pete 123, 172, 183
Mansfield, Harry 51-2, 133, 169
Mantell, Frank 46-7, 60-2, 91, 99, 168-9, 171, 182
Marshall, Young 21, 166
Martinez, Rudy 134, 174

Index of Persons

McAvoy, Eddie 25, 167
McCann, Hugh 21, 166
McCarron, Jack 88, 107, 116, 118–9, 120–1, 172, 183
McGoorty, Eddie 53, 75–6, 78, 81, 94, 98, 169, 179, 180
McMahon, Tom 49, 50, 168, 179
Meehan, Willie 19, 116–8, 121, 128, 172, 183
Miller, Peck 71, 74, 169, 180
Miller, Yong Herman 101, 108, 114, 121, 134, 144, 171–2, 174, 182
Moha, Bob 45, 51, 64, 68, 71, 78, 105, 169, 179
Moore, Frankie 22, 166
Moore, Reddy 22, 24, 166
Murray, Billy 41, 68, 90–2, 94, 133, 170, 181

Nelson, Dick 37, 168, 178
Nitchie, Young 28–9, 33–4, 39, 167

O'Dowd, Dan 139, 174
O'Keefe, Tommy 23, 27, 30–2, 166–7, 177
Otto, Young 43–4, 168

Papke, Billy 45, 48, 51–2, 58–9, 62, 64, 66–7, 71, 74–6, 78, 80, 169, 179, 180
Parks, Sam 21–22, 166
Perron, Frank 38–9, 168, 178

Quill, Tommy 44, 46, 77, 168

Ramsey, Harry 8, 52–3, 62, 64, 169
Reck, Jack 107, 109, 171, 182
Revoire, Eddie 106–7, 112, 133, 171, 173
Rogers, Al 80, 102–3, 170–1, 181

Samson, George KO 131, 133–4, 173–4, 184
Schupp, Lew 144, 146, 174
Sieger, Joe 27–8, 43, 167, 178

Smith, Dave 76–8, 169, 180
Smith, Gunboat 121–2, 172, 183
Smith, Jeff 45, 122, 135, 172, 183
Smith, Sgt. Ray 144, 174, 185
Sullivan, KO 135, 174

Theil, Al 129, 173
Thomas, Joe 58, 62, 169, 179
Toland, Jack 97, 170, 181
Tunney, Gene 1, 10, 135–6, 161, 174
Turner, Clay 121, 128, 130, 172, 183

Wagner, Emmett Kid 76, 78, 96, 170, 181
Wiggins, Chuck 118, 120, 138, 172, 183
Willetts, Johnny 39, 168
Williams, Larry 77, 128, 130, 139, 141–2, 170, 173, 184
Wilson, Johnny 120–1, 163, 172

Zulu Kid 126, 173, 184

www.ingramcontent.com/pod-product-compliance
Lightning Source LLC
Chambersburg PA
CBHW081559300426
44116CB00015B/2934